T0252988

IET COMPUTING SERIES 61

Access Control and Security Monitoring of Multimedia Information Processing and Transmission

The IET International Book Series on Multimedia Information Processing and Security

Call for Authors

Multimedia data (and more generally multimodal data) stands as one of the most demanding and exciting aspects of the information era. The processing of multimedia has been an active research area with applications in secure multimedia content on social networks, digital forensics, digital cinema, education, secured e-voting systems, smart healthcare, automotive applications, the military, insurance, and more. The advent of the Internet of Things (IoT), big data, cyber-physical systems (CPSs), robotics as well as personal and wearable devices now provide many opportunities for the multimedia community to reach out and develop synergies.

This book series comprehensively defines the current trends and technological aspects of multimedia research with a particular emphasis on interdisciplinary approaches. The authors will review a broad scope to identify challenges, solutions, and new directions The published books can be used as references by practicing engineers, scientists, researchers, practitioners, and technology professionals from academia, government, and industry working on state-of-the-art multimedia processing, analysis, search, mining, management, and security solutions for practical applications. It will also be useful to senior undergraduate and graduate students.

Proposals for coherently integrated international co-authored or multi-authored edited research monographs will be considered for this book series. Each proposal will be reviewed by the book series editors with additional peer reviews from independent reviewers. Please contact:

- Dr. Amit Kumar Singh, Department of Computer Science & Engineering, National Institute of Technology Patna, India; Emails: amit_245singh@yahoo.com; amit.singh@nitp.ac.in
- Prof. Stefano Berretti, Media Integration and Communication Center (MICC) & Department of Information Engineering (DINFO), University of Florence, Italy; E-mail: stefano.berretti@unifi.it

Access Control and Security Monitoring of Multimedia Information Processing and Transmission

Edited by
Zhihan Lyu, Jaime Lloret and Houbing Herbert Song

The Institution of Engineering and Technology

Published by The Institution of Engineering and Technology, London, United Kingdom

The Institution of Engineering and Technology is registered as a Charity in England & Wales (no. 211014) and Scotland (no. SC038698).

The Institution of Engineering and Technology
Futures Place
Kings Way, Stevenage
Hertfordshire SG1 2UA, United Kingdom

www.theiet.org

British Library Cataloguing in Publication Data
A catalogue record for this product is available from the British Library

ISBN 978-1-83953-693-9 (hardback)
ISBN 978-1-83953-694-6 (PDF)

Typeset in India by MPS Limited

Cover Image: Weiquan Lin / Moment via Getty Images

Contents

About the editors

Zhihan Lyu is an associate professor at Uppsala University, Sweden, where he specializes in virtual and augmented reality, computer vision and visualization, and the Internet of Things. He has successfully completed several projects on PC, website, smartphone, and smart glasses. He is editor-in-chief of *Internet of Things* and *Cyber-Physical Systems(KeAi)*, an associate editor of *IEEE TITS, IEEE TNSM, IEEE TCSS, IEEE TNSE,* and *ACM TOMM*. He is the general chair, co-chair, or TPC of 50 conferences. Zhihan has two granted patents. He is an IEEE senior member, British Computer Society fellow, ACM distinguished speaker, and full member of Sigma Xi. He received his PhD degree in computer applied technology from Ocean University of China in Qingdao of China.

Jaime Lloret is a full professor at the Polytechnic University of Valencia, Spain. He is the chair of the Integrated Management Coastal Research Institute (IGIC). He received his BSc+MSc in Physics in 1997, his BSc+MSc in Electronic Engineering in 2003, and his PhD in telecommunication engineering (Dr. Ing.) in 2006. He is a Cisco certified network professional instructor and he has seven Cisco Networking Academy Certifications. He also has the Hewlett-Packard IT Architect Certification. He worked as a network designer and administrator in several enterprises. He was the founder of the "Communications and Networks" research group of the IGIC and he is the head (and founder) of the "Active and collaborative techniques and use of technologic resources in the education (EITACURTE)" Innovation Group. He is the director of the University Diploma "Redes y Comunicaciones de Ordenadores" and he has been the director of the University Master "Digital Post Production" for the term 2012–2016. He was vice-chair for the Europe/Africa Region of Cognitive Networks Technical Committee (IEEE Communications Society) for the term 2010–2012 and vice-chair of the Internet Technical Committee (IEEE Communications Society and Internet Society) for the term 2011–2013. He has been the Internet Technical Committee chair (IEEE Communications Society and Internet Society) for the term 2013–2015. He has authored 15 books and has more than 800 research papers published in national and international conferences, and international journals (more than 400 with Clarivate Analytics JCR).

He has been the co-editor of 54 conference proceedings and guest editor of several international books and journals. He is editor-in-chief of the "Ad Hoc and Sensor Wireless Networks" (with Clarivate Analytics Impact Factor), the international journal "Networks Protocols and Algorithms", and the International Journal of Multimedia Communications. Moreover, he is associate editor of *Sensors* in the Section Sensor Networks, and in Wireless Communications and Mobile Computing, he is an advisory board member of the *International Journal of Distributed Sensor Networks* (all with Clarivate Analytics Impact factor), and he is IARIA Journals Board Chair (8 Journals). Furthermore, he is (or has been) associate editor of 46 international journals (16 of them with Clarivate Analytics Impact Factor). He has led many local, regional, national, and European projects. He was the chair of the Working Group of the Standard IEEE 1907.1 from 2013 to 2018. Since 2016 till today he has been the Spanish researcher with the highest h-index in the TELECOMMUNICATIONS journal list according to Clarivate Analytics Ranking. Moreover, he has been included in the world's top 2% of scientists according to the Stanford University List since 2020. He has been involved in more than 500 program committees of international conferences, and more than 160 organization and steering committees. He has been the general chair (or co-chair) of 78 international workshops and conferences. He is an IEEE senior member, ACM senior member, IARIA fellow, and EAI fellow.

Houbing Herbert Song (PhD, IEEE fellow), is the director of security and optimization for the Networked Globe Laboratory (SONG Lab, http://songlab.us/) and a professor in the Department of Information Systems at the University of Maryland, Baltimore County, USA. His research interests include cyber-physical systems, the Internet of Things, cybersecurity and privacy, AI and machine learning, big data analytics, edge computing, unmanned aircraft systems, connected vehicles, smart and connected health, and wireless communications and networking. His research has been sponsored by federal agencies (including the US National Science Foundation, US Department of Transportation, Federal Aviation Administration, US Department of Defense, and Air Force Research Laboratory) and the industry. He serves as associate technical editor for several IEEE journals and magazines. He is the editor of eight books, author of over 100 articles, and inventor of two patents (US & WO). He is an IEEE fellow and an ACM distinguished member. He is an ACM distinguished speaker (2020–present), an IEEE Vehicular Technology Society (VTS) distinguished lecturer (2023–present) and an IEEE systems council distinguished lecturer (2023–present). He has been a highly cited researcher identified by Clarivate^{TM} (2021, 2022). He received Research.com Rising Star of Science Award in 2022, 2021 Harry Rowe Mimno Award bestowed by IEEE Aerospace and Electronic Systems Society, and 10+ Best Paper Awards from major international conferences. He received his PhD degree in Electrical Engineering from the University of Virginia, USA.

Foreword

Multimedia (and more generally multimodal data) stands as one of the most demanding and exciting aspects of the information era. The processing of multimedia has been an active research area with applications in secure multimedia content on social networks, digital forensics, digital cinema, education, secured e-voting systems, smart healthcare, automotive applications, the military, finance, insurance, and more. The advent of the Internet of Things (IoT), cyber-physical systems (CPSs), robotics as well as personal and wearable devices now provide many opportunities for the multimedia community to reach out and develop synergies.

Our book series comprehensively defines the current trends and technological aspects of multimedia research with a particular emphasis on interdisciplinary approaches. The authors will review a broad scope to identify challenges, solutions, and new directions. The published books can be used as references by practicing engineers, scientists, researchers, practitioners, and technology professionals from academia, government, and industry working on state-of-the-art multimedia processing, analysis, search, mining, management, and security solutions for practical applications. It will also be useful to senior undergraduate and graduate students as well as PhD students and Postdoc researchers.

This book focuses on state-of-the-art research and innovations as well as future perspectives for the access control and security monitoring of multimedia information processing and transmission. The authors present cybersecurity and control methods and technologies including anti-virus and encryption techniques, forger identification, steganography, reciprocation, and transmission supported by Virtual Reality, multimedia copyright protection, and digital content copyright services with blockchain and multimedia AI. The unique contribution of this volume is to bring together researchers from distinct domains that seldom interact to identify theoretical, technological, and practical issues related to the access control and security monitoring of multimedia data. The book is intended to enhance the understanding of opportunities and challenges in access control and security monitoring of multimedia information processing and transmission and its applications at the global level. We hope the readers will find this book of great value in its visionary words.

Dr. Amit Kumar Singh, Book Series Editor
Department of Computer Science and Engineering
National Institute of Technology Patna 800005 India

Prof. Stefano Berretti, Book Series Editor
Department of Information Engineering
University of Florence 50139 Italy

Chapter 1

Introduction

Zhihan Lyu[1]

With the exponential growth of information technology, multimedia digital technology has become an indispensable part of people's daily lives. However, multimedia data security issues are particularly prominent in the current Internet of Things (IoT) environment. Issues such as user privacy leakage, malicious data tampering, and infringement of intellectual property rights of multimedia data on platforms are not uncommon. Strengthening technical research and exploration is necessary to effectively solve the security issues of multimedia data. In this context, digital watermarking technology and encryption algorithms have become the main means of protecting multimedia data security. This study classifies the contents of multimedia and analyzes multimedia security technology based on the background information of multimedia technology. After summarizing the basic concepts of multimedia encryption technology, this study reviews the literature on multimedia watermarking and encryption technology. Furthermore, this study combines multimedia digital signature technology and multimedia authentication technology to analyze the network system structure of multimedia security. The research results demonstrate that digital watermarking technology and digital encryption algorithms can improve the application security of multimedia digital technology to a certain extent. The findings of this study hold practical reference value for optimizing the network structure of multimedia information security. By providing a comprehensive analysis of multimedia security technology, this study highlights the significance of technical research and exploration in addressing security issues surrounding multimedia data in the current IoT environment.

1.1 Introduction

Multimedia technology has revolutionized modern society by enabling a wide range of applications, including audio and video transmission, gaming, and film production, among others [1,2]. However, with the proliferation and advancement of multimedia technology, the volume of data has also increased, leading to complex security challenges. These challenges include copyright infringement, identity

---

[1]Department of Game Design, Faculty of Arts, Uppsala University, Sweden

theft, data tampering, and forgery. Consequently, there is a pressing need to develop effective solutions to enhance multimedia data security, protect users' interests, and safeguard intellectual property [3–5].

In the field of multimedia security, advanced solutions include digital watermarking technology, encryption technology, digital signature technology, and secure transmission technology. Digital watermarking technology can achieve functions such as copyright protection and identity verification by embedding invisible data. Encryption technology can protect the confidentiality of multimedia data through symmetric/asymmetric encryption algorithms. Digital signature technology ensures the integrity and authenticity of multimedia data. The implementation of these multimedia security technologies can effectively ensure the security and integrity of multimedia data and provide users with a more reliable and secure usage environment.

Multimedia security solutions, such as digital watermarking and digital signature technology, have been widely used to ensure the integrity, authenticity, and confidentiality of multimedia data. However, these technologies also face challenges and limitations. Digital watermarking, for example, may cause a reduction in data quality and an increase in data volume. Furthermore, some multimedia security technologies may require substantial computing resources, which can affect the efficiency of the system. In light of these challenges and the need for more adaptable and effective security measures for multimedia applications, there is a critical demand for further investigation into multimedia security solutions. Future research in this area should focus on developing innovative approaches that can effectively address the limitations of existing multimedia security technologies.

1.2   Types of multimedia content and analysis of multimedia security technology

1.2.1   *Classification of multimedia content and analysis of network attack methods*

The proliferation of multimedia content, such as images, videos, and audios, on social media platforms has intensified the need for efficient and reliable multimedia security solutions. To this end, recent studies have explored various approaches to enhancing multimedia security, as well as the classification and promotion of multimedia content. Lv *et al.* (2021) [6] examined the security threats and attack methods of the Internet of Things (IoT) edge devices and proposed several solutions, including encryption algorithms, identity authentication, and network isolation, to secure the IoT edge computing environment. Hausmann *et al.* (2018) [7] analyzed tourists' social media posts using text analysis and machine learning algorithms to predict their preferences for protected area experiences, providing insights into effective guidance and reference for tourism management. Dolan *et al.* (2019) [8] developed a framework for social media content engagement and demonstrated its effectiveness through statistical analysis and machine learning methods. The study also identified the factors influencing user participation behavior to assist social media marketing. Garg *et al.* (2019) [9] designed a hybrid anomaly detection scheme based on deep learning technologies, including multi-layer perceptron (MLP) neural networks and convolutional neural networks, to detect suspicious traffic in multimedia networks. The scheme was found to significantly improve detection accuracy. Verdoliva (2020) [10] conducted a comprehensive review of deep learning video production technologies and discussed their advantages, disadvantages, and coping strategies, as well as future research directions. Namasudra *et al.* (2020) [11] introduced a multimedia protection scheme based on deoxyribonucleic acid (DNA) encryption technology, which was found to be highly secure and robust in cloud computing environments. Rathee *et al.* (2020) [12] proposed a hybrid framework for multimedia data processing in IoT medical care that demonstrated superior data security and privacy protection, as well as efficient multimedia data processing capabilities.

Zalisham *et al.* (2021) [13] employed expert survey and data analysis methodologies to examine issues related to network security maintenance and management, and proposed solutions to address them. The study's outcomes demonstrate the effectiveness of the proposed solution in resolving current organizational security management challenges. Shang *et al.* (2021) [14] designed a computer-based multimedia security protection system, based on a proactive defense model for network security, and verified its feasibility and effectiveness using software simulation technology. The investigation revealed that the system can provide more flexible and efficient protection for multimedia data security. Khan *et al.* (2022) [15] proposed a face recognition method that utilizes artificial intelligence and genetic algorithms for multimedia digital forensics. The authors used a considerable amount of experimental data to validate the practicality and effectiveness of the proposed method. The results demonstrate that the method can accurately identify faces, shorten the time for multimedia forensics, and improve the efficiency of forensics. Tolba *et al.* (2022) [16] introduced a deep learning-based multimedia network attack scheme for the security assessment of multimedia data. The study employed deep learning techniques and experimental data to demonstrate that the proposed project can more accurately evaluate multimedia security. Cecchinato *et al.* (2022) [17] developed a real-time multimedia stream transmission scheme for drone networks, which employs Advanced Encryption Standard encryption to ensure secure and efficient multimedia transmission. The researchers verified the scheme's feasibility and effectiveness through experimental data and found that it can achieve safe and efficient multimedia transmission in military tasks. Li *et al.* (2023) [18] conducted a security analysis and improvement of a dual watermarking framework for multimedia privacy protection and content authentication. The study employed mathematical analysis and experimental results to evaluate the framework's safety and efficiency and provided detailed improvement suggestions.

Figure 1.1 shows a structural analysis of multimedia content classification and network attack modes.

The aforementioned studies highlight the increasing importance of multimedia data in the network and the diverse security threats and management challenges it

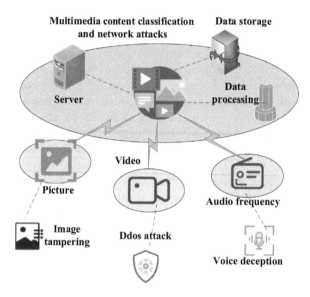

Figure 1.1   Multimedia content classification and network attack structure

poses. While scholars have conducted extensive research in this area, a more comprehensive and systematic approach is required to safeguard the security of multimedia data and enhance its classification and promotion on the network. Future research could focus on developing more effective and secure multimedia data management systems, as well as leveraging advanced techniques to assess and address multimedia security concerns.

1.2.2   Overview and research of multimedia security technology

The rapid advancement and extensive use of information technology have led to the emergence of emotion-aware multimedia systems and e-learning systems, which have become an integral part of people's lives. However, these systems encounter several security and sustainability issues threatening users' privacy and data security. To address these concerns, scholars are exploring new security schemes and critical success factor models to safeguard users' data privacy and enable seamless usage. For instance, Zhang *et al.* (2018) [19] discussed the security challenges of emotion-aware multimedia systems and proposed a security scheme based on obfuscated encryption technology. They employed emotion recognition technology to authenticate users during key data transmission. Ahmad *et al.* (2018) [20] investigated the critical success factors for enhancing the sustainability and efficiency of e-learning systems. They modeled the critical success factors through structural equation modeling and multiple regression analysis and examined their influence on system sustainability and performance. In another study, Hu *et al.* (2018) [21] introduced a technique for quantifying security risk situations using threat prediction, which is applicable to multimedia communication networks. The researchers quantitatively assessed the security risks of the system by developing threat models and threat assessment methods. KM *et al.* (2019) [22] explored multimedia adaptation layer technology for underwater sensor networks. The researchers utilized multi-band and multimedia data, along with dynamic adjustment mechanisms, to enhance data transmission efficiency and system reliability and performance. In a recent study, Chen *et al.* (2020) [23] presented a social multimedia security detection technology based on deep learning. They combined convolutional neural networks and recurrent neural networks to detect suspicious activities accurately. Shandilya *et al.* (2022) [24] proposed an artificial intelligence-assisted computer network test platform, combined with nature-heuristic network security, for adaptive defense simulation and analysis. Experimental results showed that the platform could improve the intelligence level and defense capabilities of network security.

In a further study, Zhang *et al.* (2022) [25] introduced a multi-symbol non-coherent learning detection method for identifying coded signals in wireless multimedia networks. They enhanced recognition accuracy and performance by optimizing the algorithm. Safhi *et al.* (2022) [26] summarized the primary security challenges encountered by social networks and presented the main defense strategies, such as multi-factor authentication, encryption technology, and network security monitoring. Sathish *et al.* (2022) [27] developed a computer network test platform, augmented with artificial intelligence and nature-inspired network security, to enable adaptive defense simulation and analysis. Their experimental results demonstrated that this platform can enhance the intelligence level and defense capabilities of network security. To enhance multimedia encryption, Al-Hazaimeh *et al.* (2022) [28] offered an overview of the application and development of chaotic cryptography in multimedia encryption. They presented various chaotic encryption algorithms and their application in network and internet security. Furthermore, Gadde *et al.* (2023) [29] proposed a cloud multimedia data security protection scheme based on optimization-assisted encryption technology. They optimized the algorithm to enhance encryption speed and efficiency while preserving data confidentiality and privacy. Lastly, Nawaz *et al.* (2023) [30] reviewed the security threats and solutions faced by online social networks. They analyzed and summarized the current network security challenges and future research directions. Figure 1.2 depicts the system structure of multimedia encryption technology and multimedia security.

In summary, the aforementioned literature abstracts encompass diverse facets of security challenges and solutions in network domains, including multimedia networks, social networks, and computer networks. Researchers have proposed novel and effective methods and technologies while enhancing the defense capabilities and intelligence levels of network security through algorithm optimization and artificial intelligence. These research outcomes advance the research and practical proficiency in the network security domain and facilitate the safeguarding of personal information security and the preservation of social order.

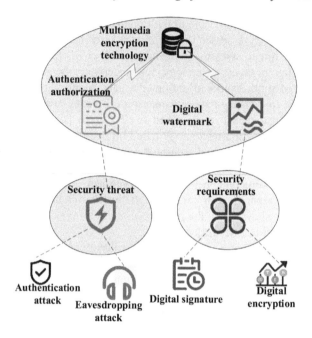

Figure 1.2   System structure of multimedia encryption technology and multimedia security

1.3   Multimedia watermark technology and multimedia security

1.3.1   *Principle and application of multimedia watermarking technology*

With the rise of the digital age, the safeguarding of multimedia data has become increasingly vital. Multimedia watermarking technology has gained more attention as an effective method for digital copyright protection and information hiding. Zear *et al.* (2018) [31] proposed a multiple digital watermarking technique for healthcare applications using discrete cosine transform and discrete wavelet transform techniques. The study showed the effectiveness and feasibility of the technique in information protection, robustness, and error control through experiments. Kumar *et al.* (2018) [32] conducted a review of image watermarking techniques and their applications in e-governance, covering various techniques and algorithms and discussing key issues related to embedding and extracting watermarks. This study proves that watermarking technology has important application value in the field of electronic governance. Menendez-Ortiz *et al.* (2019) [33] reviewed and analyzed the application of reversible watermarking technology in multimedia content protection, introducing different reversible watermarking methods and embedding algorithms and studying the robustness and tolerance of these methods to verify their feasibility. Thakur *et al.* (2019) [34] proposed a multi-layered security method of chaotic encryption and digital watermarking for medical data in TV health applications, adopting wavelet transform and discrete cosine transform technology. Experiments proved its feasibility and effectiveness in data protection and privacy protection. Singh (2019) [35] proposed an image double watermarking method based on joint wavelet transform, optimizing the embedding process with polynomial fitting technology and improving robustness and error tolerance with error correction code technology. Experimental results proved that the technology is feasible and robust. Ray *et al.* (2020) [36] conducted a review of the application of image watermarking technology in copyright protection, analyzing the advantages and disadvantages of various technologies. The study believes that different technologies should be selected according to different application requirements and security levels and emphasizes the importance of watermarking technology in digital copyright protection.

Kaur *et al.* (2020) [37] reviewed the characteristics, applications, and attacks of robust multimedia watermarking, analyzing the advantages and disadvantages of various watermarking techniques from multiple aspects. This research demonstrates the effectiveness of robust watermarking and encryption techniques in protecting multimedia content and guaranteeing digital rights. Faragallah *et al.* (2020) [38] proposed an efficient video integrity verification scheme using hashes and keys for encryption and verification, adopting high-efficiency video codec technology based on hardware. The experiment proves that it has a good application prospect in multimedia network security. Anand *et al.* (2021) [39] reviewed watermarking techniques for medical data authentication and evaluated their robustness and protection. This study demonstrates the application prospect and importance of watermarking technology in medical data management and security. Singh *et al.* (2021) [40] provide a comprehensive review of techniques for image watermarking using soft computing techniques, analyzing the characteristics and effects of various algorithms and techniques and comparing the advantages and disadvantages of various techniques. The study demonstrates the significant value of soft computing techniques in securing multimedia content. Zainol *et al.* (2021) [41] provided a comprehensive review and comparison of image watermarking techniques based on singular value decomposition, exploring the characteristics, strengths, weaknesses, and application scenarios of various approaches and evaluating the effectiveness and robustness of these techniques for multimedia protection and digital copyright. Sridhar *et al.* (2021) [42] analyzed the usage and effect of watermarking technology in multimedia communication, comparing the characteristics and effects of various algorithms and technologies and proposing suggestions for further optimization and improvement. This research proves the application prospect and importance of watermarking technology in multimedia communication. Figure 1.3 illustrates the relationship structure between multimedia watermarking technology and multimedia security technology.

The above-reviewed studies clearly demonstrate the significant application value of watermarking technology in protecting multimedia content and digital copyright. Each watermarking technology possesses unique characteristics and

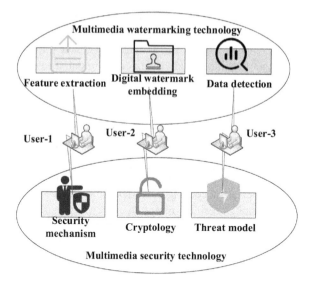

Figure 1.3   Correlation between multimedia watermarking technology and multimedia security technology

applicable scenarios. For example, robust watermarking and encryption technology can be employed in combination to enhance security; hardware-based high-efficiency video codec technology can enable video integrity verification; and soft computing technology can be applied for image watermarking. Furthermore, watermarking technology also holds crucial application value in medical data management and security. It is essential to continuously improve and optimize watermarking technology and strengthen its combination with other security technologies to better safeguard the security of multimedia content and digital copyright in the future.

1.4   Multimedia encryption technology and multimedia security

1.4.1   *Principle and application of multimedia encryption technology*

As information technology continues to advance, ensuring the security and privacy of digital data is becoming increasingly crucial. Encryption technology has emerged as a popular tool for safeguarding digital data, but the ever-evolving landscape of attack techniques and encryption vulnerabilities has challenged the security of many encryption schemes. Thus, investigating the security and robustness of encryption technology has become a paramount concern. In this regard, Li *et al.* (2018) [43] conducted a cryptographic attack on an image encryption algorithm employing automatic blocking and ECG techniques and proposed a new key-guessing method for reconstructing the encrypted image without knowledge of the key. The experimental results revealed that the encryption effect of this algorithm is inadequate in terms of security. Cox *et al.* (2018) [44] provided a comprehensive review of digital watermarking techniques, outlining the definition, application scenarios, classification, and primary embedding and extraction methods of watermarks. Furthermore, the authors analyzed and discussed the security and robustness of digital watermarking technology. Shifa *et al.* (2019) [45] proposed a video encryption scheme based on lightweight cryptography that employed matrix permutation and lightweight scrambling algorithms, effectively enhancing encrypted images' security while reducing the encryption space ratio. In addition, Han (2019) [46] proposed an image encryption algorithm that utilized a modified Logistic chaotic map to generate a random key. The algorithm segmented the image into equal-sized blocks and leveraged the entropy value of the Logistic chaotic map to ensure the encryption algorithm's security. Sivakumar *et al.* (2019) [47] introduced an image encryption method based on laser chaos. This method utilized a laser spot to scan the image and converted the laser chaotic sequence into a random key stream to guarantee the image's security during encryption. Experimental results showed that this method had excellent encryption effectiveness. Finally, Xiong *et al.* (2019) [48] proposed a chaotic encryption algorithm based on the Jiugongge diagram, which transformed a color image into a Gray image and used the Jiugongge diagram to generate random numbers for encryption. The experimental results showed that the algorithm had high security and efficiency.

Hamad *et al.* (2020) [49] proffered an intriguing image encryption algorithm based on the permutation principle and obfuscation technology. Through the permutation and obfuscation of the image matrix, the authors achieved efficient and safe encryption of the image. The experimental results of the proposed algorithm demonstrate the ability to guarantee the security and reliability of image encryption, and the encryption process has high speed and efficiency. Bhat *et al.* (2020) [50] have proposed a novel image encryption algorithm using a combination of inter-mapping, permutation, and pixel replacement methods. The experimental results exhibit that the proposed algorithm can effectively protect the confidentiality of images and maintain minimal impact on transmission bandwidth, making it an ideal candidate for image encryption applications on mobile devices. Tariq *et al.* (2020) [51] have introduced a hybrid encryption method based on the chaotic Lorenz system and logarithmic key generation. The method combines chaotic cryptography and analysis methods, ensuring strong encryption and recovery capabilities. The experimental results demonstrate the reliability of the proposed method in terms of encryption effectiveness. Lamiche (2020) [52] has presented a digital image encryption technique using chaotic maps. The algorithm combines grayscale transformation, interchange, and XOR technology to provide ample image security and robustness. The experimental results highlight the good encryption performance of the proposed algorithm. Koppanati *et al.* (2020) [53] have proposed a multimedia encryption technique based on polynomial congruence and applied it in cloud computing. The experimental results demonstrate that the encryption technology can provide reliable security protection for multimedia data.

Abdelfatah *et al.* (2020) [54] have proposed a digital multimedia encryption method based on chaotic maps. The authors have considered the balance between encryption cost and effect while ensuring security. The experimental results demonstrate that the proposed method has a better encryption effect and is suitable for various encryption scenarios.

In light of the above-discussed digital image and multimedia encryption techniques, the selection of an appropriate encryption algorithm according to the specific situation is crucial for data protection. Additionally, the encryption process must take into account multiple factors such as security, speed, and effect to ensure the rationality and reliability of the encryption effect. With the continuous development of network technology, digital image, and multimedia encryption technology will undoubtedly face more challenges and opportunities. Therefore, continuous innovation and improvement are essential to adapt to the ever-changing network environment and meet the data security requirements.

1.5   Multimedia digital signature technology and multimedia authentication technology

1.5.1   *Multimedia digital signature technology and multimedia security*

The current literature examines various aspects of multimedia security and its applications. Pooja *et al.* (2018) [55] discussed the relationship between multimedia digital signature technology and multimedia security, and introduce the basics of digital signatures. The authors conducted an overview of the definition, process, characteristics, and algorithm of digital signatures and discussed the problems encountered in their application and realization. Arora (2018) [56] presented a robust digital watermarking algorithm for digital images based on wavelet transform and singular value decomposition. The author conducts a comparative experiment on the algorithm. The results demonstrated its effectiveness in protecting the privacy of image content and the reliability of the watermark, with good robustness and undetectability. Bejan *et al.* (2018) [57] explored the application of multimedia information and communication technology in reminiscence therapy for the elderly and found that multimedia therapy can improve the self-expression ability of the elderly, enhance their sense of participation, and improve their mental health. The authors offered new ideas for the application of information and communications technology in the care and treatment of the elderly. Al Hashimi *et al.* (2019) [58] proposed a multimedia-based teaching method that can enhance students' creativity and self-confidence and significantly positively impact their educational effectiveness and interpersonal relationships. The method can also support students' independent learning, enhance their hands-on and collaboration abilities, and improve their comprehensive quality and future development potential. Hurrah *et al.* (2019) [59] introduced an intricate multimedia framework for ensuring privacy protection and content authentication based on double digital watermarking. To fortify the framework, the author fused multiple algorithms, including the discrete wavelet transform and the discrete cosine transform, to boost the watermark's robustness and heighten the authentication efficacy. The framework proficiently accomplished the double protection of multimedia information by encrypting confidential data and appending digital watermarks for content authentication. In the realm of online education, copyright protection has become an increasingly critical issue. To address this concern, Guo *et al.* (2020) [60] proposed a digital rights management (DRM) scheme built on a blockchain platform. The scheme aims to protect copyright and prevent infringement of online educational multimedia resources. It achieves this by guaranteeing the identity of copyright, access control, and the integrity of the transmission path for various resources. The experimental results demonstrated that the DRM scheme effectively reduces the occurrence of copyright infringement and plagiarism, promoting the healthy development of online education.

Kumar *et al.* (2020) [61] provided a comprehensive overview of the recent research progress in digital watermarking in multimedia and database applications. The authors introduced the classification, principle, and application fields of digital watermarking algorithms and analyzed and compared existing algorithms according to their application fields. Additionally, they discussed the future development directions and challenges of digital watermarking technology. Yilmaz *et al.* (2022) [62] conducted a bibliometric analysis to explore the research trends in the field of foreign language teaching in preschool education. Their analysis reveals the research hotspots in multilingual learning, teaching strategies, and assessment methods, as well as identifying unresolved issues and future research directions in this area. Li *et al.* (2022) [63] proposed a blockchain-based privacy-preserving authentication system for protecting the authenticity of multimedia content. They used the zero-knowledge proof mechanism to enhance security and provide an authentication service for content integrity and privacy protection in a decentralized environment. The experimental results demonstrated that the proposed system is effective and capable of protecting multimedia content. In their recent study, Wang *et al.* (2022) [64] put forth an innovative multimedia data auditing scheme that operates on a blockchain platform for IoT cloud computing. The authors suggested a structured audit approach that includes a data audit protocol based on smart contracts, enabling IoT devices to perform more efficient and secure audit functions. The experimental results indicated that the proposed scheme performs well in both time and space efficiency, signifying its potential to address the challenges of multimedia data auditing in IoT cloud computing. Alagheband *et al.* (2022) [65] put forward a cutting-edge privacy protection and trust management technology, which is based on digital signatures and applied in hierarchical distributed IoT. The authors extensively categorized advanced applications of digital signatures and rigorously analyzed their capabilities and goals. Their experimental results indicated that this technology is effective in safeguarding data privacy, enhancing data trust, and driving forward the development of IoT technology. Li *et al.* (2023) [66] proposed a defense method against deep neural network watermarking attacks using a linear functional equivalence attack method and a neuron mapping defense method. This defense

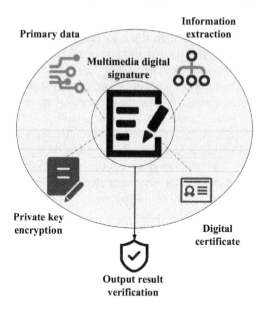

Figure 1.4   *Network structure of multimedia digital signature technology*

method could significantly enhance the confidentiality and security of network watermarking.

Furthermore, multimedia digital signature technology is commonly used for result verification through different links, such as raw material extraction, information collection, private key encryption, and digital certificate authentication. Figure 1.4 shows the specific network structure of multimedia digital signature technology.

To synthesize, the aforementioned studies have investigated the implementation and prospective trajectory of digital security across diverse domains. Notably, investigations have been conducted on various issues within the realm of digital security, and multiple approaches have been proposed to address these issues. Among the areas that have been explored are digital watermarking, privacy preservation, and digital signature, and these approaches are crucial in various application fields. Moreover, certain studies have examined the hurdles and upcoming paths of digital security technologies. These inquiries have made noteworthy strides toward safeguarding data privacy and integrity, elevating data trust, and boosting data auditing efficiency.

1.5.2   *Multimedia authentication technology and multimedia security*

Several studies have been conducted in different fields to elucidate the intricate relationship between multimedia authentication technology and multimedia security. Mishra *et al.* (2018) [67] proposed an efficient authentication protocol based on a key exchange scheme for multimedia communication security of IoT wireless sensor networks, which achieved reliable and efficient authentication of communication data under the condition of low computational overhead. In the intelligent industrial environment, Sajjad *et al.* (2019) [68] proposed a security authentication method based on image hashing to ensure privacy protection and reliable identification and authentication of industrial data. Fadi *et al.* (2020) [69] developed a comprehensive authentication scheme for intelligent industrial application systems, which integrated multi-factor authentication technology and ensured system data security. Hasan *et al.* (2021) [70] embedded identification protection into the image based on digital watermarking technology, which ensured the reliability of the authenticity and integrity of image data. Mehraj *et al.* (2021) [71] designed a security authentication scheme for social networks using protection motivation and multi-factor authentication technology, which improved the security and privacy protection of user data. Ogundokun *et al.* (2021) [72] combined image steganography and other technologies to ensure the confidential transmission of medical text information and improve the security protection level of text data transmission in the medical field. These studies demonstrate the diverse applications of multimedia authentication technology and its potential for enhancing multimedia security in different fields.

Gautham *et al.* (2021) [73] proposed a security authentication method based on convolutional neural networks for wireless multimedia devices, improving the security of wireless devices. Dolan *et al.* (2022) [74] designed a hotspot network user authentication system, improving network security and ensuring reliable identification of hotspot network user identities. Rusdan *et al.* (2022) [75] provided a user identity authentication method based on multi-factor authentication technology for wireless distribution systems, ensuring multi-directional identification and authentication of wireless network user identities and ensuring network data security. Tosun *et al.* (2022) [76] introduced a new assessment tool called the "Safety Social Networking Assessment Scale" for assessing the security status of social network users, which has high accuracy and practicability. Kim *et al.* (2022) [77] proposed a security authentication protocol for the multi-access edge computing environment, improving the security and reliability of mobile multimedia services. Raut *et al.* (2022) [78] employed the elliptic curve Diffie-Hellman (ECDH) algorithm security authentication protocol for the Internet of Vehicles, improving the security and data privacy protection of the Internet of Vehicles system.

Multimedia authentication technology covers various links, such as data security broadcasting, data security storage, multimedia content analysis, and security management strategy optimization. A schematic representation of the specific structural process is shown in Figure 1.5.

In summary, the aforementioned studies have primarily focused on discussing security authentication methods and technical applications in the wireless internet environment. These investigations have encompassed several domains and aspects, including device identification, user identity authentication, security assessment, mobile multimedia services, and the Internet of Vehicles. The importance of these studies lies in their ability to enhance the security of wireless networks and devices,

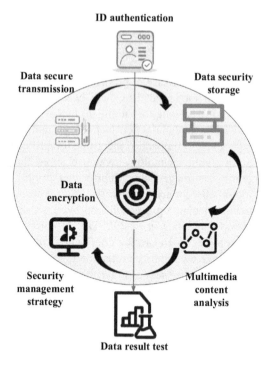

Figure 1.5   *Structural flow of multimedia authentication technology and multimedia security*

safeguard the confidentiality and privacy of user data, enhance network availability and stability, and guarantee the dependability of network interactions.

1.6   Chapter introduction

1.6.1   *Preserving multimedia information security through the use of fractal-based cryptosystems*

Unquestionably, the multimedia information security applications and trends are advancing at a high speed of light, despite all malicious threats and intentions of hackers. From the cryptosystem design to the hardware implementation, the cryptographic applications continue to attest its efficiency and various aptitudes of use in several sensitive sectors such as the medical and military ones, requiring indeed a high performance of security, privacy conservation, and low energy consumption. Nevertheless, the information security field continues to attract hackers who never skip the opportunity of interfering and stealing or damaging confidential data.

This chapter provides a brief overview of recent works and solutions suggested for efficient multimedia information security using various theories such as the chaos theory, cellular automata structures, and algebraic operators alongside some reconfigurable technologies-based approaches. Throughout this chapter, a secure application combining fractal bases, cellular structures, and chaotic attractors is proposed, to be an efficient approach for multimedia information security with low power consumption and high-speed processing competence in data safe storage and transmission.

1.6.2   Security of an image utilizing modified use of DWT and SVD along with multiple watermarking

In the case of digital communication, the security of a signal is the most important factor. Security can be ensured by several techniques. In this chapter, the security of an image is developed by using digital watermarking. In the proposed technique image as well as audio signals are used as watermarks which are the proofs of the true owner of the image being sent. To embed the watermarks into the host image, the total energy of both the host and the watermark signals are divided several times. These energy divisions are performed by using discrete wavelet transform (DWT) and singular value decomposition (SVD). The energy divisions are incorporated for utilizing the total energy distribution of the host signal for embedding the watermarks. For this, the developed technique ensures the insertion of a large piece of information into the host signal. Apart from that, the developed technique distributes the energy of the watermark signals into the entire region of the host signal which will create difficulty in removing or destroying the watermarks by the unwanted parties. The proposed technique offers a PSNR (Peak Signal to Noise Ratio) of 63.7525 dB and normalized cross-correlation (NC) close to 0.9. The robustness is tested not only against conventional attacks but also against real-life scenarios.

1.6.3   Machine/deep learning techniques for multimedia security

Multimedia security based on machine learning (ML)/deep learning (DL) is a research field that focuses on using ML/DL technology to protect multimedia data such as images, videos, and audio from unauthorized access, manipulation, or theft. Developing and implementing algorithms and systems that use ML/DL technology to detect and prevent security vulnerabilities in multimedia data is the main topic in this field. These systems use technologies such as watermarking, encryption, and digital signature verification to protect multimedia data. The advantages of using ML/DL in multimedia security include improved accuracy, scalability, and automation. The ML/DL algorithm can improve the accuracy of detecting security threats and help identify multimedia data vulnerabilities. In addition, the ML model can be enlarged to handle a large amount of multimedia data, thus helping to protect the big dataset. Finally, the ML/DL algorithm can automate the multimedia security process, making protecting multimedia data easier and more efficient. The drawbacks of using ML/DL in multimedia security include data availability, complexity, and black box models. ML and DL algorithms require a large amount of data to train models, which can be challenging at times. Developing and implementing ML algorithms can also be complex and require professional skills and knowledge. Finally, ML/DL models are usually black-box models, which means it is difficult to understand how they make decisions. This can be a challenge when explaining decisions to stakeholders or auditors. Overall, multimedia security based on ML/DL is a promising research field with many potential benefits. However, it also presents challenges that must be addressed to ensure the security and privacy of multimedia data.

The rapid development of multimedia technology has brought new difficulties to maintaining the integrity and authenticity of digital media information. This chapter investigates the concept of multimedia security, with a focus on identifying deepfakes, which are fake media generated using DL methods. We have discussed many methods and ML strategies to address these security issues. News, entertainment, and politics are just a few industries that face serious threats from deepfakes, as they may be used to influence and mislead audiences. To maintain the credibility and reliability of multimedia materials, deep forgery detection is essential. The dangers associated with deepfakes can now be identified and mitigated through the use of ML algorithms. We study the Supervised learning, Unsupervised learning, and Mixture model used in deep forgery detection and other ML technologies. Cellular neural network and neural network, two types of Supervised learning methods, have proved promising results in separating actual materials and manipulating materials. These models are trained using labeled datasets to develop their ability to distinguish between actual and fraudulent samples. Deep forgery detection also uses Unsupervised learning techniques like generative adversarial networks (GANs). The discriminator network that attempts to distinguish between real and fraudulent samples and the generator network that generates synthetic media form GAN. GANs can learn to create increasingly realistic media while continuously enhancing generator and discriminator networks to achieve precise deep forgery detection. To improve the effectiveness of deep forgery detection system, the Mixture model combines the advantages of supervised and Unsupervised learning methods. These models can improve the generalization ability and resistance to adversarial attacks by combining labeled and unlabeled data. The value of dataset management and expansion in training deep forgery detection models was also introduced. For the model to be trained that can successfully identify deepfakes in actual environments, various representative datasets must be provided. The ability of the model to promote and identify previously unrecognized depth forgery variants can also be improved by using data enhancement techniques such as image and comparison of video converters. The deep forgery detection technology based on ML has achieved encouraging results, but there are still some problems. An important obstacle is adversarial attacks, where deep forgers attempt to deceive detection models. Research is currently underway to create more resilient models that can survive such attacks and adapt to new deep forgery generation methods.

In summary, deep forgery detection is crucial for ensuring the effectiveness and reliability of multimedia materials. Multimedia security is an important issue in the current digital age. ML methods (such as Supervised learning, Unsupervised learning, and Mixture model) can be used to identify and mitigate the danger of deep forgery. By utilizing various carefully planned datasets and data augmentation techniques, these models can achieve higher accuracy and resilience. However, to counter the constantly evolving adversarial attacks and deep forgery generation technologies, further research and development are needed.

1.6.4   Blockchain-envisioned arbitrable multimedia data auditing based on post quantum computing paradigm in IoT

With many users hoping to outsource large multimedia data from Internet of Things (IoT) devices to the cloud, data auditing has become increasingly important. This is because it allows users to confirm the accuracy of their outsourced data. However, most of the existing data audit technologies cannot ensure comprehensive data integrity, which is an important prerequisite to meet the security requirements of valuable multimedia services. In addition, when cloud service providers (CSPs) tamper with outsourced data, users do not receive timely compensation due to a lack of fair competition.

This chapter introduces a blockchain-driven approach to achieve arbitrable data auditing. In the proposed system, users typically only need to perform private audits, and only when the verification of private audits is unsuccessful will smart contracts be triggered to perform public audits. The proposed hybrid audit method prevents users from paying audit fees and quickly recovering when CSP destroys outsourced data. In addition, the proposed system can ensure 100% data integrity by using the deterministic check technology based on the Number Theory Research Unit (NTRU) lattice accumulator. In addition, when users wish to receive compensation from CSP, the proposed solution can prevent forged claims. After evaluating the safety benefits, we completed the implementation of the prototype. The test results of the proposed blockchain-based data audit system demonstrate its security, efficiency, and benefits.

1.6.5   Privacy-preserving identification for monitoring images

The camera sensor embedded in the monitoring unit or mobile phone can easily capture various personal images in daily life. Machine learning, especially deep learning, provides an elegant way to recognize images (such as character recognition, facial recognition, and facial expression recognition). However, personal images typically involve a large amount of sensitive data, such as identity, facial features, and facial expressions. Therefore, image recognition poses a serious challenge to privacy breaches such as personal identity, facial data, and facial expressions. Both GDPR (General Data Protection Regulations) and EDPS (European Data Protection Supervisory Authority) stipulate that surveillance images involve private data and are prone to violating basic privacy rights.

In this chapter, we first reviewed the privacy issues in surveillance image recognition and then formalized the privacy protection recognition of surveillance images. Next, we provide a general framework for implementing privacy protection monitoring image recognition and discuss the re-identification of privacy protection personnel based on this framework. Finally, we summarized the challenges in our research and attempted to explore some new research directions in privacy protection monitoring image recognition.

1.6.6   Analysis phases in multimedia data forensics for source identification, deleted data reconstruction, and perpetrator identification

In the field of digital forensics, the analysis of multimedia data plays a crucial role in revealing the truth behind criminal activities.

This chapter delves into the complex analysis stages used in multimedia data forensics, mainly focusing on source identification, timestamp identification, and offender identification. This chapter explores the methods and techniques for digital forensics experts to extract valuable insights from multimedia data, enabling them to identify the source of the data and, where possible, individuals responsible for cybercrime. This chapter mainly analyzes multimedia metadata. Therefore, no technical details of evidence acquisition were provided. However, this article briefly mentions appropriate evidence acquisition. Through a comprehensive study of the analysis stage in multimedia data forensics, this chapter provides valuable insights into the methods used to uncover the truth behind criminal activities and supports the development of forensic investigations in the digital age.

1.6.7   Secure interaction and processing of multimedia data in the Internet of Things based on wearable devices

The Internet of Things (IoT) has greatly improved technology by accelerating data collection, interpretation, and dissemination. In the Internet of Things network, sensor nodes or devices are connected through the use of data communication technology. Widespread applications of the Internet of Things are becoming increasingly popular, such as smart cars, smart homes, smart agriculture, and smart industries. However, these networks face various challenges, including adaptability, compatibility, and security. Due to the exchange and transmission of personal data by users, security always comes first. There are various types of security threats in these networks.

This chapter explores security threats, attacks, and other vulnerabilities in these networks. This chapter also introduces detection and prevention methods designed for multimedia data security. Due to the limited equipment resources of IoT networks, these networks require lightweight security solutions. This chapter summarizes the findings on preventing these networks from any type of security violation and provides a roadmap for new researchers in the field.

1.6.8   Violence detection in videos: a review on hand-crafted and deep-learning techniques

Violence is a widespread destructive force in society, causing physical and mental harm to victims and their families. The impact of violence is not limited to individuals but also has broader social consequences, including increased medical costs, decreased productivity, and decreased quality of life. To address this issue, an intelligent closed-circuit television (CCTV) system has been developed to prevent violent incidents in public and private places. These systems use advanced technologies such as computer vision and machine learning to analyze human behavior and detect violent behavior.

In recent years, people have become increasingly interested in developing automatic violence recognition systems that can accurately identify violent behavior in real-time. These systems use a range of technologies, from traditional manual methods to state-of-the-art deep learning algorithms, to analyze video clips and detect violent behavior. The purpose of this book chapter is to comprehensively review violence identification methods, including their advantages and limitations.

In addition to discussing the technical aspects of violence recognition systems, this chapter also investigates publicly available violence datasets for experimentation and evaluation. These datasets are crucial for training and testing brute force recognition algorithms, and their availability has led researchers to make significant progress in this field.

Finally, this chapter discusses the remaining challenges in developing effective violence recognition systems, including issues related to real-time reasoning, generalization capabilities, and the need for more diverse datasets. Future research directions in this field were also introduced, emphasizing the potential of new technologies to enhance violence recognition capabilities.

Overall, this chapter of the book provides a comprehensive overview of methods for identifying violence and emphasizes the importance of continuing research in this field to address the persistent issues of violence in society.

1.6.9   Image compression-encryption scheme using SPIHT and 2D-BCM

With the advancement of network technology, data sharing on the internet has also significantly increased. Images are the most shared data on the internet. However, certain information is sensitive and requires secure storage or transmission, especially when communicating over insecure channels. Digital images typically exhibit high data correlation, where compression can be performed to reduce the load on transmission channels and storage memory.

To address the above issues, this chapter proposes an algorithm that combines image compression and encryption techniques. The algorithm uses Partition of a set (SPIHT) technology in a hierarchical tree for image compression. After compression, the algorithm continues to encrypt the compressed image. It achieves this by processing chaotic sequences generated using two-dimensional beta chaotic maps (2D-BCM) and permutation diffusion structures. Based on experimental results and security analysis, the compression encryption algorithm has high sensitivity and security. Therefore, this algorithm demonstrates its ability to resist selected plaintext attacks.

1.6.10   Enhancing medical image security: a look into crypto-watermarking method via LabVIEW

This chapter proposes a new method for watermarking and encrypting medical images using Haar discrete wavelet transform (DWT). The proposed system aims to securely embed the patient's private information into medical images, and then encrypt the watermarked images using a chaotic-based cryptographic system to enhance robustness. Our method uses standard grayscale to embed the patient's private data, and the insertion block follows the Haar DWT process. The encryption stage combines the SHA-2 hash function and Rossler chaotic system for key generation, ensuring confusion and diffusion to enhance security. This system includes transmitting encrypted data with watermarks to the cloud, enabling authorized parties to securely access and retrieve watermarked data. The proposed system was successfully implemented using LabVIEW on the MyRIO board, demonstrating its practicality and functionality. The performance is evaluated through various attacks on the system, including compression, noise, filtering, and geometric transformation. The experimental results show that the watermark process has low distortion, strong robustness, and enhanced security during the encryption phase.

1.6.11   Detection of secret information in the processing of multimedia information

This chapter introduces the overview of steganography and the requirements for JPEG compression resistance. In addition, we also analyze the JPEG compression resistance of steganography using the correlation characteristics of the DCT domain proposed by us. Surprisingly, we found that our proposed steganography is likely to minimize the file size of the steganography image while maintaining the secret information recovery performance by setting the quality factor to a specific area slightly higher than all embedding strengths.

1.6.12   Trustworthy grant-free random access in an untrusted shared network: dilemma, solution, and evaluation

The proliferation of Internet of Things (IoT) applications has made traditional cloud-centric network architectures inadequate. It is divided by multiple non-cooperative operators, hindering the scalability of future IoT development. However, the lack of trust within multiple operator networks has led to a rogue dilemma, where rogue devices may skip the required backoff, gaining an unfair advantage and potentially leading to network congestion. Therefore, there is an urgent need for groundbreaking access protocols tailored to untrustworthy multi-operator networks. In this chapter, we introduce Hash Access, a trusted unauthorized random access protocol that enables multi-operator networks without shared authentication. By using hash access, IoT devices can be forced to comply with access rules and regulate data traffic, effectively reducing the loss of network efficiency caused by selfish behavior among rogue devices. We further established a comprehensive analysis model for hash access to comprehensively evaluate the performance of various aspects. The simulation results validate the effectiveness of hash access and provide practical design guidelines.

References

[1] Febriyanti, BD: 'Nilai Karakter Dalam Film Tanah Surga Katanya Sebagai Alternatif Media Pembelajaran', *Jurnal Pendidikan*, 2023, 11, (1), pp. 32–45.

[2] Rindawati, T., Thamrin, L., Lusi, L.: 'Penggunaan Media Audio Visual Film Kartun dalam Pembelajaran Kosakata Bahasa Mandarin pada Siswa SD LKIA', *Jurnal Tunas Bangsa*, 2022, 9, (1), pp. 1–10.

[3] Hao, Y., Ba, N., Ren, S., *et al.*: 'How does international technology spillover affect China's carbon emissions? A new perspective through intellectual property protection', *Sustainable Production and Consumption*, 2021, 25, pp. 577–590.

[4] Bamakan, SMH, Nezhadistani, N., Bodaghi, O., *et al.*: 'Patents and intellectual property assets as non-fungible tokens; key technologies and challenges', *Scientific Reports*, 2022, 12, (1), pp. 1–13.

[5] Koh, D., Santaeulàlia-Llopis, R., Zheng, Y.: 'Labor share decline and intellectual property products capital', *Econometrica*, 2020, 88, (6), pp. 2609–2628.

[6] Lv, Z.: 'Security of internet of things edge devices', *Software: Practice and Experience*, 2021, 51, (12), pp. 2446–2456.

[7] Hausmann, A., Toivonen, T., Slotow, R., *et al.*: 'Social media data can be used to understand tourists' preferences for nature-based experiences in protected areas', *Conservation Letters*, 2018, 11, (1), pp. e12343.

[8] Dolan, R., Conduit, J., Frethey-Bentham, C., *et al.*: 'Social media engagement behavior: a framework for engaging customers through social media content', *European Journal of Marketing*, 2019, 53, (10), pp. 2213–2243.

[9] Garg, S., Kaur, K., Kumar, N., *et al.*: 'Hybrid deep-learning-based anomaly detection scheme for suspicious flow detection in SDN: a social multimedia perspective', *IEEE Transactions on Multimedia*, 2019, 21, (3), pp. 566–578.

[10] Verdoliva, L.: 'Media forensics and deepfakes: an overview', *IEEE Journal of Selective Topics in Signal Processing*, 2020, 14, (5), pp. 910–932.

[11] Namasudra, S., Chakraborty, R., Majumder, A., *et al.*: 'Securing multimedia by using DNA-based encryption in the cloud computing environment', *ACM Transactios on Multimedia Computing, Communications, and Applications*, 2020, 16, (3s), pp. 1–19.

[12] Rathee, G., Sharma, A., Saini, H., *et al.*: 'A hybrid framework for multimedia data processing in IoT-healthcare using blockchain technology', *Multimedia Tools Applications*, 2020, 79, (15–16), pp. 9711–9733.

[13] Zalisham, FABHAM, Jali, MNN: 'Preliminary study on IT security maintenance management in Malaysia organizations', *PalArch's Journal of Archaeology Egypt/ Egyptology*, 2021, 18, (1), pp. 4061–4073.

[14] Shang, Y., Zhang, J.: 'Computer multimedia security protection system based on the network security active defense model', *Advances in Multimedia*, 2021, 2021, pp. 1–9.

[15]   Khan, AA, Shaikh, AA, Shaikh, ZA, *et al.*: 'IPM-Model: AI and metaheuristic-enabled face recognition using image partial matching for multimedia forensics investigation with genetic algorithm', *Multimedia Tools Applications*, 2022, 81, (17), pp. 23533–23549.

[16]   Tolba, Z., Derdour, M., Ferrag, MA, *et al.*: 'Automated deep learning BLACK-BOX attack for multimedia P-BOX security assessment', *IEEE Access*, 2022, 10, pp. 94019–94039.

[17]   Cecchinato, N., Toma, A., Drioli, C., *et al.*: 'A secure real-time multimedia streaming through robust and lightweight AES encryption in UAV networks for operational scenarios in military domain', *Procedia Computer Science*, 2022, 205, pp. 50–57.

[18]   Li, M., Yue, Y.: 'Security analysis and improvement of dual watermarking framework for multimedia privacy protection and content authentication', *Mathematics*, 2023, 11, (7), pp. 1689.

[19]   Zhang, Y., Qian, Y., Wu, D., *et al.*: 'Emotion-aware multimedia systems security', *IEEE Transactions Multimedia*, 2018, 21, (3), pp. 617–624.

[20]   Ahmad, N., Quadri, NN, Qureshi, MRN, *et al.*: 'Relationship modeling of critical success factors for enhancing sustainability and performance in e-learning', *Sustainability*, 2018, 10, (12), pp. 4776.

[21]   Hu, H., Zhang, H., Yang, Y.: 'Security risk situation quantification method based on threat prediction for multimedia communication network', *Multimedia Tools and Applications*, 2018, 77, pp. 21693–21723.

[22]   KM, DR Yum, SH, Ko, E., *et al.*: 'Multi-media and multi-band based adaptation layer techniques for underwater sensor networks', *Applied Sciences*, 2019, 9(15), pp. 3187.

[23]   Chen, JIZ, Smys, S.: 'Social multimedia security and suspicious activity detection in SDN using hybrid deep learning technique', *Journal of Information Technology*, 2020, 2(02), pp. 108–115.

[24]   Shandilya, SK, Upadhyay, S., Kumar, A., *et al.*: 'AI-assisted computer network operations testbed for nature-inspired cyber security based adaptive defense simulation and analysis', *Future Generation Computer Systems*, 2022, 127, pp. 297–308.

[25]   Zhang, G., Ma, C., Chen, K., *et al.*: 'Multiple-symbol noncoherent learning detection of coded QAM signals in IEEE 802.15.3 wireless multi-media networks', *Physical Communication*, 2022, 55, pp. 101922.

[26]   Safhi, A., Al-Zahrani, A., Alhibbi, M.: 'Major security issue that facing social networks with its main defense strategies', *Tehnički glasnik*, 2022, 16 (2), pp. 205–212.

[27]   Sathish, C., Rubavathi, CY: 'A survey on Blockchain mechanisms (BCM) based on internet of things (IoT) applications', *Multimedia Tools and Applications*, 2022, 81(23), pp. 33419–33458.

[28]   Al-Hazaimeh, OM, Abu-Ein, AA, Al-Nawashi, MM, *et al.*: 'Chaotic based multimedia encryption: a survey for network and internet security', *Bulletin of Electrical Engineering and Informatics*, 2022, 11(4), pp. 2151–2159.

[29] Gadde, S., Amutharaj, J., Usha, S.: 'Cloud multimedia data security by optimization-assisted cryptographic technique', *Internation Journal of Image and Graphics*, 2023, 10.1142/S0219467824500104.

[30] Nawaz, NA, Ishaq, K., Farooq, U., *et al.*: 'A comprehensive review of security threats and solutions for the online social networks industry', *PeerJ Computer Science*, 2023, 9, e1143.

[31] Zear, A., Singh, AK, Kumar, P.: 'Multiple watermarking for healthcare applications', *Journal of Intelligent Systems*, 2018, 27(1), pp. 5–18.

[32] Kumar, C., Singh, AK, Kumar, P.: 'A recent survey on image watermarking techniques and its application in e-governance', *Multimedia Tools and Applications*, 2018, 77, pp. 3597–3622.

[33] Menendez-Ortiz, A., Feregrino-Uribe, C., Hasimoto-Beltran, R., *et al.*: 'A survey on reversible watermarking for multimedia content: a robustness overview', *IEEE Access*, 2019, 7, pp. 132662–132681.

[34] Thakur, S., Singh, AK, Ghrera, SP, *et al.*: 'Multi-layer security of medical data through watermarking and chaotic encryption for tele-health applications', *Multimedia Tools and Applications*, 2019, 78, pp. 3457–3470.

[35] Singh, AK: 'Robust and distortion control dual watermarking in LWT domain using DCT and error correction code for color medical image', *Multimedia Tools and Applications*, 2019, 78, pp. 30523–30533.

[36] Ray, A., Roy, S.: 'Recent trends in image watermarking techniques for copyright protection: a survey', *International Journal of Multimedia Information Retrieval*, 2020, 9(4), pp. 249–270.

[37] Kaur, A., Singh, P., Nayyar, A.: 'Robust multimedia watermarking: characteristics, applications, and attacks', in *Handbook of Research on Multimedia Cyber Security*, 2020, pp. 73–89.

[38] Faragallah, OS, Afifi, A., El-Sayed, HS, *et al.*: 'Efficient HEVC integrity verification scheme for multimedia cybersecurity applications', *IEEE Access*, 2020, 8, pp. 167069–167089.

[39] Anand, A., Singh, AK: 'Watermarking techniques for medical data authentication: a survey', *Multimedia tools and applications*, 2021, 80, pp. 30165–30197.

[40] Singh, OP, Singh, AK, Srivastava, G., *et al.*: 'Image watermarking using soft computing techniques: a comprehensive survey', *Multimedia tools and applications*, 2021, 80, pp. 30367–30398.

[41] Zainol, Z., Teh, JS, Alawida, M., *et al.*: 'Hybrid SVD-based image watermarking schemes: a review', *IEEE Access*, 2021, 9, pp. 32931–32968.

[42] Sridhar, B., Syambabu, V.: 'Analysis of watermarking techniques in multimedia communications', *Serbian Journal of Electrical Engineering*, 2021, 18(3), pp. 321–332.

[43] Li, C., Lin, D., Lü, J., *et al.*: 'Cryptanalyzing an image encryption algorithm based on autoblocking and electrocardiography', *IEEE multimedia*, 2018, 25 (4), pp. 46–56.

[44]　Cox, IJ, Miller, ML, Linnartz, JPMG, *et al.*: 'A review of watermarking principles and practices 1', *Digital signal processing for multimedia systems*, 2018, pp. 461–485.

[45]　Shifa, A., Asghar, MN, Noor, S., *et al.*: 'Lightweight cipher for H. 264 videos in the Internet of multimedia things with encryption space ratio diagnostics', *Sensors*, 2019, 19(5), pp. 1228.

[46]　Han, C.: 'An image encryption algorithm based on modified logistic chaotic map', *Optik*, 2019, 181, pp. 779–785.

[47]　Sivakumar, T., Li, P.: 'A secure image encryption method using scan pattern and random key stream derived from laser chaos', *Optics & Laser Technology*, 2019, 111, pp. 196–204.

[48]　Xiong, Z., Wu, Y., Ye, C., *et al.*: 'Color image chaos encryption algorithm combining CRC and nine palace map', *Multimedia tools and applications*, 2019, 78(22), pp. 31035–31055.

[49]　Hamad, AS, Farhan, AK: 'Image encryption algorithm based on substitution principle and shuffling scheme', *Engineering and Technology Journal*, 2020, 38(3B), pp. 98–103.

[50]　Bhat, SA, Singh, A.: 'A novel image encryption algorithm using multiple encryption techniques for mobile devices', *International Journal of Sensors Wireless Communications and Control*, 2020, 10(2), pp. 123–142.

[51]　Tariq, S., Khan, M., Alghafis, A., *et al.*: 'A novel hybrid encryption scheme based on chaotic Lorenz system and logarithmic key generation', *Multimedia Tools and Applications*, 2020, 79, pp. 23507–23529.

[52]　Lamiche, C.: 'An Effective Encryption Scheme Based on Chaotic Maps Applied to Digital Image', *Multimedia Security Using Chaotic Maps: Principles and Methodologies*, 2020, pp. 187–198.

[53]　Koppanati, RK, Kumar, K.: 'P-MEC: polynomial congruence-based multimedia encryption technique over cloud', *IEEE Consumer Electronics Magazine*, 2020, 10(5), pp. 41–46.

[54]　Abdelfatah, RI, Nasr, ME, Alsharqawy, MA: 'Encryption for multimedia based on chaotic map: several scenarios', *Multimedia Tools and Applications*, 2020, 79, pp. 19717–19738.

[55]　Pooja, M., Yadav, M.: 'Digital signature', *International Journal of Scientific Research in Computer Science, Engineering and Information Technology (IJSRCSEIT)*, 2018, 3(6), pp. 71–75.

[56]　Arora, SM: 'A DWT-SVD based robust digital watermarking for digital images', *Procedia Computer Science*, 2018, 132, pp. 1441–1448.

[57]　Bejan, A., Gündogdu, R., Butz, K., *et al.* 'Using multimedia information and communication technology (ICT) to provide added value to reminiscence therapy for people with dementia: lessons learned from three field studies', *Zeitschrift fur Gerontologie und Geriatrie*, 2018, 51(1), pp. 9–15.

[58]　Al Hashimi, S., Al Muwali, A., Zaki, Y., *et al.* 'The effectiveness of social media and multimedia-based pedagogy in enhancing creativity among art, design, and digital media students', *International Journal of Emerging Technologies in Learning (iJET)*, 2019, 14(21), pp. 176–190.

[59] Hurrah, NN, Parah, SA, Loan, NA, *et al.* 'Dual watermarking framework for privacy protection and content authentication of multimedia', *Future generation computer systems*, 2019, 94, pp. 654–673.

[60] Guo, J., Li, C., Zhang, G., *et al.* 'Blockchain-enabled digital rights management for multimedia resources of online education', *Multimedia Tools and Applications*, 2020, 79, pp. 9735–9755.

[61] Kumar, S., Singh, BK, Yadav, M. 'A recent survey on multimedia and database watermarking', *Multimedia Tools and Applications*, 2020, 79, pp. 20149–20197.

[62] Yilmaz, RM, Topu, FB, Takkaç Tulgar, A. 'An examination of the studies on foreign language teaching in pre-school education: a bibliometric mapping analysis', *Computer Assisted Language Learning*, 2022, 35(3), pp. 270–293.

[63] Li, X., Wei, L., Wang, L., *et al.* 'A blockchain-based privacy-preserving authentication system for ensuring multimedia content integrity', *International Journal of Intelligent Systems*, 2022, 37(5), pp. 3050–3071.

[64] Wang, S., Zhang, Y., Guo, Y. 'A blockchain-empowered arbitrary multimedia data auditing scheme in IoT cloud computing', *Mathematics*, 2022, 10 (6), pp. 1005.

[65] Alagheband, MR, Mashatan, A. 'Advanced digital signatures for preserving privacy and trust management in hierarchical heterogeneous IoT: taxonomy, capabilities, and objectives', *Internet of Things*, 2022, 18, pp. 100492.

[66] Li, FQ, Wang, SL, Liew, AWC 'Linear functionality equivalence attack against deep neural network watermarks and a defense method by neuron mapping', *IEEE Transactions on Information Forensics and Security*, 2023, 18, pp. 1963–1977.

[67] Mishra, D., Vijayakumar, P., Sureshkumar, V., *et al.* 'Efficient authentication protocol for secure multimedia communications in IoT-enabled wireless sensor network KS', *Multimedia Tools and Applications*, 2018, 77, PP. 18295–18325.

[68] Sajjad, M., Haq, IU, Lloret, J., *et al.* 'Robust image hashing based efficient authentication for smart industrial environment', *IEEE Transactions on Industrial Informatics*, 2019, 15(12), pp. 6541–6550.

[69] Fadi, ALT, Deebak, BD 'Seamless authentication: for IoT-big data technologies in smart industrial application systems', *IEEE Transactions on Industrial Informatics*, 2020, 17(4), pp. 2919–2927.

[70] Hasan, BMS, Ameen, SY, Hasan, OMS 'Image authentication based on watermarking approach', *Asian Journal of Research in Computer Science*, 2021, 9(3), pp. 34–51.

[71] Mehraj, H., Jayadevappa, D., Haleem, SLA, *et al.* 'Protection motivation theory using multi-factor authentication for providing security over social networking sites', *Pattern Recognition Letters*, 2021, 152, pp. 218–224.

[72] Ogundokun, RO, Abikoye, OC 'A safe and secured medical textual information using an improved LSB image steganography', *International Journal of Digital Multimedia Broadcasting*, 2021, 2021, pp. 1–8.

[73] Gautham, SK, Koundinya, A. 'CNN-based security authentication for wireless multimedia devices', *Int. J. Wirel. Microw. Technol*, 2021, 11(4), pp. 1–10.

[74] Dolan, E., Widayanti, R. 'Implementation of authentication systems on hotspot network users to improve computer network security', *International Journal of Cyber and IT Service Management*, 2022, 2(1), pp. 88–94.

[75] Rusdan, M., Sabar, M. 'Design and analysis of wireless network with wireless distribution system using multi-factor authentication-based user authentication'. 2022.

[76] Tosun, N., Gecer, A. 'A development, validity and reliability of safe social networking scale', *Athens Journal of Mass Media Communications*, 2022, 8, pp. 179–200.

[77] Kim, J., Han, DG, You, I. 'Design of secure authentication handover protocol for innovative mobile multimedia services in 5G MEC environments', *Journal of Internet Technology*, 2022, 23(6), pp. 1245–1261.

[78] Raut, UK, Vishwamitra, LK 'Multi-level ECDH-based authentication protocol for secure software-defined VANET interaction', *International Journal of Mobile Computing and Multimedia Communications (IJMCMC)*, 2022, 13(1), pp. 1–28.

Chapter 2

Detection of secret information in the processing of multimedia information

Sumiko Miyata[1]

This chapter describes an overview of steganography and the need for JPEG compression resistance. Moreover, we analyze the JPEG compression resistance of steganography using the correlation properties of the Discrete Cosine Transform (DCT) domain that we have proposed. Surprisingly, we found that our proposed steganography has the potential to minimize the file size of stego images while maintaining the secret information recovery performance by setting the quality factor slightly above a certain region for all embedding strengths.

2.1 Introduction

Recently, many users upload and share multimedia information via social network services [1]. Thus, steganography that hides secret information in multimedia is also increasingly being used [2]. Steganography is such a technology and enables secure confidential communication by concealing confidential data in multimedia data such as images, video, music, and text [3]. Steganography is similar to encryption technology in terms of protecting information. Encryption converts data using a numerical sequence called a key, which is used for sending and receiving data. The encrypted data appears as a character string that cannot be understood by humans. Thus, a third party may easily determine that the encrypted data contain secret information. Steganography differs from encryption [4] in a way that important data are hidden in seemingly unimportant multimedia data, thus reducing the risk of attracting the attention of third parties.

Another technology that is similar to steganography is watermarking. Watermarking enables various functions such as copyright claiming and information tampering detection [5]. Watermarking also hides information in multimedia data; however, the requirements are different [6]. Table 2.1 lists the requirements for each technology. Note that this table shows a general summary and not for all cases. In both technologies, the following three factors are mainly considered.

[1]Department of Information and Communications Engineering, Shibaura Institute of Technology, Japan

Table 2.1   *Differences between steganography and*
watermarking

	Steganography	Watermarking
Embedding capacity	High	Low
Robustness	Low	High
Imperceptibility	High	High

The first is "embedding capacity", which is how much information can be embedded in the multimedia data. Since watermarking only needs to hide data, such as copyright, data to protect multimedia data, the priority of embedding capacity is low. In steganography, however, multimedia data are used as a communication medium, so the larger the embedding capacity, the better. The second is "robustness", which is how resistant the embedded data are to attacks such as common signal-processing operations. Since the data embedded in a watermark are intended to protect multimedia data, they must not be deleted. Therefore, the priority for robustness is high. Since the purpose of steganography is to communicate confidentially, it is acceptable for the data to be deleted. However, it is useful to have compression resistance so that the file size can be reduced. The third is "imperceptibility", which is how difficult the embedded data are to detect. Both watermarking and steganography should be prevented from being detected because it is easy to tamper or remove the data if detected.

Pictures using the steganographic method is called stego image, these stego images are compressed by using JPEG because these stego images are transmitted in the network with limited bandwidth [7]. Thus, stego images with JPEG compression need to detect secret information correctly. Some steganographic methods considering JPEG compression were proposed by JPEG UNIversal WAvelet Relative Distortion (J-UNIWARD) [8], uniform embedding revisited distortion (UERD) [9]. However, an embedding method is not proposed because these methods propose a kind of cost function [10].

There are many embedding methods for steganography such as Wavelet Obtained Weights (WOW) [11], High-pass, Low-pass, and Low-pass (HiLL) [12], and Minimizing the Power of Optimal Detector (MiPOD) [13]. However, these methods need to embed secret information in the texture region. Typically, when the secret information is concealed within texture regions of steganographic images and these images are compressed using JPEG, it becomes challenging to discern the hidden information.

As we mentioned, it is generally preferable to embed the largest possible amount of secret information in steganography. However, the more secret information is embedded in a cover image, the degradation in image quality becomes more pronounced. In other words, embedding capacity and carrier-image quality are in a trade-off relationship. Unnaturally degraded images are undesirable as they may attract the attention of third parties. Thus, we must attempt to embed the largest possible amount of secret information without image degradation.

In our previous study [14], we proposed a steganographic method that is an extension of the method used for watermarking [15]. We call this method correlation-based steganography. This method uses a Discrete Cosine Transform (DCT) and pseudo-random noise (PN) sequence such as an M-sequence, which has good correlation properties. However, a PN sequence is also used with spread spectrum image steganography (SSIS), which is a method based on code division multiple access (CDMA) [16]. The difference between SSIS and correlation-based steganography is how secret information is represented. With SSIS, secret information is transformed and represented by multiplying PN sequences with the binary secret information. With correlation-based steganography, secret information is represented by cyclic shifting PN sequences based on the decimal secret information. As a result, correlation-based steganography can increase the amount of information that can be represented by one PN sequence.

With correlation-based steganography, the main factor of image-quality degradation is the intensity factor multiplied by an M-sequence. Correlation-based steganography requires computing correlations to extract the information embedded in an image. In other words, the intensity factor is necessary for the accurate detection of embedded information. However, the larger the intensity factor, the more the image quality degrades.

To extend the watermarking method to steganography, we have to consider image-quality degradation. Steganography needs to be able to embed more information than watermarking. Therefore, it is necessary to consider an embedding method that can embed more information with less image degradation. In our previous study [17], we introduced the Reed-Solomon (RS) code and suppressed image-quality degradation by reducing the intensity factor.

On the other hand, if the stego image is a photograph, lossy compression formats such as JPEG are more natural and less likely to be suspected of having secret information embedded. Also, the image may be automatically lossy compressed again in the transmission path from sender to receiver. Moreover, if the secret information is not lost in JPEG compression, the file size of the stego image can be reduced while maintaining the probability of recovery, thus reducing storage and network usage. From the above, the resistance to JPEG compression determines the practicality of the steganography method. Therefore, we investigate the JPEG tolerance of the conventional method [17] in this chapter.

2.2   Framework of our correlation-based steganography

2.2.1   Overview

The conventional SSIS method uses an M-sequence to represent secret information in terms of the number of shifts and has been used for watermarking [15]. In our previous studies [14,17], we proposed a method that extends the conventional SSIS method to steganography. Our previous method, called correlation-based steganography, represents the secret information in M' sequences and embeds it in the DCT domain. Let W^0 be the original generated sequence of the M' sequence. It also

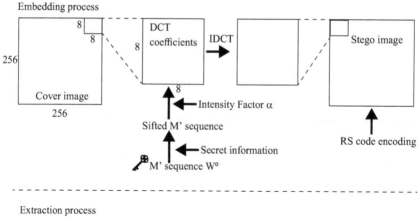

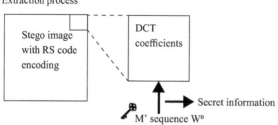

Figure 2.1   Overview of our method

recovers the secret information by correlating the M′ sequence with embedded DCT coefficients. There are two differences between correlation-based steganography and SSIS. The first is how the secret information is represented. The second is how the secret information is extracted because we use cyclic shifting PN sequences. The amount of information that can be represented in one sequence can be larger than with SSIS.

As shown in Figure 2.1, in our method, we use the introduced RS code and suppressed image quality degradation by intensity factor to detect secret information correctly. Note that a conventional watermarking [15] is not used because the image quality level with stego image needs to maintain a high level instead of watermarking image. In the extraction process, we can detect secret information by multiple M′ sequences W^0 and DCT coefficient with stego image.

2.2.2   Preliminaries

First, we explain important words and equations for our method.

2.2.2.1   Discrete Cosine Transform (DCT)

DCT is a common signal transformation algorithm used in the compression of coded data such as JPEG and MP4. It is also used in steganography. Specifically, DCT transforms the signal type from the spatial domain to the frequency domain.

With frequency-domain methods, to embed data in a carrier image, it is necessary to transform the carrier image, and DCT is a means of doing this. Generally, an image is divided into 8×8 blocks and transformed into the DCT domain, and the secret information is embedded in the non-zero coefficient of the DCT coefficient matrix [18,19]. The DCT coefficients are divided into high-, middle-, and low-frequency bands. Low-frequency bands significantly degrade image quality. Therefore, embedding information into low-frequency bands should be avoided. High-frequency bands do not significantly degrade image quality but are removed by compression. Therefore, middle-frequency bands are generally used for embedding [16].

2.2.2.2   M-sequence

An M-sequence is a periodic binary signal of length $L = 2^m - 1$ generated by the maximal-length linear-feedback shift register of degree m [20]. An M-sequence is characterized by the fact that the number of 1's and 0's is almost equal and the auto-correlation function is close to the delta function [21]. Namely, an M-sequence has good auto-correlation properties. Let $\{a_i\} = (a_0, a_1, ..., a_{L-1}, a_0, a_1, ...)$ be an M-sequence with $L = 2^m - 1$. This sequence is derived by the following m-th-order linear-regression equation:

$$\{a_i\} \equiv \sum_{l=1}^{m} c_l a_{i-l} \quad (\text{mod} \quad 2), \quad i = m, m+1, ... \tag{2.1}$$

A necessary and sufficient condition for a_i to be an M-sequence is that the polynomial is a primitive polynomial:

$$f(x) = \sum_{l=0}^{m} c_l x^l, \tag{2.2}$$

$$c_0 = c_m = 1, \quad c_l = 0, 1, \tag{2.3}$$

$$0 < l < m. \tag{2.4}$$

2.2.2.3   Representing secret information

In this study, we used the bit value 1 as $+1$ and the bit value 0 as -1 in an M-sequence. To represent the number up to $2^m - 1$, we add -1 to the end of the generated M-sequence. In this situation, the length of the sequence is $L = 2^m$. We call this M-sequence when $L = 2^m$ an M′ sequence. Then, let W^{t_M} ($M = 1, 2, ...; 0 \leq t_M \leq 2^m - 1$) be the generated M′ sequence, which shifts all elements, t_M times, to the right. Note that t_M is a decimal number and M is the number of M′ sequences. We assume that the number of times the generated M′ sequence is shifted directly represents secret information t_M. Figure 2.2 shows an example of converting secret information into an M′ sequence. To represent secret information "B" using an M′ sequence of length $L = 8$, we divide a 1-byte character into 3 bits and convert each 3 bit into a decimal number. We then shift W^0 twice, as shown in Figure 2.2, to represent the right bit sequence as an M′ sequence. In this case, W^{t_M} is W^2. By doing this for each bit sequence, a character can be represented by three M′ sequences.

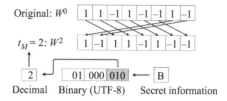

Figure 2.2   Secret information represented by M' sequence

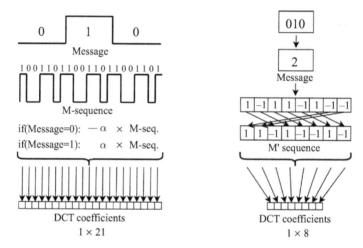

Figure 2.3   Comparison between SSIS and correlation-based steganography

The difference between correlation-based steganography and SSIS is that correlation-based steganography represents secret information in terms of the number of shifts. With SSIS, secret information is represented in binary and multiplied by the sequence; however, with correlation-based steganography, the sequence is shifted based on the decimal number. Figure 2.3 shows the representation and embedding of secret information with SSIS and correlation-based steganography. In this example, 1 bit is represented by an M-sequence of length 7, as shown in Figure 2.3(a). In other words, 21 DCT coefficients need to be changed to embed 3 bits of information in the image. With correlation-based steganography, 3 bits can be represented by a sequence of length $L = 8$, as shown in Figure 2.3(b). In other words, eight DCT coefficients need to be changed to embed 3 bits of information in the image. Therefore, with correlation-based steganography, the amount of information that can be represented in one sequence is larger than with SSIS.

2.2.2.4   Intensity factor

The intensity factor α is also called a scaling parameter [22] or gain factor [23]. The role of α differs depending on the method. With correlation-based steganography, α affects the correlation properties. As shown in Figure 2.1, we need to calculate α

to embed secret information because DCT coefficients can range from less than one to several hundred. On the other hand, the M′ sequence representing the secret information is composed of "1" and "-1". The larger the DCT coefficients of the embedding target, the smaller the impact of the M′ sequence. Therefore, it becomes difficult to obtain the correct correlation.

The M′ sequence is multiplied by α, as shown in (2.5) and (2.6), in the embedding process, so that the correct correlation can be obtained. However, multiplying α means that the amount of change in the DCT coefficients to be embedded will also increase. As a result, the image quality will degrade. According to Garg *et al.* [16], when α is 1, the peak signal-to-noise ratio (PSNR) is 48 dB. However, when α is 5, it drops to 34 dB, and when it is 10, the PSNR drops to 28 dB. As α increases, the correlation characteristics improve; however, image quality deteriorates significantly. In other words, there is a trade-off between image quality and correlation characteristics, which is a major issue. Thus, we also analyze the characteristic of our method when α changes.

2.2.2.5   Extraction of secret information

To recover the secret information represented by the M′ sequence, we compute the correlation between W^0 and the shifted M′ sequence W^{t_M}. If the correct correlation is obtained, the position of the peak appears at the number of shifts t_M. The position of peak t_M can be recovered as secret information. Taking Figure 2.2 as an example, we can recover the information t_M as "2" by calculating the correlation between W^2 and W^0.

The manner of extracting secret information differs between the two methods. With SSIS, a threshold is set for the correlation value, and from the threshold, the value is determined by a binary value of 1 or 0. With correlation-based steganography, the position of the correlation peak is defined as secret information.

2.2.3   *Embedding process*

The basic embedding process of correlation-based steganography is shown in Figures 2.4 and 2.5. Note that DC_M means the DCT coefficients that are modified in the embedding process. The flow of the process is as follows.

1.   All secret information is divided into m bits and represented as t_M. Then, each t_M is converted into an M′ sequence. Note that, the length of the M′ sequence is $L(= 2^m)$.

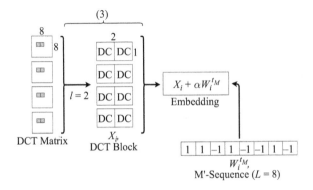

Figure 2.4   Embedding process: $l \leq L$

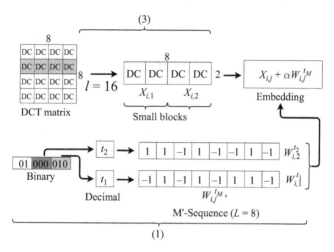

Figure 2.5   Embedding process: l > L

2. The cover image I_c is divided into pixel blocks of size 8×8 and DCT is executed on each to obtain DCT matrices.

3. DCT coefficients of length l are extracted to be embedded from each DCT matrix and concatenated to form a DCT block X_i (or $X_{i,j}$). Note that the range l is ($1 \leq l \leq 64$). Let i be the DCT block number and j the number of small blocks that separate the DCT block by length L. Note that j is used when more than two M' sequences are embedded in one DCT block ($l > L$), as shown in Figure 2.5. Let s be the position of the first coefficient to be extracted from the DCT matrix and let this be the starting position of the embedding. Note that the position number of the DCT coefficients goes up in the order of zigzag scan. The range of the DCT matrix that is being modified is s to $s + l - 1$, and the range of possible values for s is ($1 \leq s \leq 64 - l + 1$) for an 8×8 DCT.

4. The M' sequence is shifted t_M times and W^{t_M} is embedded using the intensity factor α with the following equations. Modified DCT blocks S_i (or $S_{i,j}$) are then obtained.

$$S_i = X_i + \alpha W_i^{t_M}, \quad \text{if} \quad l \leq L, \tag{2.5}$$

$$S_{i,j} = X_{i,j} + \alpha W_{i,j}^{t_M}, \quad \text{if} \quad l > L. \tag{2.6}$$

Note that α increases until all M' sequences can obtain the correct correlation value.

5. A stego image I_s with embedded secret information is obtained by executing inverse DCT (IDCT) to S_i (or $S_{i,j}$) and reconstructing the image.

Equations (2.5) and (2.6) are switched depending on the number of coefficients to be extracted from each DCT matrix l and the length of the M' sequence L. Equation (2.5) is for $l \leq L$, as shown in Figure 2.4. In this case, the number of DCT coefficients of X_i and L are the same. For example, in Figure 2.4, two coefficients are extracted from each DCT matrix, so $l = 2$. The L of the M' sequence to be

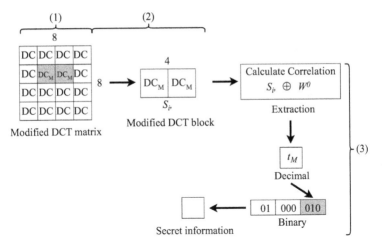

Figure 2.6   Extraction process

embedded is 8. In the embedding process, one M' sequence can be embedded by concatenating two DCT coefficients extracted from each block to form X_i of length 8. Equation (2.6) is for $l > L$, as shown in Figure 2.5. In this case, the number of DCT coefficients of $X_{i,j}$ is an integer multiple of L. For example, in Figure 2.5, 16 coefficients are extracted from each DCT matrix, so $l = 16$. Also, the L of the embedded M' sequence is 8. In this case, the number of DCT coefficients of $X_{i,j}$ is $2L$, so two M' sequences can be embedded.

2.2.4   Extraction process

This section describes the extraction of secret information. The extraction process is shown in Figure 2.6. Note that the $\oplus$ means cross-correlation. The details of this process are as follows.

1.   A stego image I_s is divided into pixel blocks of size 8×8 and DCT is executed on each.
2.   Modified DCT coefficients are extracted from the sth to $s + l - 1$th in each modified DCT matrix and concatenated to form S_i (or $S_{i,j}$).
3.   The secret information is extracted by calculating the correlation between W^0 and S_i (or $S_{i,j}$).

In the extraction of the secret information, we compute the cross-correlation values of W^0 and all shifted M' sequences W^{t_M}s. As a result, a peak appears at the position of t_M, which is represented as secret information and extracted.

2.3   Proposed methods

As mentioned earlier, the intensity factor multiplied during embedding is necessary to correctly extract secret information. However, this degrades image quality. Since there is a trade-off between image quality and embedding capacity, achieving the smallest possible intensity factor leads to an increase in embedding capacity. Therefore, the intensity factor is an important issue in correlation-based steganography. Our method is correlation-based steganography that uses the RS code [17] and is considered the intensity factor.

Our method uses the RS code, which is a type of error-correcting code and is based on the Galois field theory, and the encoding processes the bits string of r [bits] as one symbol. If the block length of the RS code is $N(= 2^r - 1)$, one codeword, which combines all information symbols and parity symbols, is $r \times N$ [bits]. Note that the symbol is an element of the Galois extension field GF(2^r). The RS coding is the calculation of parity symbols. For example, let $D = \{d_1, d_2, ..., d_K\}$ be the set of the information symbols. Then, let $P = \{p_1, p_2, ..., p_{N-K}\}$ be the set of the parity symbols. The encoder takes D and make N symbols the codeword $C = \{d_1, d_2, ..., d_K, p_1, p_2, ..., p_{N-K}\}$ by adding parity symbols P. The number of correctable symbols Q is represented as

$$Q = \lfloor \frac{N - K}{2} \rfloor, \quad 2^r > N > K > 0. \tag{2.7}$$

We used the following RS codes. The new processes added to Method 2 from Method 1 are RS encoding and parity embedding to the carrier image. Let $T_{n,M} = \{t_1, t_2, ..., t_K\}$ be the set of information symbols grouped by the number of K secret information pieces t_M. Then let $P_{n,M} = \{p_1, p_2, ..., p_{N-K}\}$ be the set of parity symbols. The encoder takes $T_{n,M}$ and makes N symbol codeword $C_{n,M} = \{t_1, t_2, ..., t_K, p_1, p_2, ..., p_{N-K}\}$ by adding parity symbol $P_{n,M}$. The generated $P_{n,M}$ is extracted from $C_{n,M}$, converted to binary numbers, and embedded in the least significant bit (LSB) of the image. In the extraction process, the extracted temporary secret information $\overline{T_{n,M}}$ and $P_{n,M}$ are combined, and error correction is executed. We then obtain the correct divided $T_{n,M}$. Therefore, this method combines the frequency and spatial domains.

The point of this method is that α can be reduced. Because for each $\overline{T_{n,M}}$, since the Q of secret information pieces can be corrected, it is sufficient to determine α such that the number of $K - Q$ M' sequences can obtain the correct correlation value. Note that α is the same for all $T_{n,M}$. That is, it is minimum such that the number of secret information pieces to be modified for each $T_{n,M}$ is at most Q.

Figures 2.7 and 2.8 show the parity embedding and error-correction processes for Method 2, the details of which are as follows.

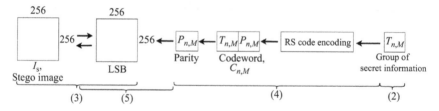

Figure 2.7 Embedding process of the parity of our method

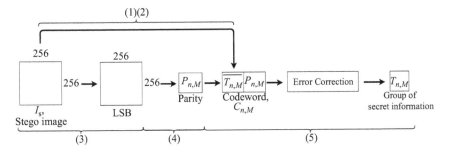

Figure 2.8   Error correction process of our method

Embedding process for Method 2:

1. Execute the embedding overview process 1 to 5.
2. The t_M is divided into K pieces, and we make one group $T_{n,M}$.
3. The LSB is extracted from stego image I_s.
4. RS encoding is executed for each $T_{n,M}$, and we obtain the codeword $C_{n,M}$. Then, $P_{n,M}$ is extracted from $C_{n,M}$.
5. $P_{n,M}$ is converted to binary numbers and embedded in the LSB.

Extraction process for Method 2:

1. Execute steps 1 to 3 of the overview extraction process.
2. The temporary secret information $\overline{t_M}$ is divided into K pieces, and we make one group $\overline{T_{n,M}}$.
3. The LSB is extracted from I_s.
4. $P_{n,M}$ is extracted from the LSB.
5. Codeword $C_{n,M}$ is obtained by adding $P_{n,M}$ to the end of $\overline{T_{n,M}}$. Then, error correction is executed, and we obtain $T_{n,M}$.

2.4   Experimental result

2.4.1   Experimental setup

This subsection describes the images, metrics, and parameters used for our evaluation of the proposed methods.

To verify the effectiveness of the proposed methods, the M′ sequence is conducted on several carrier images. We used some uncompressed grayscale images, such as Boat.bmp and Barbara.bmp of size $I^2 = 256^2$ pixels as a cover image.

The PSNR is a measure based on the perceptual sensitivity of the noise component caused by coding. This is often used as an evaluation index for image quality. Let I_c be the carrier image and I_s be the stego image, and each image has a size of I^2 pixels and 256 shades. The PSNR is represented by the following equation using mean squared error (MSE).

It is said that an acceptable PSNR is 30 dB or higher [24] and that for a high-quality stego image should be 40 dB or higher [4].

The structural similarity index measure (SSIM) is a measure of structural similarity based on brightness, contrast, and structure, which matches the human visual system [25]. Therefore, this index is closer to the human senses than the PSNR. Setiadi [26] recommends evaluating with SSIM. SSIM is designed by modeling image distortion as a combination of three factors: loss of correlation, luminance distortion, and contrast distortion. The SSIM for 8-bit grayscale images is represented by

$$SSIM = \frac{(2\mu_x\mu_y + C_1)(2\sigma_{xy} + C_2)}{(\mu_x^2 + \mu_y^2 + C_1)(\sigma_x^2 + \sigma_y^2 + C_2)},\tag{2.8}$$

$$C_1 = (255K_1)^2, \quad C_2 = (255K_2)^2,\tag{2.9}$$

$$K_1 \ll 1, \quad K_2 \ll 1,\tag{2.10}$$

where,

x, y = nonnegative image signals
μ_x, μ_y = mean intensity of x, y
σ_x^2, σ_y^2 = variance of x, y
σ_{xy} = covariance x and y
C_1, C_2 = constant values

Note that C_1 and C_2 are used to avoid instability when the denominator is very close to zero. Wang *et al.* [25] used $K_1 = 0.01$ and $K_2 = 0.03$. The range of SSIM is from 0 to 1. The higher the SSIM, the higher the similarity between the compared images. As a rough guide to quality, a value of 0.9 or higher is considered sufficient quality [27,28].

We used an M′ sequence of length $L = 16$. Therefore, the numbers that can be represented by one M′ sequence are from 0 to 15. Moreover, the secret information to be embedded is divided into 4 bits and converted into one M′ sequence.

There are three types of secret information to be embedded: 512-byte, 1,024-byte, and 2,024-byte. In this case, the number of DCT coefficients for each block l are $l = 16$, $l = 32$, and $l = 64$. This means that there are L, $2L$, and $4L$ M′ sequences embedded in one DCT matrix, respectively.

The embedding start number s is the first number of the DCT matrix used for embedding. In this study, s was set to $64 - l + 1$ to evaluate the characteristics of image-quality degradation caused by s. Note that s increases in the order of zigzag scan, so a smaller value means lower frequency, and a higher value means higher frequency. As a rough guide to the low-, mid-, and high-frequency bands, $l = 5$ or less is a low-frequency band, $l = 5$ to around 20 is a mid-frequency band, and above that is a high-frequency band.

We used the RS code with codeword length $N = 255$. Moreover, the message symbol length was $K = 127$. Therefore, Q was 64. Intensity factor is set from 0 to 40. Moreover, quality factor in JPEG is set from 40 to 98.

2.4.2 Experimental results and discussion

Figures 2.9–2.26 show the PSNR, SSIM, and BER for each intensity factor G for varying JPEG quality factors, using "Boat" and "Barbara" as cover images. As

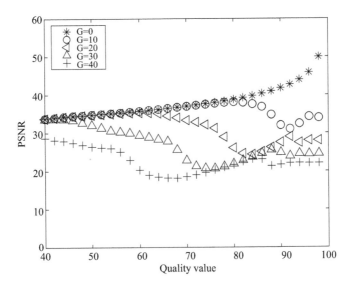

Figure 2.9   BOAT.bmp PSNR $s_{info}= 512$ byte

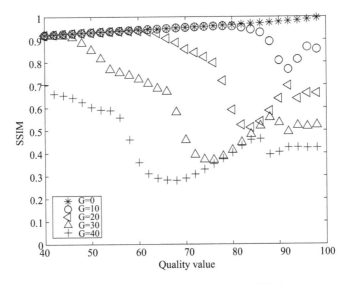

Figure 2.10   BOAT.bmp SSIM $s_{info}= 512$ byte

shown in Figures 2.9, 2.12, and 2.15, when no secret information is embedded ($G= 0$), PSNR and SSIM are monotonically increased by the increase of quality factor. On the other hand, when secret information is embedded ($G> 0$), as the quality factor increases, the PSNR initially decreases (denoted as region A), then begins to increase (denoted as region B), and remains unchanged in the region

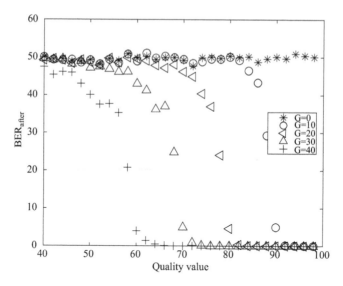

Figure 2.11   BOAT.bmp BER s_{info}= 512 byte

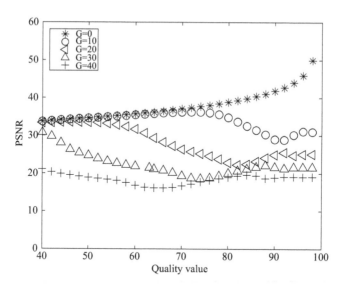

Figure 2.12   BOAT.bmp PSNR s_{info} = 1024 byte

where the QF is close to 100 (denoted as region C). The SSIM results in Figures 2.10, 2.13, and 2.16 show a similar trend.

First, let us consider region A. The reason for this tendency can be assumed to be that the embedded secret information is preferentially removed from the DCT

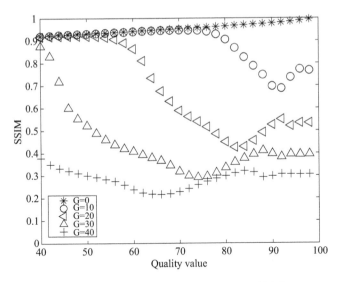

Figure 2.13   BOAT.bmp SSIM $s_{info} = 1024$ byte

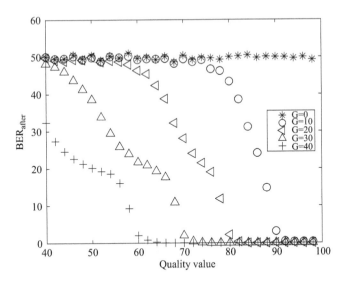

Figure 2.14   BOAT.bmp BER $s_{info} = 1024$ byte

coefficients derived from the original image due to low-quality factor (= coarse quantization). Figures 2.11, 2.14, and 2.17 show that the bit error rate (BER) approaches the chance rate (50%) in region A. This indicates that the embedded secret information is gradually removed in region A, supporting our assumption.

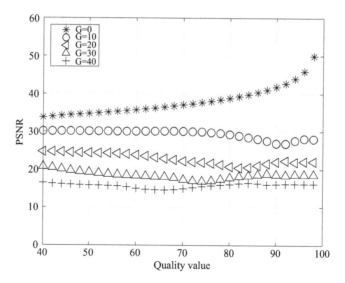

Figure 2.15　BOAT.bmp PSNR $s_{info} = 2048$ byte

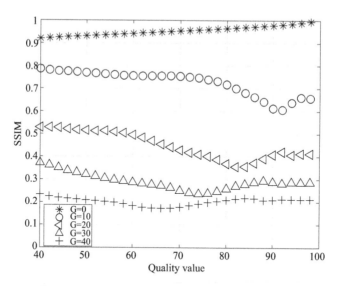

Figure 2.16　BOAT.bmp SSIM $s_{info} = 2048$ byte

The SSIM results in Figures 2.10, 2.13, and 2.16 show a similar trend. Figures 2.11, 2.14, and 2.17 show the BER in region A, the BER increases rapidly and is close to the chance rate (50%). This indicates that the embedded secret information is completely removed in region A, supporting the aforementioned hypothesis. In

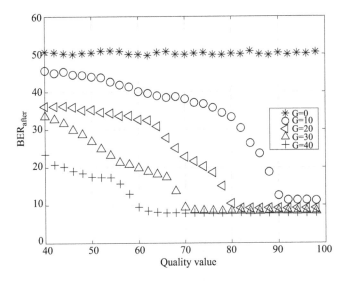

Figure 2.17   BOAT.bmp BER $s_{\text{info}} = 2048$ byte

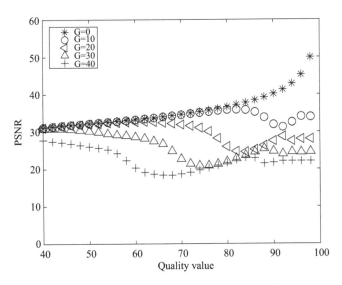

Figure 2.18   BARBARA.bmp PSNR $s_{\text{info}} = 512$ byte

contrast, the deletion of the original information in the original image by lowering the quality factor within region A increases more slowly than the deletion of secret information. This "difference in the speed at which information is lost" produces the seemingly strange phenomenon of PSNR and SSIM increasing as the quality factor is lowered.

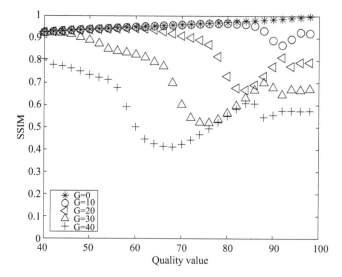

Figure 2.19   BARBARA.bmp SSIM $s_{info} = 512$ byte

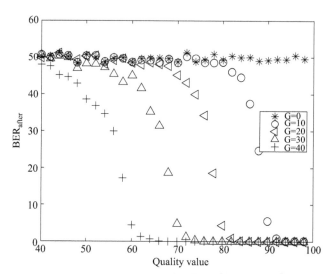

Figure 2.20   BARBARA.bmp BER $s_{info} = 512$ byte

Then, we discuss region B. In region B, PSNR and SSIM do not improve even if the quality factor is increased. This is because the gap between the original image and the cover image caused by the embedding of secret information is not resolved even if the quantization step width is narrowed above a certain level. The above

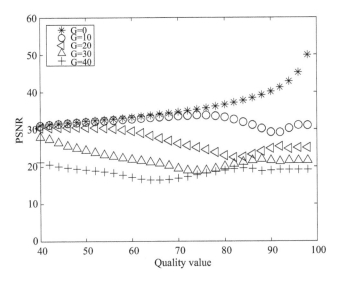

Figure 2.21   *BARBARA.bmp PSNR* $s_{\text{info}} = 512$ *byte*

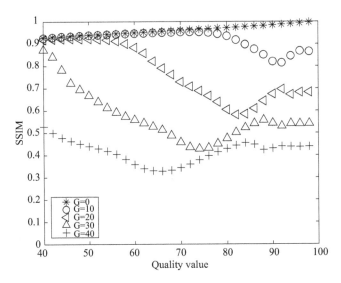

Figure 2.22   *BARBARA.bmp SSIM* $s_{\text{info}} = 512$ *byte*

trend is also quite similar when the image "BARBARA" is used as a cover image (Figures 2.18–2.26), and it can be said that this trend is independent of the cover image. From the above discussion, we can conclude that our proposed steganography method can minimize the file size of stego-images while maintaining the

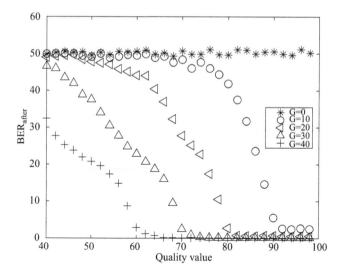

Figure 2.23   BARBARA.bmp BER $s_{info} = 512$ byte

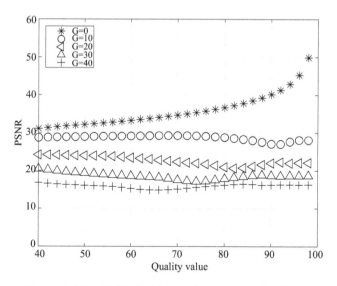

Figure 2.24   BARBARA.bmp PSNR $s_{info} = 2048$ byte

recovery performance of secret information by setting the quality factor slightly above region A for all embedding intensities. The region A varies depending on the image and embedding strength. In future work, we will establish a method to estimate this point without actually embedding the image.

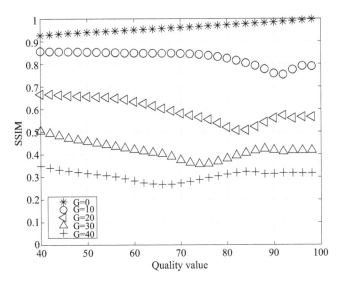

Figure 2.25   BARBARA.bmp SSIM $s_{\text{info}} = 2048 \; byte$

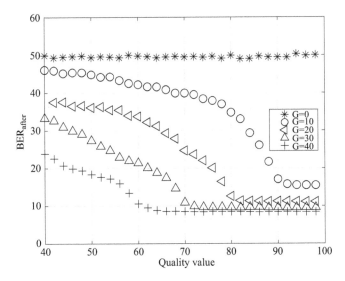

Figure 2.26   BARBARA.bmp BER $s_{\text{info}} = 2048 \; byte$

2.5   Conclusion

In this chapter, we analyze the JPEG tolerance of the conventional method. Our proposed steganography has the potential to minimize the file size of stego-images while maintaining the recovery performance of secret information by setting the quality factor slightly above region A for all embedding intensities. The region A varies depending on the image and embedding strength. In future work, we will establish a method to estimate this point without actually embedding the image.

Acknowledgment

These research results were obtained from the commissioned research (No.05201) by National Institute of Information and Communications Technology (NICT), Japan. This work was supported by JSPS KAKENHI Grant Numbers 19K1194722K1201522K12036. Moreover, Mr. Kaito Onuma made an enormous contribution to this chapter and Mr. Yuki Yokota gave insightful comments and suggestions.

References

[1]   Zhang J, Zhao X, He X, *et al.* Improving the robustness of JPEG steganography with robustness cost. *IEEE Signal Processing Letters.* 2022;29:164–168.

[2]   Zhu L, Luo X, Yang C, *et al.* Invariances of JPEG-quantized DCT coefficients and their application in robust image steganography. *Signal Processing.* 2021;183:108015. Available from: https://www.sciencedirect.com/science/article/pii/S0165168421000542.

[3]   Zebari DA, Zeebaree DQ, Saeed JN, *et al.* Image steganography based on swarm intelligence algorithms: a survey. *Test Engineering & Management.* 2020;7(8):9.

[4]   Cheddad A, Condell J, Curran K, *et al.* Digital image steganography: survey and analysis of current methods. *Signal Processing.* 2010;90(3):727–752.

[5]   Sari CA, Rachmawanto EH, Setiadi DRIM. Robust and imperceptible image watermarking by DC coefficients using singular value decomposition. In: *2017 4th International Conference on Electrical Engineering, Computer Science and Informatics (EECSI).* IEEE; 2017. p. 1–5.

[6]   Evsutin OO, Melman AS, Meshcheryakov RV. Digital steganography and watermarking for digital images: a review of current research directions. *IEEE Access.* 2020;8:166589–166611. DOI: 10.1109/ACCESS.2020.3022779.

[7]   Mehta D, Bhatti D. Blind image steganography algorithm development which resistant against JPEG compression attack. *Multimedia Tools and Applications* 2022;1–21.

[8]   Holub V, Fridrich J. Digital image steganography using universal distortion. In: *Proceedings of the First ACM Workshop on Information Hiding and Multimedia Security. IH MMSec'13.* New York, NY: Association for Computing Machinery; 2013. p. 59–68. Available from: https://doi.org/10.1145/2482513.2482514.

[9]   Guo L, Ni J, Su W, *et al.* Using statistical image model for JPEG steganography: uniform embedding revisited. *IEEE Transactions on Information Forensics and Security.* 2015;10(12):2669–2680.

[10]   Chen K, Zhou H, Zhou W, *et al.* Defining cost functions for adaptive JPEG steganography at the microscale. *IEEE Transactions on Information Forensics and Security.* 2019;14(4):1052–1066.

[11]   Holub V, Fridrich J. Designing steganographic distortion using directional filters. In: *2012 IEEE International Workshop on Information Forensics and Security (WIFS)*; 2012. p. 234–239.

[12]   Li B, Wang M, Huang J, *et al.* A new cost function for spatial image steganography. In: *2014 IEEE International Conference on Image Processing (ICIP)*; 2014. p. 4206–4210.

[13]   Sedighi V, Cogranne R, Fridrich J. Content-adaptive steganography by minimizing statistical detectability. *IEEE Transactions on Information Forensics and Security.* 2016;11(2):221–234.

[14]   Onuma K, Miyata S. A proposal for correlation-based steganography using Shamir's secret sharing scheme and DCT domain. In: *2021 International Conference on Information Networking (ICOIN)*; 2021. p. 255–260.

[15]   Koda H, Furuta H. A note on a correlation-based scheme of digital watermarking for images embedding the RDS in DCT domain (in Japanese). *Bulletin of the University of Electro-Communications.* 2018;30(1):62–70.

[16]   Garg S, Singh R. An efficient method for digital image watermarking based on PN sequences. *International Journal on Computer Science and Engineering.* 2012;4(9):1550.

[17]   Onuma K, Miyata S. A study of steganography based on error correction code and secret sharing scheme. In: *2020 3rd International Conference on Signal Processing and Information Security (ICSPIS)*. IEEE; 2020. p. 1–4.

[18]   Kaur B, Kaur A, Singh J. Steganographic approach for hiding image in DCT domain. *International Journal of Advances in Engineering & Technology.* 2011;1(3):72.

[19]   Saidi M, Hermassi H, Rhouma R, *et al.* A new adaptive image steganography scheme based on DCT and chaotic map. *Multimedia Tools and Applications.* 2017;76(11):13493–13510.

[20]   Golomb SW, *et al. Shift register sequences.* Aegean Park Press, Laguna Hills, CA, USA; 1967.

[21]   Engelberg S, Benjamin H. Pseudorandom sequences and the measurement of the frequency response [instrumentation notes]. *IEEE Instrumentation & Measurement Magazine.* 2005;8(1):54–59.

[22]   Cox IJ, Kilian J, Leighton FT, *et al.* Secure spread spectrum watermarking for multimedia. *IEEE transactions on image processing.* 1997;6(12):1673–1687.

[23]   Singh RP, Khan MAA, Khan M, *et al.* Spread spectrum image steganography in multimedia messaging service of mobile phones. *International Journal of Electronics Engineering.* 2010;2(2):365–369.

[24]   Chatterjee A, Ghosal SK, Sarkar R. LSB based steganography with OCR: an intelligent amalgamation. *Multimedia Tools and Applications.* 2020;p. 1–19.

[25]   Wang Z, Bovik AC, Sheikh HR, *et al.* Image quality assessment: from error visibility to structural similarity. *IEEE transactions on image processing.* 2004;13(4):600–612.

[26]   Setiadi DRIM. PSNR vs SSIM: imperceptibility quality assessment for image steganography. *Multimedia Tools and Applications.* 2021;80:8423–8444.

[27]   Al-Mansoori S, Kunhu A. Robust watermarking technique based on DCT to protect the ownership of DubaiSat-1 images against attacks. *International Journal of Computer Science and Network Security (IJCSNS).* 2012;12(6):1.

[28]   Cuervo E, Wolman A, Cox LP, *et al.* Kahawai: high-quality mobile gaming using gpu offload. In: *Proceedings of the 13th Annual International Conference on Mobile Systems, Applications, and Services*; 2015. p. 121–135.

Chapter 3

Machine/Deep learning techniques for multimedia security

Arash Heidar[1], Nima Jafari Navimipour[2] and Poupak Azad[3]

Multimedia security based on *Machine Learning* (ML)/*Deep Learning* (DL) is a field of study that focuses on using ML/DL techniques to protect multimedia data such as images, videos, and audio from unauthorized access, manipulation, or theft. Developing and implementing algorithms and systems that use ML/DL techniques to detect and prevent security breaches in multimedia data is the main subject of this field. These systems use techniques like watermarking, encryption, and digital signature verification to protect multimedia data. The advantages of using ML/DL in multimedia security include improved accuracy, scalability, and automation. ML/DL algorithms can improve the accuracy of detecting security threats and help identify multimedia data vulnerabilities. Additionally, ML models can be scaled up to handle large amounts of multimedia data, making them helpful in protecting big datasets. Finally, ML/DL algorithms can automate the process of multimedia security, making it easier and more efficient to protect multimedia data. The disadvantages of using ML/DL in multimedia security include data availability, complexity, and black box models. ML and DL algorithms require large amounts of data to train the models, which can sometimes be challenging. Developing and implementing ML algorithms can also be complex, requiring specialized skills and knowledge. Finally, ML/DL models are often black box models, which means it can be difficult to understand how they make their decisions. This can be a challenge when explaining the decisions to stakeholders or auditors. Overall, multimedia security based on ML/DL is a promising area of research with many potential benefits. However, it also presents challenges that must be addressed to ensure the security and privacy of multimedia data.

[1]Department of Software Engineering, Haliç University, Istanbul, Turkey
[2]Department of Computer Engineering, Kadir Has Universitesi, Turkey
[3]Department of Computer Science, University of Manitoba, Canada

3.1   Introduction

Multimedia content, comprising images, videos, and audio, has become integral to our daily lives [1]. With the widespread availability of advanced digital tools, there is an increasing need to ensure multimedia data's security and authenticity [2]. Multimedia security encompasses various techniques and methodologies aimed at protecting and preserving multimedia content's integrity, confidentiality, and availability. In recent years, the emergence of deepfake technology has raised significant concerns regarding the manipulation and malicious use of multimedia data [3]. Therefore, effective deepfake generation and detection mechanisms have become essential components of multimedia security [4].

Machine Learning (ML), and particularly *Deep Learning* (DL), has emerged as a powerful tool in the field of *Artificial Intelligence* (AI) [5]. It involves training computational models to learn patterns and make intelligent decisions based on large volumes of data [6]. DL algorithms, such as *Convolutional Neural Networks* (CNNs) and *Recurrent Neural Networks* (RNNs), have shown remarkable capabilities in various domains, including computer vision and *Natural Language Processing* (NLP) [7]. In the context of multimedia security, ML techniques play a crucial role in detecting and mitigating the risks posed by deepfake content [8]. The importance of DL in multimedia security cannot be overstated. DL models have demonstrated remarkable performance in deepfake detection, enabling highly accurate identification of manipulated content [9]. By leveraging the ability of *Deep Neural Networks* (DNNs) to learn complex representations and identify subtle patterns, these models can effectively distinguish between authentic and manipulated multimedia content. The integration of DL algorithms in multimedia security systems enhances their capabilities to counter the rapidly evolving deepfake techniques [10].

This book chapter aims to contribute to the field of multimedia security and ML by providing a comprehensive overview of fundamental concepts, deepfake methods, and the role of DL in addressing multimedia security challenges. The chapter will explore the history of deepfakes, their impact on society, and the different types of deepfake models, including image, video, and audio-based techniques. By presenting state-of-the-art deepfake detection methods and discussing their strengths and limitations, this chapter aims to equip researchers and practitioners with the necessary knowledge to combat the threat of deepfakes in multimedia content.

The organization of this chapter is as follows. First, we will provide a brief introduction to DL and its relevance in the context of multimedia security. This will lay the foundation for understanding the subsequent deepfake generation and detection discussions. Next, we will delve into the history and evolution of deepfakes, exploring the various techniques used to create realistic manipulations in images, videos, and audio. We will then discuss the deepfake detection models and methodologies in detail, highlighting their strengths and limitations. Finally, we will summarize the key findings and potential future directions for research in multimedia security and ML.

3.2   Core concepts and terminologies

The creation of fake content, deepfake detection, fake image and video detection, attribute switching, expression, and identity exchange, creating and detecting fake speech, domain adaptation and transfer learning, and methods for manipulating visual images are just a few of the major topics we cover in this section.

3.2.1   Fake content creation

Multiple techniques exist for altering visual content to achieve different objectives. The following section will briefly discuss the more popular and promising ones. Replicating, removing, and adding items are all frequently done operations. Copying an object from one image and moving it to another allows you to add a new object. By enlarging the backdrop to cover an existing object, or "inpainting," as in the well-known "exemplar-based inpainting," the object can be eliminated [11]. With the help of typical photo editing software, all these processes are straightforward. Additionally, suitable post-processing, such as scaling, rotation, or color correction, might enhance the item's visual attractiveness, maintain consistent perspective and scale, and better fit it to the scene. DL, multi-layer networks, and advanced computer graphics approaches have recently delivered results with enhanced semantic consistency. "Shallow fakes" or "cheap fakes" are terms that are widely used to describe manipulations that do not need the deployment of cutting-edge AI systems [12]. Its capacity to change perception, though, could be important. For instance, by removing, including, or cloning entire groups of frames, the meaning of a film may be changed. In addition to these "conventional" manipulations of certain areas of an image or video, digital signage, and computer graphics also offer a wide variety of novel ones. On rare occasions, media assets are built from scratch. Auto-encoders and *Generative Adversarial Networks* (GANs) made it possible to achieve this goal, enabling efficient solutions, notably for face synthesis, with a high level of photo-realism. A synthetic movie or image may also be created using a segmentation map. Simple drawings or text descriptions can also be used for image synthesis. A person's visage can also be altered following an audio input sequence. Frequently, the alteration modifies already-existing images or movies. Style transfer is a highly clever idea since it enables you to change a painting's style, turn peaches into oranges, or replicate a picture in a different season. Face modification has drawn much interest due to its high semantic value and variety of applications [13].

3.2.2   Deepfake detection, fake image detection, and fake video detection

Deepfake detection is often viewed as a binary arrangement issue where classifiers are employed to separate trustworthy from obfuscating videos. A large collection of real and fake films is needed to train classification models using this approach. Even if it is insufficient to provide a standard for validating different finding methodologies, the quantity of bogus videos is increasing. DL approaches, which may be divided into two detection methods: CNN-based methods and *Region Conventional Neural Networks* (RCNN)-based methods, were the subject of several earlier investigations on identifying deepfake pictures or videos [14]. CNN-based methods produce an image-level output by feeding face images from video frames into the CNN for training and prediction. Therefore, these algorithms only use spatial information from a single frame in deepfake films. On the other hand, RCNN-based approaches need a set of video frames for training to create a video-level output. RNN and CNN are combined in this method, referred to as RCNN. Consequently, deepfake videos' spatial and temporal information might be completely used by RCNN-based algorithms. A *Support Vector Machine* (SVM) is used as a classifier, and handcrafted properties, such as biological signals, are extracted and used as a classifier for several deepfake detection algorithms. Face swap may be used to replace faces in pictures with ones from a collection of stock photos, which has various compelling applications in video compositing, portrait modification, and, most importantly, identity protection. But imposters utilize it as one of their strategies to get entry to authentication systems. Face shots have also grown more challenging for forensics since DL techniques like CNN, GAN, SVM, random forest, and multi-layer perceptron can maintain the images' location, facial features, and lighting. Since GAN can learn the supply of input data and produce new results with the same input distribution, its DL pictures may be the most challenging to distinguish from actual, high-quality photographs [15]. Even though GAN is always improving and new variations are routinely presented, most studies on the recognition of GAN-creating samples do not look at the effectiveness of the recognition models. Numerous techniques also included an image-preparation stage. This requires the forensic classifier to examine significant associated and meaningful features with a higher simplification competence than previous image forensics methods or image stage assessment systems because it increases the statistical comparison between the real and fake images at the pixel level. Additionally, maximal image-based deepfake recognition approaches cannot be used with videos due to the strong deprivation of frame data that results from audio-visual compression. Additionally, the different temporal features that differ between groups of frames in films make it difficult for algorithms meant to identify specific false pictures. This topic focuses on techniques for identifying deep fake videos and separates them into two categories: those that look at chronological traits and those that look at visual artifacts inside frames [16].

Meanwhile, certain deepfake video generation models cannot synthesize all of the textures of the face, leading to some fake faces that are a little rough. For instance, it is impossible to replicate the fine lines on the face precisely. The formed face is fused with the background in the last stage of producing the fake frame. Border irregularities caused by this procedure, which cause the loss of facial texture details, are usually reduced using smoothing methods [17]. A frame from the authentic films VidTIMIT dataset is shown in Figure 3.1(a), whereas a frame from the face-manipulation movies DeepFake-TIMIT dataset is shown in Figure 3.1(b). Following the figure, human eyes find it challenging to determine whether the frame is real. However, the texture of the genuine frame is more

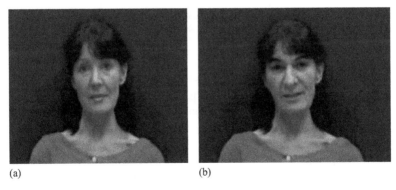

(a)   (b)

Figure 3.1   Real and fabricated frames are shown. (a) Is a genuine frame, whereas (b) is a fake [18].

lifelike, with characteristics like double eyelids and wrinkles around the eyes, whereas the texture of the fake frame is lacking [19].

3.2.3   Attribute switching, expression, and identity exchange

In identity swap techniques, the face of one person in a video is replaced with the face of another person. Traditional computer graphics-based solutions like FaceSwap and revolutionary deepfakes techniques like the current ZAO smartphone app are the two strategies that are frequently taken into consideration. Additionally, you may discover quite lifelike instances of this kind of alteration on commercial websites like YouTube [20]. The entertainment business, among others, may benefit from such a change. However, it might also be employed for evil purposes, such as the creation of celebrity pornographic movies, fraud, and financial fraud, to mention a few. Traditional computer graphics-based solutions like FaceSwap and revolutionary deepfakes techniques like the current ZAO smartphone app are the two strategies that are frequently taken into consideration. Additionally, you may discover quite lifelike instances of this kind of alteration on commercial websites like YouTube. The entertainment business, among others, may benefit from such a change. However, it might also be employed for evil purposes, such as the creation of celebrity pornographic movies, fraud, and financial fraud, to mention a few. Face reenactment is a sort of manipulation that also involves changing a person's facial expression. The most well-known methods, Face2Face and NeuralTextures, which replace one person's facial expression in a video with that of another, are the ones this group focuses on, even though several modification approaches are suggested in the literature, such as at the image level using well-known GAN architectures. If this kind of deceit is used, the results might be disastrous [21].

3.2.4   Making fraudulent speech and detecting fake speech

The topic of synthetic speech creation has been studied for a long time and in a variety of approaches. As a result, many techniques in the literature produce fantastic results; there is no one reliable way to create a synthetic voice recording. *Text-to-Speech* (TTS) production has historically relied on concatenative waveform synthesis, which involves selecting the appropriate diphone units from a large collection of diphone waveforms and integrating them to assure acceptability. Given a text as input, the output speech is then produced. A higher level of naturalness, imitation of human prosody, and smoother transitions between diphones are all benefits of further post-processing technologies. Concatenative synthesis' main drawback is how difficult it is to adjust the sound's tonal characteristics, such as to change the speaker or add emotional resonance to the voice. Additionally, various methods are suggested to expand the variety of voice characteristics or talking patterns, such as the *Hidden Markov Models* (HMM) based speech synthesis system. These employ contextual HMMs trained using enormous auditory characteristic datasets gathered from diphones and triphones. Increased voice production is the goal of another technique known as the parametric TTS synthesis technique. Given a set of speech properties, such as frequency, spectral envelope, and excitation signal, an auto-regressive process, in this case, generates a speech signal. However, compared to concatenative TTS synthesis, parametric TTS synthesis produces fewer results with a realistic sound [22]. Natural and adaptable synthetic voices have been produced via *Neural Networks* (NNs). Because voice signals sometimes count hundreds of samples per second and maintain crucial properties over a wide range of timescales, modeling audio samples by sample has historically been regarded to be highly challenging [23]. However, in recent years, CNN and RNN have made it possible to build completely auto-regressive models and directly generate raw audio waveforms. It is extremely difficult to tell if a speech recording belongs to a real person or was fabricated. Nevertheless, a variety of techniques, each with its unique set of traits, can be used to produce fake speeches. Providing a thorough forensic framework that illustrates all feasible synthetic speech techniques is challenging. Furthermore, new and enhanced approaches to producing synthetic voice recordings are frequently introduced as ML solutions gain in popularity. Because of this, it is challenging to keep up with the expansion of the speech synthesis literature. Nevertheless, the industry has created a set of detectors to stop the spread of fake audio recordings. Examining deepfake detection in the field of fake voice is one of the many objectives of this project [24].

3.2.5   *Domain adaptation and transfer learning*

An essential topic in this field is comprehending transfer learning (TL) in general and its application to deepfake detection. However, TL, a branch of DL, uses data from source domains to speed up and improve the method's ability to learn from the target domain. In the field of forensics, TL has drawn a lot of attention. It is simple for TL to load ImageNet's pre-trained weight to the model before training. On discrepancy measurement, the bulk of research utilizing deep domain adaptation relies on these. Some initiatives also focus on discrepancy assessment and domain-adversarial learning [25]. Therefore, TL is a method for completing a new task (seemingly related or unrelated) utilizing model knowledge that has already been learned with minimum need for retraining or fine-tuning. Compared to

Table 3.1   *Image manipulation, forgeries, tampering with images, and image production definitions.*

Terminology	Definition
Image manipulation	Editing or changing digital photos using computer-based means.
Image forgery	Using image manipulation to produce bogus visual materials that offer deceptive information.
Image tampering	A particular type of image scam where the manipulator changes numerous scenes inside a single image.
Image generation	Employing DL algorithms to create photos that don't exist but contain real-world items.

conventional ML techniques, DL needs more training data. The time needed to train for a domain-specific issue is significantly decreased when employing TL. A TL-based DL strategy is used to reduce the dataset's complexity. Finding them has become a major concern in the current situation due to the scary proliferation of deepfakes on the internet. Researchers in this field are trying very hard to create some perspective TL mechanisms that may help to lessen the difficulties in such a situation [26].

3.2.6   Techniques for manipulating visual images

The phrase "Visual Imagery" covers both still photos and moving pictures. Using computer software or digital tools like smartphones and tablets, *Imagery Manipulation* (IM) includes manipulating pictures or videos. Image editing is another name for it. Nowadays, mobile devices have replaced cameras and can take high-quality digital photos that are frequently accompanied by editing software. To preserve special experiences from birthdays to weddings, digital photos have become an indispensable part of our daily lives [27]. Applications for image editing allow the addition of visual effects to enhance the aesthetic appeal of photographs and movies. Digital picture editing and "image manipulation" are terms that are frequently used interchangeably. Table 3.1 gives definitions for image manipulation, picture forgery, image tampering, and image production, whereas Figure 3.1 depicts many methods of image manipulation. Resampling, a pixel-level technique for deleting or including items in an image, is one example of an operation that may be used to manipulate images [28].

3.3   Deepfake detection methods

The DL/ML methodologies for identifying deepfakes and related conditions are covered in this section. According to their intended usage, we first categorize the approaches into four groups: The recommended taxonomy of DL-deepfake detection methods is shown in Figure 3.2, with examples of images, video, sound, and hybrid multimedia material.

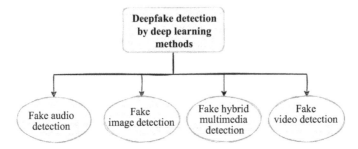

Figure 3.2   The suggested DL-deepfake detection taxonomy separated four distinct methods

3.3.1   Fake images detection

Image forgery detection is a complex and challenging task, particularly when it comes to recognizing fake facial images. The prevalence of phony identities created using manipulated images on social media platforms has raised concerns about privacy breaches and data theft. For example, the use of fake picture generators to create images depicting famous individuals engaged in questionable activities poses significant risks. This section aims to delve into using DL methods to detect and identify fraudulent photos.

One of the major advancements in image forgery is the advent of deepfake technology, which has dramatically lowered the threshold for creating manipulated faces. Deepfake leverages the power of GANs to replace a person's face in an original image with the face of another individual. These GAN models have been trained on vast datasets comprising tens of thousands of photographs, enabling them to generate highly realistic and seamless face swaps. The manipulated image can be further refined by employing appropriate post-processing techniques to enhance its realism and deceive unsuspecting viewers.

The development of DL techniques has facilitated the creation of Deepfake images and paved the way for various applications in face swapping. Beyond the realm of malicious activities, face-swap innovation has found utility in domains such as privacy protection, multimedia synthesis, and other cutting-edge applications. DL-powered face-swapping algorithms can be employed to safeguard individuals' privacy by replacing their faces with anonymized counterparts in sensitive video footage or images. Moreover, multimedia synthesis techniques can utilize face swapping to create engaging and entertaining content for artistic or creative purposes.

While DL-based methods have demonstrated impressive capabilities in identifying and analyzing fraudulent photos, it is important to acknowledge the potential risks and ethical implications associated with the misuse of such technology. The ease of generating convincing Deepfake images raises concerns about the spread of disinformation, the erosion of trust in visual media, and the potential for malicious activities. As the field continues to advance, it becomes crucial to develop robust detection mechanisms and educate users about the existence and risks of manipulated media.

In summary, the emergence of deepfake technology, driven by DL methods and GAN models, has revolutionized the landscape of image forgery and face manipulation. The widespread availability and increasing realism of manipulated images pose significant challenges to detecting and identifying fake facial images. However, DL techniques also offer opportunities for privacy protection, multimedia synthesis, and other innovative applications. As researchers and society at large navigate the complexities of this technology, striking a balance between its potential benefits and associated risks remains essential to ensure the responsible and ethical use of DL-powered face-swapping and forgery detection techniques.

3.3.2   Fake videos detection

Identifying video deepfakes poses one of the most formidable challenges in the field of multimedia forensics. With the aid of deepfake technology, an extremely sophisticated face-swap movie can be created using just a single graphics processing unit (GPU) and a vast amount of training data. This has led to the emergence of numerous live-performance videos on short video platforms, where the faces of ordinary individuals are seamlessly replaced with those of synthetic stars, giving rise to a contentious issue. The proliferation of such videos has sparked criticism and concerns. Previously, videos were widely regarded as trustworthy and admissible as video evidence in multimedia forensics. However, the advent of video deepfake technology in the digital age has undermined the public's trust in the authenticity of videos, and some even argue that it could hinder societal progress. One of the key difficulties in combating video deepfakes is the challenge of accurately distinguishing between genuine and manipulated videos. Deepfake technology, requiring only a single GPU and an extensive training dataset, can generate highly realistic face-swapped movies with remarkable precision. Technology enthusiasts have shared a plethora of live-performance videos on short video platforms, raising debates about the ethical implications and potential misuse of this technique. The use of deepfake technology has challenged long-held beliefs about the reliability of videos and their value as video evidence in multimedia forensics. In the digital era, the trust of the public in video content has been significantly undermined, potentially jeopardizing peace and security.

Traditionally, the predominant approaches for identifying video forgeries have relied on conventional methods, DL strategies, and techniques such as multimedia forensics and living body recognition in face recognition. DL methods have demonstrated the ability to generate highly convincing fake faces, detect subtle traces of undetectable forgeries, and identify manipulated videos. In contrast to conventional photo forensic methods, DL approaches offer an end-to-end solution by integrating feature extraction and classification into a network structure, enabling effective automatic feature learning and classification. However, it should be noted that standard image forensic methods are often inadequate for videos due to the significant loss of data quality during compression. Therefore, the advancement of digital forensics poses challenges to established image forensic practices. Given the widespread distribution of video deepfakes and their potential to undermine peace and security, the development of automated methods for identifying and detecting deepfake videos has become crucial. These methods aim to distinguish between genuine and manipulated videos, enabling the identification and mitigation of potential risks associated with the proliferation of deepfake technology. The ongoing research and development in this field aim to enhance the accuracy and efficiency of deepfake detection algorithms, ensure the preservation of trust in video content, and safeguard against malicious uses of this technology.

In conclusion, the rise of video deepfake technology has presented significant challenges to the field of multimedia forensics. The ease with which highly realistic face-swapped movies can be generated using deepfake techniques has eroded the public's trust in the authenticity of videos. The development of automated methods, combining conventional and DL strategies, is crucial for accurately identifying and detecting deepfake videos. As technology advances, it is imperative to develop robust and efficient techniques that can effectively address the challenges posed by video deepfakes and ensure the integrity and trustworthiness of video content in the digital era.

3.3.3   Fake sound detection

The majority of voices encountered in daily life are no longer solely human but rather artificial. With the increasing automation of technology, people are becoming more reliant on voice commands to control various aspects of their daily activities. Virtual assistants such as Google Assistant, Alexa, Siri, Bixby, and others have become commonplace, employing artificially generated or machine-created voices. Even well-known individuals, including celebrities and politicians, are not immune to the misuse of voice manipulation technology. Deepfake, an advanced technique primarily utilizing GANs, has emerged as a major concern in this context. It enables the production of synthetic audio that closely imitates real human voices, raising significant ethical and security issues. The challenge in detecting synthetic speech lies in the diverse range of methods that can be employed to generate artificial voices. Simple techniques like waveform concatenation, achieved through cut-and-paste methods, are widely available as open-source toolkits. Other approaches involve utilizing bandpass filters or voice stream source models. Recently, several CNN-based methods have been introduced, which yield remarkably realistic synthetic audio that is difficult to distinguish from natural human speech, even to human listeners. This poses a considerable challenge to the development of robust detection mechanisms.

The field of audio anti-spoofing research has explored the broader domain of synthetic speech synthesis detection. Various techniques have been proposed, ranging from manually created feature analysis to data-driven approaches. However, with the rapid advancement of CNN-based synthetic audio synthesis algorithms, many of the earlier detection methods are likely to prove ineffective. The complexity and sophistication of deepfake audio necessitate the development of novel and more sophisticated detection strategies. Efforts are underway to address the challenges posed by synthetic speech recognition and deepfake audio detection. Researchers and experts are exploring innovative approaches that leverage advanced ML algorithms and feature extraction techniques to identify synthetic voices reliably. By analyzing the unique characteristics of synthetic speech and training models on diverse datasets, it is possible to enhance the accuracy and effectiveness of detection systems.

In conclusion, the rise of artificial voices and the widespread use of deepfake techniques in synthetic speech pose significant challenges in various domains. The availability of open-source toolkits and the development of advanced CNN-based methods have made it increasingly difficult to distinguish between genuine human voices and their synthetic counterparts. The detection of synthetic speech synthesis is an active area of research, and new approaches are being developed to address this pressing issue. As technology evolves, it is crucial to stay ahead of malicious applications of voice manipulation and ensure the integrity and authenticity of voice-based interactions in both personal and professional settings.

3.3.4 Fake hybrid multimedia detection

The combination of deepfakes, which involve algorithmically altered footage, images, audio, and videos, with the rapid spread of information through social media platforms has created a significant potential for societal disruption. Deepfakes can manipulate and fabricate content, making it increasingly challenging to distinguish between real and manipulated media. To address this issue, developing effective anti-disinformation tools is crucial, including implementing deepfake detection algorithms and using immutable metadata to verify the authenticity and accuracy of digital material. When dealing with multimedia deepfake technology, it is essential to establish robust and reliable tools to accurately identify, analyze, and combat deepfake content. Deepfakes can manifest in various formats, including films, artwork, photographs, and sound recordings, making it imperative to have comprehensive solutions that encompass a wide range of multimedia content types. The ability to detect deepfakes goes beyond a single medium and requires a multidisciplinary approach combining computer vision, ML, signal processing, and forensic analysis expertise.

One of the fundamental challenges in combating deepfakes lies in the difficulty of tracking the history and origin of digital content. Even with a reliable, secure, and trusted system in place to trace the lineage of digital material, it can still be a complex task due to the ease of replication, distribution, and modification of digital assets. Deepfakes can be created and disseminated rapidly, potentially reaching millions of people before their falsity is identified. This highlights the urgent need for proactive measures that can detect deepfakes in near real-time and mitigate their potential impact. To address the challenges posed by deepfakes, researchers and technologists are continuously developing and refining deepfake detection algorithms. These algorithms leverage advanced ML techniques, including DNNs and generative models, to identify manipulated media discrepancies, artifacts, and anomalies. Additionally, efforts are being made to integrate immutable metadata into digital content, allowing for the verification of its origin and integrity. The fight against deepfakes requires a multifaceted approach that involves collaboration among researchers, technology companies, policymakers, and social media platforms. This includes developing and implementing standardized protocols, robust verification mechanisms, and educational campaigns to increase public awareness about the existence and potential dangers of deepfakes.

In conclusion, the emergence of deepfakes, in combination with the viral nature of social media platforms presents significant challenges to the integrity and authenticity of digital content. The development of effective anti-disinformation tools, including deepfake detection algorithms and the use of immutable metadata, is crucial in combatting the spread of manipulated media. However, addressing the complexities of deepfakes requires ongoing research, collaboration, and the continuous evolution of detection techniques to stay ahead of the ever-evolving landscape of digital manipulation.

3.4   Analysis of deepfake detection methods

Deepfake detection in photos uses a variety of techniques, each with unique properties. To find abnormalities brought about by deepfake manipulation, feature-based approaches focus on extracting manually created characteristics from photos, such as color, texture, or noise patterns. Since these techniques mainly concentrate on predetermined traits, they need a small to medium training size. On the other hand, statistical approaches make use of statistical analysis to find discrepancies in picture attributes. They require a medium to large training size to build robust statistical models that distinguish deepfakes from authentic images. DL methods, which employ CNNs, have gained significant attention for image deepfake detection. These approaches rely on large to very large training sizes to capture the complexity and variations of deepfakes. DL methods are particularly popular for real-time deepfake detection on social media platforms. Due to the temporal nature of video content, detecting deepfakes in videos comes with its own set of difficulties. A method that is frequently used to find inconsistencies or artifacts created by deepfake manipulation is called frame-level analysis. This strategy can combine statistical and feature-based techniques to find abnormalities at the frame level. DL techniques are essential for video deepfake identification, much like they are for image-based detection. These techniques use RNNs and CNN architectures to understand the spatiotemporal patterns connected to deepfakes. DL techniques often require a large training size due to the complexity of video footage to accurately capture the changes and subtleties of deepfake films.

While image and video deepfake detection has received significant attention, audio deepfake detection is also a critical area of research. Deepfake audio refers to synthesizing synthetic speech or manipulating existing audio to create fake recordings. The methods used for audio deepfake detection vary, including techniques such as waveform analysis, spectrogram analysis, and DL-based approaches. Waveform analysis directly analyzes audio signals to identify anomalies or inconsistencies introduced by deepfake manipulation. On the other hand, spectrogram analysis focuses on the visual representation of audio signals to detect irregularities. DL methods, particularly those based on RNNs and GANs, are gaining prominence for audio deepfake detection. These methods typically require a medium to large training size to learn and identify patterns associated with deepfake audio. Hybrid deepfake detection methods leverage a combination of techniques from image, video, and audio domains to enhance the accuracy and robustness of deepfake detection. These methods integrate various algorithms, such as feature-based, statistical, and DL approaches, to analyze multiple modalities of data. By combining the strengths of different detection techniques, hybrid models can effectively detect deepfakes across different media formats. The training size required for hybrid models varies depending on the specific algorithms and modalities used in the detection pipeline. These models find applications in various domains, including forensic analysis, media authentication, and content verification.

For deepfake identification, the *DeepFake Identification Challenge* (DFDC) dataset, CelebA, FaceForensics++, and UADFV are common options. Researchers may train and test their detection methods using these datasets, which include genuine and deepfake samples. However, the effectiveness and generalization of deepfake detection algorithms heavily depend on the accessibility and variety of datasets. To advance the state-of-the-art in deepfake identification and solve new difficulties in this discipline, larger and more diversified datasets must be created. Deepfake methods, data, characters, algorithms, etc. are displayed in Table 3.2.

Table 3.2   Deepfake techniques, information, characters, algorithms, etc.

Method	Algorithm	Required Training size	Popular Applications	Sample Datasets
Image Deepfake Detection	Feature-based Methods	Small/ Medium	Forensic analysis, early deepfake detection	CelebA, UADFV, FaceForensics++, DFDC, DeepFake TIMIT
Image Deepfake Detection	Statistical Methods	Medium/ Large	Automated detection systems, real-time monitoring	MesoNet, XceptionNet
Image Deepfake Detection	DL Methods	Large/Very Large	Real-time deepfake detection, social media platforms	DFDC, Celeb-DF, FaceForensics++, DeepFake Detection Challenge
Video Deepfake Detection	Frame-level Analysis	Medium/ Large	Forensic investigations, social media platforms	UADFV, DFDC, DeepFakeTIMIT, FaceForensics++
Video Deepfake Detection	Temporal Consistency Analysis	Large/Very Large	Video manipulation detection, real-time deepfake detection	DFDC, Celeb-DF, FaceForensics++, DeepFake Detection Challenge
Audio Deepfake Detection	Acoustic Analysis	Small/ Medium	Voice authentication, audio forensics	LibriSpeech, VoxCeleb, DeepFakeTIMIT, AVspoof
Audio Deepfake Detection	Spectral Analysis	Medium/ Large	Voice verification, speech synthesis detection	ASVspoof, VoxCeleb, DeepFakeTIMIT, LibriSpeech
Hybrid Deepfake Detection	Multimodal Fusion	Large/Very Large	Robust deepfake detection, cross-modality analysis	DFDC, Celeb-DF, FaceForensics++, VoxCeleb, DeepFakeTIMIT
Hybrid Deepfake Detection	Ensemble Methods	Large/Very Large	Improved detection accuracy, model combination	DFDC, Celeb-DF, FaceForensics++, DeepFake Detection Challenge

3.5 Criteria of DL/ML methods in multimedia security

The quality of functions is defined by mathematical metrics that show profitable feedback and analysis of a deepfake detection method's performance. We have to name a few critical parameters: accuracy, Matthews Correlation Coefficient (MCC), Confusion Matrix, recall, precision, and F1 score. Consequently, as reiterated earlier, accuracy stands as the paramount indicator, showcasing the proportion of correctly identified instances in meeting the anticipated observational requirements. In the time of combining total values in a confusion matrix, the True Negative to True Positive rate is exploited. The total quantity of patterns successfully detected is demonstrated by n, and the entire number of patterns is given by t in this equation below [29].

$$A = \frac{n}{t} * 100 \tag{3.1}$$

The given number of exact predictions is indicated by P and the rate of True Positive forecasted compared with the total positively forecasted. Moreover, S_{TP} is the representation of the sum of total true positives, when A_{FP} is the representation of total false positives [30].

$$P = \frac{S_{TP}}{S_{TP} + A_{FP}} * 100 \tag{3.2}$$

A criterion of the amount of real positive observations is demonstrated by Re_{Call} named recall which can precisely forecast. Besides, A_{FN} specifies total false negatives in equation below.

$$Re_{Call} = \frac{S_{TP}}{S_{TP} + A_{FN}} * 100 \tag{3.3}$$

In addition, the F1 score is a total functionality criterion determination of Recall and Precision and representation of Harmonic achieved by Precision and Recall.

$$F1_{score} = \frac{2 * Re_{Call} * P}{Re_{Call} + P} * 100 \tag{3.4}$$

Additionally, functionality matrix measurement which weighs forecasted and real observations is a confusion matrix that utilizes True Negatives, True positives, False Positives labels, and False Negatives. All true predictions are the total number of Positives and Negatives, so all wrong predictions are the aggregated False Negatives and False Positives.

$$\begin{vmatrix} S_{TP} & A_{FP} \\ A_{FN} & TN \end{vmatrix} \tag{3.5}$$

Further, a class that is both true and positive is predicted by True Positives. True Negatives are also wrong predictions but are Negative to a class Negatives are Negative predictions but are incorrect. Also, an individual value functionality demonstrator which encapsulates the total Confusion Matrix is the MCC. It presents a more instructive and correct result than the F1 score and accuracy in evaluating assortment challenges.

3.6 Explainable methods for multimedia security mechanisms

The purpose *of Explainable AI* (XAI) in deepfake detection techniques is to make these models' internal workings transparent and understandable. We may evaluate the reliability and trustworthiness of deepfake detection algorithms by using explainable ways to acquire insights into how they come at their judgments. Popular explainable techniques used in XAI for deepfake detection include Grad—*Gradient-weighted Class Activation Mapping* (CAM*), Local Interpretable Model-agnostic Explanations* (LIME), and SHapley Additive exPlanations (SHAP). These techniques are designed to draw attention to the crucial details and areas of the input data that influence the model's conclusion.

The use of these explicable techniques can improve deepfake detection's interpretability and comprehension. They make it possible for us to pinpoint the precise visual signals or patterns that the model uses to differentiate between authentic and false pictures or movies. We can learn more about the advantages and disadvantages of the detection model and even find holes that adversaries could take advantage of by examining these cues. While accuracy is critical for deepfake detection, other significant considerations include interpretability and explainability. If a model's decision-making is secretive and difficult to understand, it may not be as beneficial as an extremely accurate one. Interpretable models explain why decisions were taken, which promotes trust and enables the detection of biases or errors.

Researchers might concentrate on creating transparent feature extraction techniques and explainable architectures to improve interpretability and understandability. The human interpretability of the deepfake detection pipeline may be enhanced by adding interpretability techniques such as Grad-CAM, LIME, or SHAP. As both are necessary in various circumstances, achieving a balance between accuracy and interpretability is crucial. High accuracy guarantees the deepfake detection system's usefulness, while interpretability promotes confidence, identifies possible weaknesses, and enables human experts to make well-informed judgments based on the model's outputs.

3.7 Conclusion

The fast development of multimedia technology has created new difficulties in preserving the integrity and authenticity of digital media information. This chapter examined the idea of multimedia security with an emphasis on identifying deepfakes, or fake media produced with DL methods. We discussed numerous approaches and ML strategies to address these security issues. Journalism, entertainment, and politics are just a few industries that face serious threats from deepfakes since they may be used to influence and mislead viewers. For multimedia material to remain trustworthy and reliable, deepfake detection is essential. The hazards connected with deepfakes may now be recognized and mitigated with the use of ML algorithms. We looked at supervised learning, unsupervised learning, hybrid models—all employed in deepfake detection—and other ML techniques. CNNs and RNNs, two types of supervised learning approaches, have demonstrated promising results in separating actual and manipulative material. These models are trained using labeled datasets to develop their ability to distinguish between actual and fraudulent samples. Deepfake detection has also used unsupervised learning techniques like GANs. A discriminator network, which tries to tell the difference between authentic and fraudulent samples, and a generator network, which produces synthetic media, make up a GAN. GANs may learn to produce increasingly realistic media while enabling precise deepfake detection by continually enhancing the generator and discriminator networks. To improve the effectiveness of deepfake detection systems, hybrid models combine the advantages of supervised and unsupervised learning approaches. These models can improve generalization and resilience against adversarial assaults by combining labeled and unlabeled data. The value of dataset curation and augmentation in training deepfake detection models was also covered. For models to be trained that can successfully identify deepfakes in practical contexts, a variety of representative datasets must be made available. The model's capacity to generalize and identify previously unidentified deepfake variants may also be improved using data augmentation techniques like picture and video transforms. Deepfake detection techniques based on ML have shown encouraging results, however, they still have certain problems. An important obstacle is adversarial assaults, in which deepfake makers try to trick the detection models. Research is now being done to create more resilient models that can survive attacks like this and adapt to new deepfake-generating methods.

In conclusion, deepfake detection is essential to assuring multimedia material's validity and dependability. Multimedia security is a significant issue in the current digital era. Deepfake dangers may be identified and mitigated using ML approaches such as supervised learning, unsupervised learning, and hybrid models. These models can attain greater accuracy and resilience by utilizing a variety of curated datasets and data augmentation techniques. To combat the constantly developing nature of adversarial assaults and deepfake generation techniques, however, continuing study and development are required. The topic of multimedia security and deepfake detection holds promise for a safer and more reliable digital media ecosystem with continuing breakthroughs in ML and collaborative efforts among academics.

References

[1]   Noura, H.N., Azar, J., Salman, O., Couturier, R., and Mazouzi, K., A deep learning scheme for efficient multimedia IoT data compression. *Ad Hoc Networks*, 2023. **138**: p. 102998.

[2]   Cinar, A.C. and T.B. Kara, The current state and future of mobile security in the light of the recent mobile security threat reports. *Multimedia Tools and Applications*, 2023: p. 1–13.

[3]   Renaud, J., Karam, R., Salomon, M., and Couturier, R., Deep learning and gradient boosting for urban environmental noise monitoring in smart cities. *Expert Systems with Applications*, 2023: p. 119568.

[4]   Li, H., Wang, J., Xiong, N., Zhang, Y., Vasilakos, A.V., and Luo, X., A Siamese inverted residuals network image steganalysis scheme based on deep learning. *ACM Transactions on Multimedia Computing, Communications and Applications*, 2023. **19**(4): p. 1–23.

[5]   Ragab, M., Leveraging mayfly optimization with deep learning for secure remote sensing scene image classification. *Computers and Electrical Engineering*, 2023. **108**: p. 108672.

[6]   Chang, C.-C., Wang, X., Chen, S., Echizen, I., Sanchez, V., and Li, C.-T., Deep learning for predictive analytics in reversible steganography. *IEEE Access*, 2023. **6**: p. 3494–3510.

[7]   Zhang, Q., Guo, Z., Zhu, Y., Vijayakumar, P., Castiglione, A., and Gupta, B. B., A deep learning-based fast fake news detection model for cyber-physical social services. *Pattern Recognition Letters*, 2023. **168**: p. 31–38.

[8]   Waheed, S.R., Rahim, M.S.M., Suaib, N.M., and Salim, A., CNN deep learning-based image to vector depiction. *Multimedia Tools and Applications*, 2023. **82**: p. 20283–20302.

[9]   Maqsood, M., Yasmin, S., Gillani, S., Bukhari, M., Rho, S., and Yeo, S.-S., An efficient deep learning-assisted person re-identification solution for intelligent video surveillance in smart cities. *Frontiers of Computer Science*, 2023. **17**(4): p. 174329.

[10]   Minaee, S., Abdolrashidi, A., Su, H., Bennamoun, M., and Zhang D., Biometrics recognition using deep learning: a survey. *Artificial Intelligence Review*, 2023. **56**: p. 8647–8695.

[11]   Ma, Z., Yuan, X., Liang, K., *et al.*, Blockchain-escorted distributed deep learning with collaborative model aggregation towards 6G networks. *Future Generation Computer Systems*, 2023. **141**: p. 555–566.

[12]   Nie, T., Wang, S., Wang, Y., Tong, X., and Sun, F., An effective recognition of moving target seismic anomaly for security region based on deep bidirectional LSTM combined CNN. *Multimedia Tools and Applications*, 2023. https://doi.org/10.1007/s11042-023-14382-5.

[13]   Alaca, Y. and Y. Çelik, Cyber attack detection with QR code images using lightweight deep learning models. *Computers & Security*, 2023. **126**: p. 103065.

[14]   Alsubai, S., Dutta, A.K., Alkhayyat, A.H., Jaber, M.M., Abbas, A.H., and Kumar, A., Hybrid deep learning with improved Salp swarm optimization based multi-class grape disease classification model. *Computers and Electrical Engineering*, 2023. **108**: p. 108733.

[15]   Wu, Y., L. Wu, and H. Cai, A deep learning approach to secure vehicle to road side unit communications in intelligent transportation system. *Computers and Electrical Engineering*, 2023. **105**: p. 108542.

[16]   Yazdinejad, A., Kazemi, M., Parizi, R.M., Dehghantanha, A., and Karimipour, H., An ensemble deep learning model for cyber threat hunting

in industrial internet of things. *Digital Communications and Networks*, 2023. **9**(1): p. 101–110.

[17]   Garg, D., G.K. Verma, and A.K. Singh, A review of deep learning based methods for affect analysis using physiological signals. *Multimedia Tools and Applications*, 2023. **82**: p. 26089–26134.

[18]   Korshunov, P. and S. Marcel, *Deepfakes: a new threat to face recognition? assessment and detection.* arXiv preprint arXiv:1812.08685, 2018.

[19]   Goyal, A., Mandal, M., Hassija, V., Aloqaily, M., and Chamola, V., Captionomaly: a deep learning toolbox for anomaly captioning in social surveillance systems. *IEEE Transactions on Computational Social Systems*, 2023.

[20]   Sharma, P., Namasudra, S., Crespo, R.G., Parra-Fuente, J., and Trivedi, M.C., EHDHE: enhancing security of healthcare documents in IoT-enabled digital healthcare ecosystems using blockchain. *Information Sciences*, 2023. **629**: p. 703–718.

[21]   Zeng, X., Zhao, X., Zhong, X., and Liu, G., A survey of micro-expression recognition methods based on LBP, optical flow and deep learning. *Neural Processing Letters*, 2023. https://doi.org/10.1007/s11063-022-11123-x.

[22]   Zhu, Y., Wang, M., Yin, X., Zhang, J., Meijering, E., and Hu, J., Deep learning in diverse intelligent sensor based systems. *Sensors*, 2023. **23**(1): p. 62.

[23]   Kaliyar, R.K., A. Goswami, and P. Narang, FakeBERT: fake news detection in social media with a BERT-based deep learning approach. *Multimedia tools and applications*, 2021. **80**(8): p. 11765–11788.

[24]   Mohammed, A. and R. Kora, A comprehensive review on ensemble deep learning: opportunities and challenges. *Journal of King Saud University-Computer and Information Sciences*, 2023. **35**(2): p. 757–774.

[25]   Sahoo, S.R. and B.B. Gupta, Multiple features based approach for automatic fake news detection on social networks using deep learning. *Applied Soft Computing*, 2021. **100**: p. 106983.

[26]   Mridha, M.F., Keya, A.J., Hamid, M.A., Monowar, M.M., and Rahman, M. S., A comprehensive review on fake news detection with deep learning. *IEEE Access*, 2021. **9**: p. 156151–156170.

[27]   Ballesteros, D.M., Rodriguez-Ortega, Y., Renza, D., and Arce, G., Deep4SNet: deep learning for fake speech classification. *Expert Systems with Applications*, 2021. **184**: p. 115465.

[28]   Zhang, D., Li, W., Niu, B., and Wu, C., A deep learning approach for detecting fake reviewers: exploiting reviewing behavior and textual information. *Decision Support Systems*, 2023. **166**: p. 113911.

[29]   Heidari, A., Javaheri, D., Toumaj, S., Navimipour, N.J., Rezaei, M., and Unal, M., A new lung cancer detection method based on the chest CT images using federated learning and blockchain systems. *Artificial Intelligence in Medicine*, 2023. **141**: p. 102572.

[30]   Heidari, A., Navimipour, N.J., Jamali, M.A.J., and Akbarpour, S., A green, secure, and deep intelligent method for dynamic IoT-edge-cloud offloading scenarios. *Sustainable Computing: Informatics and Systems*, 2023. **38**: p. 100859.

Chapter 4

Preserving multimedia information security through the use of fractal-based cryptosystems: trends and challenges

Abbassi Nessrine[1,2] and Hajjaji Mohamed Ali[1,3]

Unquestionably, the multimedia information security applications and trends are advancing at a high speed of light, despite all malicious threats and intentions of hackers. From the cryptosystem design to the hardware implementation, the cryptographic applications continue to attest its efficiency and various aptitudes of use in several sensitive sectors such as the medical and military ones, requiring indeed a high performance of security, privacy conservation, and low energy consumption. Nevertheless, the information security field continues to attract hackers who never skip the opportunity of interfering and stealing or damaging confidential data.

This chapter provides a brief overview of recent works and solutions suggested for efficient multimedia information security using various theories such as chaos theory, cellular automata structures, and algebraic operators alongside some reconfigurable technologies-based approaches. Throughout this chapter, a secure application combining fractal bases, cellular structures, and chaotic attractors is proposed, to be an efficient approach for multimedia information security with low power consumption and high-speed processing competence in safe storage and transmission of data.

4.1 Introduction

Currently, the multimedia security field has endured a noteworthy technical modernization using several fundamental theories. Security and efficiency become a major concern, especially due to the development of internet and data availability and accessibility worldwide. Multimedia security can be treated using various techniques including steganography [1], watermarking [2,3], and cryptography [4,5]. Studying recently proposed techniques [6], cryptographic methods as one of

[1]Laboratoire d'Electronique et Microelectronique, LR99ES30, Faculty of Science of Monastir, University of Monastir, Tunisia
[2]National Engineering School of Sousse, University of Sousse, Tunisia
[3]Higher Institute of Applied Science and Technology of Sousse, University of Sousse, Tunisia

the most critical and revolutionary trends focus on two key tasks: key generation and encryption/decryption algorithm. It proved a high efficiency when it comes to data protection, safe storage, and transmission. These cryptographic methods include the application of fundamental mathematical and biological theories such as Chaos theory [7], Cellular Automaton theory [8], Fractal basis [9], and Deoxyribonucleic acid (DNA) algebraic operators [10] either in the design of high-quality pseudo-random number generators (PRNGs) or in the design of robust symmetric/asymmetric schemes. This huge amount of technical enhancement in the multimedia security field tempted the opposite forces to damage these recently developed applications, mainly software approaches, and to maliciously use confidential data. Reconfigurable platforms [11] are highly recommended to alleviate the protection of sensitive data and to stand against malevolent intentions of use.

This chapter is prepared in five sections. The next section provides a thorough review of recent works. Section 4.3 exhibits an overview of Fractal sets, chaotic attractors, and cellular structures and their utility in cryptographic applications. Section 4.4 focuses on describing meticulously the suggested approach. Experimental results are illustrated in Section 4.5, where we elaborated a comparative study with recent works to assess the efficiency of the given scheme. Finally, conclusions are given at the end of this chapter in Section 4.6.

4.2   Overview of trends and challenges

In the last few years, multimedia security techniques such as cryptography have been used in a variety of sectors: medical imaging, safe military data transmission, money transaction systems, and secret personal data conservation on social media. Nevertheless, while developing these techniques with limited and simple cryptographic primitives, the requirements of lightweight and low power consumption are always requested. The efficiency and low-cost constraints would continue to increase with the growth of the demand for new trends and approaches as technologies around safe multimedia information big data storage and transmission increase speedily.

Presently, researchers are actively engaged in the pursuit of enhancing the security and resilience of encryption methods. To achieve this, they are exploring the amalgamation of various categories of cryptographic primitives. These include chaotic systems, DNA algebraic, fractal systems, and diverse types of cellular automata (CA). The objective is to leverage the strengths and characteristics of these different primitives to bolster the overall effectiveness and robustness of encryption techniques in terms of performance, high speed, flexibility, and enhanced security within moderate power consumption ratios.

Aiming to boost the efficiency of cryptographic approaches, several works have been proposed. Some approaches were interested in software optimization while others, a few limited approaches, were focusing on hardware solutions. All the below-mentioned works tend to enhance the overall robustness of cryptographic schemes and, in hardware approaches, to reduce power consumption and resource utilization.

Zhang *et al.* [12] suggested an encryption scheme using hyperchaotic systems, the Hilbert curve fractals and H-geometric fractals. Their approach started by generating a hash value from the plain image using the SHA-3 hash function. This hash was then used as initial conditions of the hyperchaotic system formed through the combination of 3D Rössler attractor and the PWLCM chaotic map. Next, the resulting sequences from the hyperchaotic system are used to achieve global pixel position scrambling and pixel value changing. To scramble local pixel positions, the authors used the Hilbert curve and H-fractals were used twice as a diffusion technique.

Peyman *et al.* [13] proposed a fractal-based PRNG using a chaos game constructed over the 3D model of Barnsley. The encryption starts with reading the input image and the initial parameters and bases of the Barnsley system. Next, the 3D chaotic system founded on the Barnsley system with cubic organization iterates 100 times to generate (Xi, Yi, Zi) variables. Variables (Xi, Yi) are used to form a mask M for the selection of pixel location to change pixel values using a bitwise exclusive OR (XOR) operation with the variable Zi, and also to avoid pixel repetition in the Encryption/decryption processes. In addition, their scheme used two different permutation and substitution processes that depend on the current cryptographic phase whether encryption or decryption.

Masood *et al.* [14] put forward an image encryption scheme based on a Julia set of fractals and a 3D Lorenz attractor. Their approach started by reading the input image, decomposing it into separate R, G, B channels, and shuffling the obtained matrices randomly. Next, the Julia set is iterated to produce Julia fractal complex values and then modulated to retain real values. Real values from the Julia set are multiplied with previously shuffled pixels. Furthermore, the resulting values from this step are XORed with the 3D Lorenz-based streams. Encrypted R, G, B channels are concatenated to obtain the cipher image.

Ehsan *et al.* [15] proposed a cryptographic scheme built over the combination of the Julia fractal set, Hilbert curve Fractals, and variant chaotic systems. The Julia set was used to generate four fractal images used as keys. The Hilbert curve fractals are used to generate substitution boxes. In their approach, they used both a Logistic map to scramble pixel position and a Chen Hyperchaotic system to change pixel values of fractal images (Xi, Yi), and (Zi) is used to produce the index responsible for the fractal image selection. After the plain image pixel values substitution using Hilbert cure S-boxes, the cipher image is obtained using a bitwise XOR operation between the plain image pixel, the selected fractal image pixel, and the value of the previous encrypted pixel.

Khan *et al.* [16] suggested an image encryption scheme based on fractal keys using the Fibonacci series and discrete dynamical systems. The encryption started by decomposing the input image into separate RGB channels. Next, using the Mandelbrot set, a fractal image is generated having the same size as the input image. The following step is to extract the real values from this fractal image and multiply it with values generated by iterating the Fibonacci series. The Kaplan-Yorke chaotic map is then used to generate pseudo-random sequences. Fibonacci values are XORed with the Kaplan-Yorke generated sequences and with the three

RGB channels to encrypt the input image. The final cipher image is obtained through the concatenation of the three encrypted RGB channels.

The same author proposed in [17] an image cryptosystem using both Chebyshev polynomial and Fractal Tromino. The initial step of encryption involved breaking down the input image into distinct RGB channels, along with the creation of an R matrix of identical dimensions as the input image. Then, two keys, 8-bit sized each, are generated to update the R matrix and to generate the L-shaped fractal Tromino. Afterwards, the 3D Fractal Tromino is XORed with the separate R, G, B channels. Next, after being initialized, three chaotic matrices are generated using the Chebyshev Polynomial and these matrices are then subjected to an XOR operation with the previously XORed R, G, B channels. The resulting R, G, B matrices are substituted using predefined S-Boxes. Finally, to retain the cipher image an R, G, B channels concatenation is achieved.

Ye *et al.* [18] suggested an image cryptosystem using DNA algebraic operations and a fractal dynamical system (DFS) composed from the combination of IFS (iterated function system) system and Sierpinski system. Their scheme adopted mainly two processes: permutation and diffusion. The scheme started by reading the input image. Iterated for an adequate number of iterations, the DFS system is responsible for the generation of a permutation matrix applied to the input grayscale image. Afterward, the permuted image is encoded using DNA algebraic operations (DNA XOR operation) and then decoded using different DNA rules to get a DNA-processed image. Finally, the resulting image is diffused twice using a bitwise XOR operation with the pseudo-ransom sequences originating from the DFS.

Merah *et al.* [19] proposed an field programmable gate array (FPGA) implementation of a real-time image cryptosystem founded on chaotic systems. The Henon chaotic attractor was responsible for generating key streams XORed with the input image to finally obtain the cipher image. Xuenan [20] proposed a cryptographic scheme founded on both Arnold's chaotic map and multi-scroll chaotic attractors and then implemented it on an FPGA platform with 32-bit fixed point precision. The input image initially underwent a bitwise XOR operation with the generated chaotic key streams. Subsequently, the Arnold's chaotic map was employed to create confusion, effectively concealing the spatial arrangement of the pixels within the image. Ying *et al.* [21] suggested an FPGA-based implementation of a video cryptosystem capable of real-time operation. This system was built upon a newly developed multiwing chaotic system, which was derived by integrating a sawtooth wave function into the Lorenz chaotic system. The encryption process involved generating chaotic key streams and performing an XOR operation between these streams and the original input image, resulting in an encrypted image. Satyabrata in [22] proposed a Raspberry Pi implementation of an image cryptosystem founded on cellular structures. The given cryptosystem performed four algorithms using Groups of Programmable Cellular Automata resulting finally in the cipher image generation. The same author suggested in [23] an image encryption algorithm implemented on a Raspberry Pi platform. The approach utilized in this scheme involved the utilization of six algorithms to construct a symmetric block cipher. This cipher was designed based on Moore's 2D cellular automata and employed a pixel substitution process, resulting in a robust encryption method.

All the above-mentioned approaches took advantage of fundamental theories to establish software or hardware cryptographic schemes. Through the literature review, we conclude that fractal basis and chaotic attractors are sweeping the cryptographic applications. Besides, cellular structures did indeed prove their efficiency when it comes to two complex calculations, parallelism, and high-speed performances. Still, there is always room for improvement in the Multimedia Security field to keep up with recent trends and to stand against newly designed threats and attacks.

4.3   Foundational concepts: fractal systems, cellular structures, and chaotic attractors

4.3.1   Fractal systems

Fractal systems can be observed in various natural structures, including snow-flakes, clouds, mountains, tree roots, leaves, DNA, blood vessels, and river networks. These systems possess the remarkable property of exhibiting chaotic behavior, stemming from their inherent characteristics as part of nonlinear science. Fractal systems have the unique capability to simulate intricate structures with infinite nested levels, demonstrating self-similarity, high sensitivity, and non-linearity across all scales. Moreover, their iterative nature makes them highly suitable for composition using iterative methods. This feature renders fractal systems valuable in numerous cryptographic applications, as their dynamic behavior makes them ideal candidates for designing crucial primitives in encryption algorithms.

4.3.1.1   Julia set

The Julia set is a type of fractal structure that arises from the iterative application of a complex function. Named after mathematician Gaston Julia [24], the Julia set is defined as the collection of complex numbers for which the iterative process does not diverge to infinity.

To construct the Julia set, we start with a complex number, referred to as the parameter, and an initial complex number. We repeatedly apply a complex function to the previous result, generating a sequence of complex numbers. If this sequence remains bounded as the number of iterations approaches infinity, the parameter is part of the Julia set. On the other hand, if the sequence diverges towards infinity, the parameter is outside the Julia set.

The specific form of the complex function used in the iteration process determines the shape and characteristics of the Julia set. Examples of such functions include: $f(z) = z^2 + c$ or $f(z) = sin(z) + c$, where c is the parameter. By exploring different values of the parameter and visualizing the resulting Julia sets, intricate and visually appealing fractal patterns emerge.

4.3.1.2 Mandelbrot set

The Mandelbrot set is a prominent fractal structure discovered by mathematician Benoit Mandelbrot [25]. It is defined as the set of complex numbers for which an iterative process remains bounded, based on a specific mathematical formula.

$$Z_{n+1} = Z_n^2 + c$$

To construct the Mandelbrot set, we start with a complex number and iterate a formula that involves squaring the previous result and adding a constant value. The iteration begins with an initial value of zero. If, during the iteration, the magnitude of the resulting complex number remains bounded, the original complex number is considered to be part of the Mandelbrot set. However, if the magnitude grows beyond a predetermined threshold, the complex number is considered outside the set.

The visualization of the Julia set, and Mandelbrot set is often achieved by assigning colors to the points within and outside the set. Points within the set are typically colored black or a consistent hue, while points outside the set are assigned various colors based on the number of iterations required for the magnitude to exceed the threshold.

Both the Julia and Mandelbrot sets exhibit intricate self-repeating patterns, showcasing elaborate details at various scales. The boundary of the set, known as the fractal coastline, showcases fascinating structures and intricate shapes. Exploring different regions of the complex plane and visualizing the Mandelbrot set reveals a mesmerizing display of intricate fractal landscapes.

These fractal sets have captivated mathematicians, artists, and enthusiasts due to their intricate and visually striking nature, providing endless opportunities for exploration and aesthetic appreciation.

4.3.2 Chaotic attractors

Various methodologies have been developed based on chaotic systems, and we will focus on discussing two of them that leverage chaotic dynamics within cryptography. The initial approach utilizes chaotic systems to generate pseudo-random sequences, which subsequently serve as key sequences for concealing the original data through diverse methods. The second approach involves employing the original data as the initial state of the chaotic system, with the encrypted data emerging as a consequence of the generated chaotic orbits. The former approach is commonly associated with stream ciphers, while the latter is dedicated to block ciphers, applicable to both symmetric and asymmetric cryptography.

In the existing literature, simple chaotic maps [16] and multi-dimensional attractors [19] have been explored either individually [20] or in combination [8] for the development of robust PRNGs and encryption algorithms. Additionally, previous studies [8] have suggested that the use of multidimensional attractors produces the requisite random behavior necessary for generating secure key streams. In this regard, we have selected the Lorenz chaotic attractor [26], which is defined by the following set of differential equations, to construct a sophisticated PRNG:

$$\dot{x} = \partial y - \partial x$$

$$\dot{y} = \wp x - (xz + y)$$

$$\dot{z} = -\beta z + yx$$

The system consists of three state variables, namely x, y, and z, as well as three parameters: ∂, β, and $\wp$. Under certain parameter values and initial conditions ($\partial = 10$, $\beta = 8/3$, $\wp = 28$), the system exhibits chaotic behavior. To adapt this chaotic attractor for numerical applications, it is necessary to discretize it. This can be achieved by solving the aforementioned equations using Euler's forward resolution method, which is described by the equation:

$$X_{i+1} = X_i + \zeta \times E$$

In the given context, the variables are defined as follows: X_i represents the system variable, i represents the iteration index, ζ represents the time step, and E represents the differential equation that describes the chaotic system.

4.3.3   Cellular structures

Recent scientific research has been increasingly focusing on cellular structures due to their remarkable effectiveness in cryptographic applications. The simplicity and immense potential of Cellular Automata theory have contributed to its widespread popularity in studying complex systems. This discrete computational model, initially discovered by Ulam and Von Neumann in the 1940s, consists of an organized sequence of cells that evolve based on specific rules. In this context, the future state of each cell is determined by its own status as well as the statuses of its neighboring cells [27].

The 1D elementary cellular automaton, developed by Wolfram in the 1970s, is a simplistic arrangement of cells forming a linear structure. Each cell within this automaton possesses two binary states and is surrounded by its own state, its left neighbor, and its right neighbor, collectively forming its neighborhood. By applying a set of 256 evolution rules, the cells transition from their initial states to subsequent generations. The 1D rules exhibit remarkable properties that render them suitable for cryptographic applications. These notable features include:

1. Uniformity: Certain rules maintain a consistent state for each cell, with all cells remaining either 1 or 0 throughout successive generations (e.g., rule 222).
2. Repetition: Some rules generate a regular oscillation pattern, displaying repetitive behavior across generations (e.g., rule 190).
3. Randomness: Certain rules produce seemingly random patterns, making it difficult to discern any underlying order or predictability (e.g., rule 30).
4. Complexity: Rule 110 exemplifies a type of behavior where repetitive oscillations occur, but the precise locations and timing of these oscillations remain unknown, adding a level of complexity to the system.

RCA rule 90/165

First case: rule 165

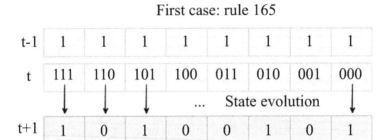

Second case: rule 90

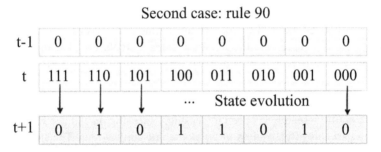

Figure 4.1   Dynamics of reversible cellular structure 90_165

These distinctive features contribute to the effectiveness of Wolfram's 1D cellular automaton in cryptographic applications. Nevertheless, in symmetric encryption, it is crucial to satisfy not only efficiency and high-security requirements but also the criterion of reversibility. Upon studying the 1D Wolfram set of rules, it has been observed that out of the 256 rules, only six are reversible [28]. To address this limitation, Fredkin proposed a technique known as the second-order cellular automaton (CA) to transform any one-dimensional cellular automaton rule into a reversible one [29]. In this method, the configuration of the future state, as depicted in Figure 4.1, is determined not only by the status of the two neighboring cells, as in the case of elementary cellular automata, but also by the current state (t) of a cell and its previous state $(t-1)$. By incorporating this additional information, reversibility can be achieved, enabling the reversibility, and ensuring data integrity.

4.4   Proposed approach

To create a cryptosystem with a high level of security, two essential elements are indispensable: a trustworthy algorithm and a resilient key generator. The proposed cryptosystem adopts a diffusion-confusion architecture complemented by a robust key generator. To achieve efficient and rapid performance, the cryptosystem

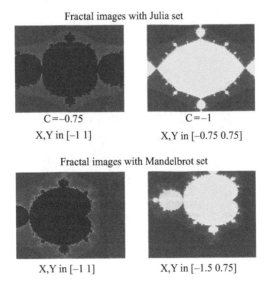

Figure 4.2 Generation of four different fractal images

employs a symmetric stream cipher encryption method, which meets the requirements for high-speed operations.

4.4.1 Fractal image generation

By altering the value of c in the Julia set of fractals, different shapes of fractals can be produced. Fractals fail to exhibit any distinct shape when c is greater than 1. However, when c is less than 1, two unique shapes of fractals are observed. In addition, the Mandelbrot set was iterated 200 times to generate two different fractal images, as depicted in Figure 4.2.

Once four distinct fractal images have been generated, they undergo modulation and conversion processes to match the format and size of the input image. This ensures consistency in the dimensions and characteristics of the images. Subsequently, these modulated fractal images are fused together, combining their features and properties. The result of this fusion is the final fractal key image (Figure 4.3).

4.4.2 Chaotic key generator

The proposed architecture for a Random Number Generator utilizing the Lorenz system is illustrated in Figure 4.4. It comprises three distinct modules:

1. Initial State Generator (ISG): The ISG module is responsible for generating the initial state of the Lorenz chaotic system. To achieve this, a 128-bit initial key is required, which is generated using a secure hash algorithm such as SHA-128.
2. Lorenz system: The Lorenz chaotic system is utilized to generate chaotic values. It takes the initial state obtained from the ISG module and evolves

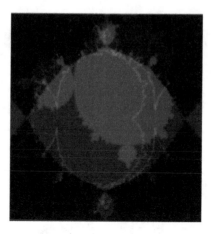

Figure 4.3   Fractal key image

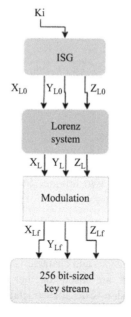

Figure 4.4   The 3D Lorenz-based PRNG

according to the Lorenz equations, producing a continuous stream of chaotic values.

3. Modulation Module: The modulation module modulates the chaotic values produced by the Lorenz to generate random numbers with a high degree of entropy.

By integrating these three modules, the PRNG architecture leverages the chaotic properties of the Lorenz system, generating random numbers with strong cryptographic characteristics. The use of modulation further enhances the randomness and diversity of the output.

4.4.3 Encryption algorithm

The cryptosystem requires several inputs, including a 256×256 grayscale input image, a fractal key image, and a 256-bit external initial key. The external initial key is generated using the SHA256 hash function (Figure 4.5).

The encryption process commences by reading a grayscale input image. Following that, the initial key Ki is generated using the SHA-256 hash function. The fractal key image is then created using the Mandelbrot and Julia sets. As a subsequent step, a diffusion process takes place by performing a bitwise XOR operation between the key fractal image and the input image.

Although the bitwise XOR operation is a straightforward logical operation, it is widely utilized as a histogram equalization technique to fortify the cryptosystem against statistical attacks. By applying the XOR operation, the pixel values are randomly redistributed, effectively mitigating high correlation, and bolstering the overall security of the system.

During the confusion phase, the randomness degree within the diffused image is increased. To generate the future cell state $(t+1)$, the encryption algorithm begins by initializing the RCA rule using the sequence X_{Lf} originating from the Lorenz PRNG.

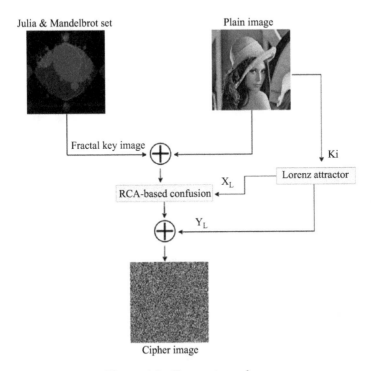

Figure 4.5 Encryption scheme

The resulting confused image undergoes another diffusion step. This diffusion is achieved by applying the bitwise XOR operation again with the sequence Y_{Lf}. The purpose of this operation is to further conceal the previous processes and make it challenging for potential intruders to discern the individual steps of the cryptosystem. By applying the XOR operation, the image becomes increasingly complex and difficult to analyze, enhancing the overall security of the system.

4.4.4   Decryption algorithm

To recover the original image, the decryption process as in Figure 4.6 utilizes the inverse of the encryption algorithm as the decryption algorithm. By reversing the operations performed during encryption, the decryption algorithm effectively undoes the transformations, allowing the original image to be retrieved. The decryption algorithm follows the reverse order of the encryption steps, applying the necessary operations in the opposite direction to restore the image to its initial state.

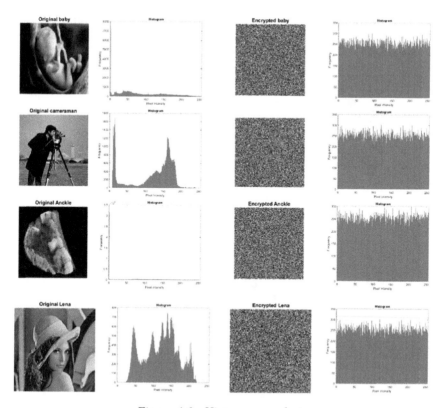

Figure 4.6   Histogram analysis

4.5   Results and discussions

4.5.1   *Key generator analysis*

As the key is the sole unknown component within the cryptosystem, it is of utmost importance to verify its efficacy in defending against brute-force attacks. Brute-force attacks involve systematically attempting every possible key combination to decrypt the data. By conducting validation procedures, the cryptosystem's ability to withstand exhaustive key search efforts can be evaluated. This validation process is essential in ensuring the robustness and integrity of the cryptosystem's security measures.

4.5.1.1   Key space

To provide robust protection against brute-force attacks, it is imperative to have a key space width of at least 2^{100}. In this research contribution, a chaotic PRNG is employed to generate a 256-bit key, resulting in a key space of size 2^{256}. A comprehensive analysis, as depicted in Table 4.1, demonstrates that this contribution outperforms previous literature works, establishing its exceptional performance and effectiveness in ensuring enhanced security measures.

The comparative study findings demonstrate that the proposed chaotic PRNG outperforms the other systems analyzed in terms of key space size. This implies that the proposed system offers a greater number of potential key combinations, resulting in enhanced resilience against exhaustive search attacks.

The overall analysis of the key space comparison underscores the superior security capabilities provided by the proposed chaotic PRNG. Its ability to generate a key with a larger key space significantly contributes to the protection of sensitive information and effectively addresses the vulnerabilities associated with brute-force attacks.

In conclusion, the comparative study conclusively establishes the superior security offered by the proposed chaotic PRNG, thereby validating its efficacy in safeguarding confidential data and mitigating the potential risks posed by brute-force attacks.

4.5.1.2   NIST SP800-22 test suite

The NIST 800-22 SP test suite is employed to verify the randomness of the 1,000-bit sized key sequences generated from the PRNG that is based on the chaotic Lorenz attractor.

Table 4.1   An examination of key space sizes:
a comparative analysis

Work	Key Space
Ref. [12]	2^{123}
Ref. [13]	2^{232}
Ref. [15]	2^{144}
Ref. [20]	10^{123}
Ref. [22]	2^{64}
This work	2^{256}

Table 4.2   The NIST 800-22 SP test suite results

Test	Value of p	State
Long runs of ones	0.66657	Valid
Status frequency	0.89568	Valid
Linear complexity (M = 500)	0.45398	Valid
Random excursions variant	0.48854	Valid
Forward cusum	0.64518	Valid
Runs	0.68539	Valid
Random excursions (x = +1)	0.93768	Valid
Spectral DFT	0.91495	Valid
Overlapping template (m = 9)	0.69824	Valid
Approximate entropy (m = 10)	0.09763	Valid
Block frequency (m = 128)	0.52823	Valid
Universal	0.08253	Valid
Binary matrix rank	0.64568	Valid
Non-overlapping template	0.45628	Valid
Reverse cusum	0.67535	Valid

The NIST SP 800-22 test suite is employed to evaluate the randomness and quality of the key sequences generated by the chaotic PRNG utilizing the Lorenz attractor. The outcomes of the test suite demonstrate the extent to which the generated key sequences conform to statistical criteria for randomness.

The obtained results in Table 4.2 indicate that all the tests produce p-values within an acceptable range, indicating that the generated key sequences exhibit randomness and successfully pass the statistical tests. This confirms that the chaotic PRNG, based on the Lorenz attractor, generates key sequences that meet the required criteria of randomness for cryptographic purposes.

In summary, these results serve as validation for the efficiency of the proposed PRNG in generating secure and dependable key sequences, thereby ensuring the integrity and confidentiality of cryptographic systems.

4.5.2   Statistical analysis

In the evaluation of cryptographic systems, statistical analysis entails employing statistical methods to evaluate the security and performance aspects of cryptographic algorithms and protocols. It involves examining data derived from experiments or simulations to assess the reliability and effectiveness of the cryptographic system.

4.5.2.1   Histogram analysis

Histogram analysis is a statistical method utilized to explore the frequency distribution of data points for a given dataset. When applied to cryptographic systems, histogram analysis becomes a useful tool for examining specific characteristics or properties of the data, such as the occurrence of values or patterns. By creating a histogram, which visually represents the data's distribution, valuable insights can be gained regarding the behavior and nature of the cryptographic system. This analytical approach enables the detection of irregularities, patterns, or potential weaknesses within the system, thereby aiding in the evaluation of its security and performance.

The uniform histogram, as depicted in Figure 4.6, indicates that pixel intensities are equally distributed across the image. In this case, the original and cipher image histograms exhibit dissimilar patterns, implying that the encryption process introduced distortions to the pixel distribution.

4.5.2.2 Correlation coefficient analysis

Correlation coefficient analysis is a valuable tool in the evaluation of cryptographic systems as it allows for the investigation of the relationships between various components. By assessing the interdependencies among elements such as encryption algorithms, key generation techniques, and data transformation processes, correlation coefficient analysis aids in determining the system's resilience and efficacy. It also helps in uncovering potential vulnerabilities or weaknesses that could arise from significant or unintended correlations between variables. This analysis is essential for ensuring the overall security and reliability of cryptographic systems.

The formula provided below is utilized for computing the correlation coefficients:

$$\varsigma_{xy} = \varphi(x,y)/\sqrt{\theta(x)}\sqrt{\theta(y)}$$

The correlation coefficient computed between the grayscale values (x,y) of two adjacent pixels within the image, the covariance estimation between (x,y), and the estimations of variance in x and y are denoted as ς_{xy}, $\varphi(x,y)$, and $(\theta(x), \theta(y))$, respectively (Table 4.3).

When comparing the correlation coefficient value of the cipher image to that of other recent works, a lower value closer to 0 suggests a stronger encryption scheme. This indicates that the cipher image (Table 4.4) demonstrates a lack of significant

Table 4.3   An examination of the correlation coefficient values of test images

Images	Direction	C.C value of original image	C.C value of cipher image
Baby medical	Horizontal	0.9984	0.0033
	Vertical	0.9665	−0.0029
	Diagonal	0.9810	0.0021
Lena	Horizontal	0.9723	−0.0012
	Vertical	0.9945	−0.0041
	Diagonal	0.9901	0.0022
Ankle	Horizontal	0.9746	−0.0002
	Vertical	0.9571	0.0029
	Diagonal	0.9733	−0.0011
Cameraman	Horizontal	0.9311	−0.0042
	Vertical	0.9820	0.0033
	Diagonal	0.9852	0.0029

correlation with the reference images, resulting in a higher level of security and confidentiality. In such cases, the cipher image is distinct and does not reveal any noticeable patterns or relationships, enhancing its overall effectiveness in protecting sensitive information.

4.5.2.3 Information entropy

Shannon information entropy, also referred to as Shannon entropy, serves as a metric to gauge the average information or uncertainty within a given dataset. In the realm of cryptography, it is utilized to evaluate the randomness and unpredictability of data, such as cryptographic keys or cipher images, calculated as follows:

$$\varepsilon(I) = \sum_{i=1}^{N} (P(x_i)\log_2 P(x_i))$$

The pixel intensity value, denoted as x, represents the value associated with a specific pixel in an image. The probability of a pixel having a particular intensity value x is represented by $P(x)$.

By determining the entropy value based on the probabilities associated with various outcomes within the data. A lower entropy value suggests a higher level of order or predictability that may indicate potential vulnerabilities or weaknesses within the encryption scheme.

As demonstrated in Table 4.5 the higher entropy value signifies a greater degree of randomness and unpredictability, indicative of stronger encryption and heightened resilience against cryptographic attacks.

Table 4.4   An examination of correlation coefficients values of cipher Lena image: a comparative analysis

Work	C.C Values		
	Horizontal	Vertical	Diagonal
Ref. [12]	0.0015	−0.0014	−0.0028
Ref. [13]	−0.0031	−0.0293	0.0077
Ref. [15]	0.0603	0.0005	−0.0019
This work	−0.0012	−0.0041	0.0022

Table 4.5   An examination of the global Shannon entropy values of test images

Images	Global entropy of original image	Global entropy of cipher image
Baby medical	3.2633	7.9979
Lena	7.4116	7.9976
Ankle medical	6.9837	7.9967
Cameraman	7.0097	7.9975

Table 4.6   *An examination of the global Shannon entropy values of cipher Lena image: a comparative analysis*

Work	Global entropy value
Ref. [12]	7.997
Ref. [17]	7.9973
Ref. [18]	7.997
Ref. [22]	7.9646
This work	7.9976

The entropy value of the ciphered Lena image surpasses the entropy values found in recent studies, signifying that the encryption scheme being evaluated demonstrates a commendable level of randomness and offers an adequate degree of security (Table 4.6).

4.5.3   Differential attack analysis

The NPCR (Number of Pixel Change Rate) is a quantitative measure utilized for assessing the degree of diffusion accomplished by an encryption algorithm. It quantifies the proportion of pixels that undergo a change in their values when a single bit of the encryption key is modified, comparing the original image with the encrypted image.

$$NPCR = 1/A \sum \psi(i,j) \times 100\%$$

The size of the image is denoted by A, while the logical value ψ is determined using the equation specified as follows:

$$\psi(i,j) = 1, p_1(i,j) = p_2(i,j)$$

or

$$\psi(i,j) = 0, p_1(i,j) \neq p_2(i,j)$$

Whereas The UACI (Unified Average Changing Intensity) metric is employed to assess the diffusion achieved by an encryption algorithm. It quantifies the average variation in intensity between corresponding pixels of the original image and the encrypted image resulting from modifying a single bit of the encryption key.

$$UACI = 1/A \sum \sigma/G \times 100\%$$

σ represents the disparity observed between two pixels sharing identical coordinates within the image, calculates as in:

$$\sigma = p_1(i,j) - p_2(i,j)$$

In this study, we introduced a modification by changing a single pixel in the input image. Specifically, we set pixel (1,5) to a grayscale value of 0. Subsequently, we

Table 4.7   *An examination of the NPCR and UACI values of test images*

Images	NPCR (%)	UACI (%)
Baby medical	99.6246	33.263
Lena	99.6170	33.6674
Ankle medical	99.6521	33.215
Cameraman	99.6246	33.1968

Table 4.8   *An examination of the global Shannon entropy values of cipher Lena image: a comparative study*

Work	NPCR (%)	UACI (%)
Ref. [12]	99.6231	33.5312
Ref. [13]	99.6100	33.4515
Ref. [17]	99.63	33.47
Ref. [18]	99.61	33.47
Ref. [22]	99.7834	33.841
This work	99.6170	33.6674

computed the UACI and NPCR values to evaluate the impact of this alteration on the encryption algorithm.

The UACI value serves as a valuable indicator for evaluating the diffusion capabilities and confidentiality of an encryption algorithm. A higher UACI value signifies a stronger level of diffusion, which is a critical aspect in ensuring the resilience of cryptographic systems.

When analyzing NPCR values, a higher value is desirable as it indicates enhanced diffusion and increased resilience against attacks.

Through careful analysis of the UACI and NPCR values, one can gain insights into the effectiveness of the encryption algorithm in achieving a desirable level of diffusion and maintaining the security of the encrypted data (Table 4.7).

The UACI and NPCR values of a cipher Lena image in Table 4.8 exceed those found in recent studies, this suggests that the evaluated encryption scheme demonstrates enhanced diffusion and improved resistance against attacks. As a result, the encryption algorithm offers a heightened level of security and confidentiality compared to other existing systems.

4.6   Conclusion

In this research paper, an innovative technique for preserving multimedia information is proposed. The encryption process involves a collaborative approach between Fractal sets, cellular structures, and the Lorenz chaotic attractor. The scheme utilizes the Mandelbrot and Julia sets of fractals to generate a fractal key image, which is then employed to diffuse the input image. The 3D Lorenz attractor acts as a pseudo-random generator, while cellular structures are utilized for the confusion process.

Through a comprehensive security analysis, it has been demonstrated that this model exhibits resistance against known attacks. Several metrics, including the histogram, correlation coefficients, and entropy of the cipher image, have been computed, yielding promising results. The optimal key space for encryption in this scheme is a 256-bit chaotic key.

As a continuation of this research, the proposal includes the hardware implementation of this encryption scheme and its application to large-scale images and video signals. This expansion aims to further enhance the practicality and versatility of the proposed technique.

References

[1] Subramanian, Nandhini, Omar Elharrouss, Somaya Al-Maadeed, and Ahmed Bouridane. "Image steganography: A review of the recent advances." *IEEE Access* 9 (2021): 23409–23423. DOI: 10.1109/ACCESS.2021. 3053998

[2] Nazari, Mahboubeh, and Mahshid Mehrabian. "A novel chaotic IWT-LSB blind watermarking approach with flexible capacity for secure transmission of authenticated medical images." *Multimedia Tools and Applications 80.7* (2021): 10615–10655. https://doi.org/10.1007/s11042-020-10032-2.

[3] Hajjaji, Mohamed Ali, Mohamed Gafsi, and Abdellatif Mtibaa. "Discrete cosine transform space for hiding patient information in the medical images." 2019 IEEE International Conference on Design & Test of Integrated Micro & Nano-Systems (DTS). IEEE, 2019. DOI: 10.1109/DTSS.2019.8914880.

[4] N. Abbassi, A. Mtibaa, M. Gafsi and M. A. Hajjaji, "An enhanced ECA/ Chaotic-based PRNG: Hardware design and Implementation," 2022 IEEE 21st International Conference on Sciences and Techniques of Automatic Control and Computer Engineering (STA), Sousse, Tunisia, 2022, pp. 249–254, DOI: 10.1109/STA56120.2022.10019236.

[5] N. Abbassi, A. Mtibaa, M. Gafsi and M. A. Hajjaji, "An enhanced ECA/ Chaotic-based PRNG: Hardware design and Implementation," 2022 IEEE 21st International Conference on Sciences and Techniques of Automatic Control and Computer Engineering (STA), Sousse, Tunisia, 2022, pp. 249–254, DOI: 10.1109/STA56120.2022.10019236.

[6] M. Gafsi, N. Abbassi, R. Amdouni, M. A. Hajjaji and A. Mtibaa, "Hardware implementation of a strong pseudo-random numbers generator with an application to image encryption," 2022 IEEE 9th International Conference on Sciences of Electronics, Technologies of Information and Telecommunications (SETIT), Hammamet, Tunisia, 2022, pp. 510–515, DOI: 10.1109/SETIT54465.2022.9875453.

[7]   M. Gafsi, R. Amdouni, N. Abbassi, M. A. Hajjaji and A. Mtibaa, "Implementation of a symmetric chaos-based cryptosystem for image security in real time," 2022 IEEE 9th International Conference on Sciences of Electronics, Technologies of Information and Telecommunications (SETIT), Hammamet, Tunisia, 2022, pp. 138–142, DOI: 10.1109/SETIT54 465.2022.9875573.

[8]   Abbassi, Nessrine, Mohamed Gafsi, Rim Amdouni, Mohamed Ali Hajjaji, and Abdellatif Mtibaa. "Hardware implementation of a robust image cryptosystem using reversible cellular-automata rules and 3-D chaotic systems." *Integration* 87 (2022): 49–66. https://doi.org/10.1016/j.vlsi.2022.06.007

[9]   Agarwal, Shafali. "Designing a pseudo-random bit generator using generalized cascade fractal function." *Chaos Theory and Applications* 3, no. 1 (2021): 11–19. https://doi.org/10.51537/chaos.835222

[10]   Amdouni, Rim, Mohamed Gafsi, Nessrine Abbassi, Mohamed Ali Hajjaji, and Abdellatif Mtibaa. "Robust hardware implementation of a block-cipher scheme based on chaos and biological algebraic operations." *Multimedia Tools and Applications* (2023): 1–34. DOI: 10.1007/s11042-023-15027-3

[11]   Gafsi, Mohamed, Nessrine Abbassi, Mohammed Ali Hajjaji, Jihene Malek, and Abdellatif Mtibaa. "Xilinx Zynq FPGA for hardware implementation of a chaos-based cryptosystem for real-time image protection." *Journal of Circuits, Systems and Computers* 30, no. 11 (2021): 2150204. https://doi.org/ 10.1142/S0218126621502042

[12]   Zhang, Xuncai, Lingfei Wang, Zheng Zhou, and Ying Niu. "A chaos-based image encryption technique utilizing hilbert curves and H-fractals." *IEEE Access* 7 (2019): 74734–74746. DOI: 10.1109/ACCESS.2019.2921309

[13]   Ayubi, Peyman, Saeed Setayeshi, and Amir Masoud Rahmani. "Deterministic chaos game: a new fractal based pseudo-random number generator and its cryptographic application." *Journal of Information Security and Applications* 52 (2020): 102472. https://doi.org/10.1016/j.jisa.2020.102472

[14]   Masood, Fawad, Jawad Ahmad, Syed Aziz Shah, Sajjad Shaukat Jamal, and Iqtadar Hussain. "A novel hybrid secure image encryption based on julia set of fractals and 3D Lorenz chaotic map." *Entropy* 22, no. 3 (2020): 274. https://doi.org/10.3390/e22030274

[15]   Hasanzadeh, Ehsan, and Mahdi Yaghoobi. "A novel color image encryption algorithm based on substitution box and hyper-chaotic system with fractal keys." *Multimedia Tools and Applications* 79 (2020): 7279–7297. https:// doi.org/10.1007/s11042-019-08342-1

[16]   Khan, Majid, Fawad Masood, and Abdullah Alghafis. "Secure image encryption scheme based on fractals key with Fibonacci series and discrete dynamical system." *Neural Computing and Applications* 32 (2020): 11837–11857. https://doi.org/10.1007/s00521-019-04667-y

[17]   Khan, Majid, Ammar S. Alanazi, Lal Said Khan, and Iqtadar Hussain. "An efficient image encryption scheme based on fractal Tromino and Chebyshev polynomial." *Complex & Intelligent Systems* 7, no. 5 (2021): 2751–2764. https://doi.org/10.1007/s40747-021-00460-4

[18] Ye, Ruisong, and Huiqing Huang. "An Adaptive Image Encryption Scheme Using Fractal Dynamical System and DNA Operations." In 2021 IEEE International Conference on Electronic Technology, Communication and Information (ICETCI), pp. 284–289. IEEE, 2021. DOI: 10.1109/ICETCI53161.2021.9563513

[19] Merah, Lahcene, Adda Ali-Pacha, and Naima Hadj-Said. "Real-time cryptosystem based on synchronized chaotic systems." *Nonlinear Dynamics* 82, no. 1 (2015): 877–890. https://doi.org/10.1007/s11071-015-2202-2

[20] Peng, Xuenan, and Yicheng Zeng. "Image encryption application in a system for compounding self-excited and hidden attractors." *Chaos, Solitons & Fractals* 139 (2020): 110044. https://doi.org/10.1016/j.chaos.2020.110044.

[21] Ying Li, Zhijun Li, Minglin Ma and Mengjiao Wang. "Generation of grid multi-wing chaotic attractors and its application in video secure communication system." *Multimedia Tools and Applications* 79. (2020): 29161–29177. https://doi.org/10.1007/s11042-020-09448-7

[22] Roy, Satyabrata, Umashankar Rawat, Harsh Ajay Sareen and Sanjeet Kumar Nayak. "IECA: an efficient IoT friendly image encryption technique using programmable cellular automata." *Journal of Ambient Intelligence and Humanized Computing* 11 (2020): 5083–5102. https://doi.org/10.1007/s12652-020-01813-6

[23] Roy, Satyabrata, Manu Shrivastava, Umashankar Rawat, Chirag Vinodkumar Pandey, and Sanjeet Kumar Nayak. "IESCA: an efficient image encryption scheme using 2-D cellular automata." *Journal of Information Security and Applications* 61 (2021): 102919. https://doi.org/10.1016/j.jisa.2021.102919.

[24] Gaston Julia. "On Iteration of Rational Functions." *American Journal of Mathematics*, 40, no. 4 (1918) 169–218.

[25] Benoit B. Mandelbrot. *The Fractal Geometry of Nature*, Publisher: W. H. Freeman and Company,1982 ISBN: 0-7167-1186-9.

[26] Özkaynak, F. and Özer, A.B., "A method for designing strong S-Boxes based on chaotic Lorenz system." *Physics Letters A* 374, no. 36 (2010); 3733–3738.

[27] Wolfram, Stephen. "Cryptography with cellular automata." Conference on the Theory and Application of Cryptographic Techniques. Springer, Berlin, Heidelberg, 1985. https://doi.org/10.1007/3-540-39799-X_32

[28] Kumaresan, G., and N. P. Gopalan. "An analytical study of cellular automata and its applications in cryptography." *International Journal of Computer Network and Information Security* 11, no. 12 (2017): 45. DOI: 10.5815/ijcnis.2017.12.06.

[29] Morita, Kenichi. "Reversible cellular automata." *Theory of Reversible Computing*. Springer, Tokyo, 2017. 261–298. https://doi.org/10.1007/978-3-540-92910-9_7

Chapter 5

Secure interaction and processing of multimedia data in the Internet of Things based on wearable devices

Kashif Naseer Qureshi[1], Aizaz Raziq[2] and Gwanggil Jeon[3]

The advancement of technology has been significantly propelled by the Internet of Things (IoT), which has accelerated the processes of data collection, interpretation, and dissemination. In IoT networks, the sensor nodes or devices are connected by using data communication technologies. A wide range of IoT applications have gained popularity like smart cars, smart homes, smart agriculture, and smart industries. However, these networks have various challenges including adaptability, compatibility, and security. Security is always on the top due to users' personal data exchange and transmission. Various different types of security threats exist in these networks. This chapter explores the security threats, attacks, and other vulnerabilities in these networks. This chapter also presents the detection and prevention methods designed for multimedia data security. As these networks need lightweight security solutions due to limited resources enabled by devices of IoT networks. The chapter concludes with findings to prevent these networks from any type of security violations and provides a roadmap to the new researchers in this domain.

5.1 Introduction

Internet of Things (IoT) is one of the smart technology where devices are connected for data communication. The sensor nodes or physical things are equipped with transmitters and receivers and embedded technologies for data communication. The small devices can communicate with infrastructure and backbone networks by using long- and short-range communication standards [1]. Heterogeneous wireless standards and technologies are adopted such as Bluetooth, and Wi-Fi for data transmission [2]. Multimedia data is one of the interactive mediums that offer the user a variety of attractive methods to represent information such as text, sound,

[1]Department of Electronic & Computer Engineering, University of Limerick, Ireland
[2]Department of Social and Media Sciences, Shaheed Zulfikar Ali Bhutto Institute of Science and Technology (SZABIST), Pakistan
[3]Department of Embedded Systems Engineering, Incheon National University, South Korea

Figure 5.1   Multimedia files for wearable devices

and video. Users can interact and transfer multimedia data by using smart devices. Education, reference materials, training, corporate presentations, documentaries, and advertising are a few areas that mostly use multimedia data. The term "multimedia" combines the words "multi" and "media," which refers to a variety of media (sound, text, video) used to convey information. Video, audio, images, and text data are combined during data transmission to navigate, interact, create, and communicate [3].

The definition of a multimedia file is constantly being improved due to the rapid development of multimedia technology and network transmission efficiency. Numerous studies have been done on multimedia, including social media, multimedia retrieval, and multimedia security [1]. Figure 5.1 shows different types of multimedia files needed for wearable devices.

In recent decades, wearable technology has surged in popularity, capturing considerable attention from both academic and industrial circles, thanks to the smart and cost-effective services enabled by the Internet of Things (IoT). Wearable computing is emerging as the next major area of ubiquitous computing. The wearable devices market, valued at $9 billion in 2014, was projected to expand to over $30 billion by 2018 and further reach $70 billion by 2024 [2]. Wearable technology encompasses electronic devices designed to be worn or attached to the human skin, allowing continuous and close monitoring of an individual's actions without impeding or restricting the user's movements. Using smart wearables can improve applications' efficiency and optimization, improve people's quality of life, and boost productivity and safety [3].

Some wearables devices work without physical contact with the user, even though the majority are linked with clothing or worn on the body. Wearable devices

have advanced features and computational sensing capabilities, opening new services and scenarios. There are some similarities between the value proposition of
wearables and other areas of research such as Wireless Body Area Networks
(WBANs). However, to provide high and precise monitoring of human health,
WBAN's objective is much broader since it aims to network together many wearable sensors and actuators, including medically implanted devices [4].

Computers, smart tags, or cell phones can still track users' activities. Other
wearable devices are used to track body movement by using smart sensors and
accelerometers, while some utilize optical sensors to measure glucose levels or
heart rate. For example, the Brain Sensing Headband tracks brain activity and
wirelessly sends the data to a laptop, smartphone, or tablet. These technological
wearables devices have one thing in common: they continuously monitor data. The
main components of wearable devices are microprocessors, batteries, and internet
connectivity, which enables the synchronization of the acquired data with other
electronics like computers or mobile devices. Figure 5.2 shows the classification of
wearable devices.

These devices are not powerful due to limited resources and because of their
application, implementation, and design limitations. There are various difficulties
in using and deploying wearable technologies, such as developing sophisticated
functionality with limited processing resources, extending battery life, resolving
issues with the human–computer interface, reducing the size, and overcoming other

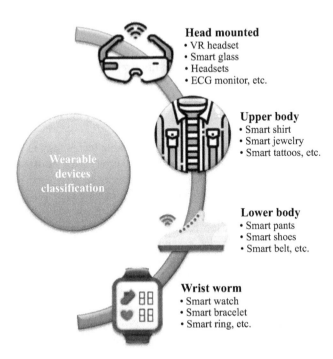

Head mounted
• VR headset
• Smart glass
• Headsets
• ECG monitor, etc.

Upper body
• Smart shirt
• Smart jewelry
• Smart tattoos, etc.

Lower body
• Smart pants
• Smart shoes
• Smart belt, etc.

Wrist worm
• Smart watch
• Smart bracelet
• Smart ring, etc.

Wearable
devices
classification

Figure 5.2   Classification of wearable devices

form restrictions. While many researchers and engineers consider these issues, security is somehow neglected. Due to the limited capabilities of wearable devices, traditional security solutions are not feasible and suitable.

Despite the substantial upward trajectory of the wearable industry, concerns regarding data security and privacy persist. Wearable devices are used in unsafe settings, vulnerable to Man-in-the-Middle attacks like Bluesnarfing, eavesdropping, and packet injection [2]. The Pentagon confirmed that the fitness-tracking software Strava had disclosed the locations of US troops in war-torn Syria and Iraq. The Strava fitness tracking app's "heatmap" tool was able to locate US military installations in Syria and other war areas. A user's identity, speed, and even heart rate could be revealed by de-anonymizing user-shared data made available by Strava [5].

Attackers can compromise wearable devices to exploit functionality and steal sensor data. Unauthorized access to wearable devices provides access to other connected IoT networks and leads to vulnerabilities in the networks. In addition, unauthorized users may have access to data on wearables; for instance, a wearable device that is connected to medical centers and central servers. Another issue is the validity (i.e., trustworthiness) of the devices and their activities.

However, due to a lack of storage, processing, and battery power resources, these devices are experiencing serious security difficulties in authentication, integration, secure data transfer, and key management.

5.2 Applications

The wearable devices are available in various shapes and sizes, including jewelry, accessories, medical equipment, and clothing-related items. Smartwatches, VR headsets, smart jewelry, fitness trackers, Bluetooth headsets, and web-enabled glasses are popular wearable devices [6], as shown in Figure 5.3. In addition, wearables function differently depending on the area they fall under, such as health, fitness, or entertainment [7].

One of the most well-liked categories of wearable technology is smartwatches. Smartphone applications are used with features like receiving notifications such as SMS, voice control, phone calls, social media application alert, email, and weather updates, and performing other tasks. Some other wearable technology applications like smartwatches have features like setting reminders, sending data, and taking voice commands, which are used for data communication and notification. The majority of smartwatches can track certain human medical and health conditions. As a result, they can be used for monitoring heart rate and fitness and help users keep track of daily activities, including automatically timing workouts, calories burned, and total step counts. The gathered data is delivered to a smartphone or cloud for better displaying the reports in the dashboard for making decisions for further consultations with doctors [8].

The other well-liked group of wrist-worn wearables is wrist bands. While wristbands and smart watches share certain characteristics, wristbands are made primarily to track a specific set of fitness activities, GPS tracking, and health. As a

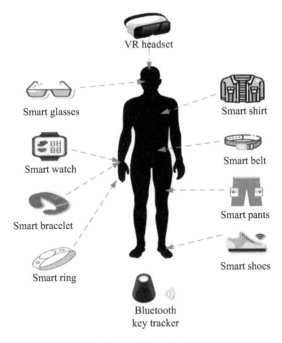

Figure 5.3   Wearable device types

result, unlike smartwatches, which are meant to replace traditional timepieces, most wristbands need a display screen for notifications or have a limited function and design [8]. On the other hand, a smart ring contains the same as a wristband component, including an near-field communication (NFC) chip and sensors that are used to track everyday human activities. Because of this, smart rings make a cool substitute for smartwatches and fitness bands. In addition, the wristbands and smart ring embedded device design ensures that their longer battery life satisfies the need for frequent outside use during sports like cycling, running, and hiking. On the other side, such designs restrict user interaction.

Spectacles or contact lenses with sensing, wireless connection, or other features like virtual or augmented reality are considered and known as smart glasses. The concept of augmented reality is when a human user can view both the real-world surroundings and the virtual contents displayed in the display in real-time [9,10]. Smart glasses have suffered from difficult problems as compared to smartphones, such as a smaller display, a smaller input interface, less processing power, shorter battery life, and security concern. A device worn on the head fully encloses the eyes to provide a 3D virtual experience known as Virtual Reality (VR) headset. The user's motion is detected by VR headsets using a combination of a gyroscope, proximity sensor magnetometer, and accelerometer.

Shirts, pants, belts, and undergarments are the most common smart clothing items. A variety of such products are available for biomechanics and monitoring human physiological signals. Specially designed garments with conductive silver-coated fibers serve as GPS tracking and health monitoring sensors, transmitting data to a smartphone or real-time devices. Many smart clothing options use Bluetooth or Wi-Fi to link to software on a different device. For example, smart shoes can identify and capture information from the user's regular activities. For the wearer's comfort and benefit, these smart shoes are built with vibrating motors, sensors, wireless Bluetooth systems, GPS, and various other sensors.

5.3   Security challenges

Security, energy, and computing power are still major challenges for research and commercial wearables development. These wearable devices depend on numerous wireless communication protocols that support various communication ranges, such as Bluetooth and Wi-Fi. A condensed version of the conventional Bluetooth protocol called Bluetooth Low Energy (BLE) was created to communicate with small, power-constrained electronics. BLE is the preferred standard for wearable devices to interact with mobile applications on more powerful smartphones, largely because of the minimal power needs.

Communication security is very important, yet most application developers must pay more attention to protecting the data created or collected by these devices. It also covers the logical security of software programs, administrative and access controls, and physical security. In this context, "physical security" refers to the protection of the hardware and storage components, and "logical security" refers to the defense of the software programs. Some of these devices contain extremely private information, such as financial, health, personal data, or other private transactions. These devices must be protected from wireless multimedia data access security issues. One of the biggest drawbacks is the security risk of storing sensitive data in a single database.

Resource limitations are some other frequent constraints for the adoption of advanced secure communication methods in the form of restricted central processing unit (CPU), battery, memory, and device size from the factory. Therefore, it is critical to identify any possible security gaps in wearable wireless communications and create workable safeguards against hardware, software, and communication-related security threat. IoT devices are a prime target for hackers because if any one device is hacked or compromised access to other networks is easy. Before transmitting sensitive information, a wearable device must verify the user's identity. These devices cannot use conventional encryption methods because the devices have limited memory to support modern cryptography methods and storage requirements. Several well-known attacks, known as replay, impersonations, ephemeral secret leakage attacks, man-in-the-middle, and stolen wearable devices, are suspected to occur in a wearable communication environment. Figure 5.4 shows different types of threats in wearable devices.

Major security threats for wearable devices are related to confidentiality, integrity, and availability. When an attacker uses any technique or attack during

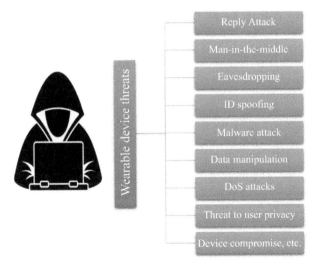

Figure 5.4   Wearable device threats

data communication between two devices, such as eavesdropping to gain unauthorized access to information, that is a breach of confidentiality. The illegal real-time interception of private communication is known as eavesdropping. These attacks offer serious security risks to wearable devices because they can reveal users' sensitive information to an adversary [8]. Adversaries can get the information transferred between wearable devices by passively monitoring data flows on wearable devices. As a result, the information gathered can be utilized to carry out significant information-gathering operations like breaking the key exchange wearable device pairing or collecting sensitive details about the user's other devices, like cell phones [11].

When an attacker modifies resources or information without authorization that is a breach of integrity and these attacks are replay attacks, masquerade attacks, and modification attacks. It is critical to make sure that data is only received by authorized devices and is not altered while in transit. When attackers take action to prevent services between wearable devices communication which are authorized to use them, this is a breach of availability. Location attacks offer a serious risk to people and organizations in terms of authenticity, secrecy, integrity, and availability. Malicious people can track users' whereabouts or previous locations to launch phishing attempts to distribute viruses. Other security threats or vulnerabilities are weak passwords, a lack of communication encryption, no security update mechanisms, insecure data management, outdated software or components, lack of privacy protection, and code injection.

There are several options; however, because of the various communication technologies and limited device resources, more than one solution might be needed to secure everything.

5.4   Existing solutions to protect wearables devices

Acar *et al.* [12] proposed the Wearable-Assisted Continuous Authentication (WACA) framework, which uses the motion sensors of wearables to authenticate a user continually. It employs sensor-based keystroke dynamics in which the user's typing speed is recorded by the motion sensors of the smartwatch they are wearing. Keystroke dynamics is a type of behavior biometric that uses users' typing habits to characterize them. Preprocessing, Feature Extraction, user profiling, and decision module are the four key phases of WACA. First, the raw data gathered by wearables is cleaned up by filtering during the preprocessing stage. Next, a collection of features is extracted from the input data. The properties of the current user profile are represented by this group of features, called a feature vector. Finally, the decision module receives the requested user profile from the authentication server. To determine whether the current user's authentication is successful or unsuccessful, the decision module calculates a similarity score between the returned and specified profiles.

Srinivas *et al.* [13] presented a novel user authentication method for secure medical data authentication in the cloud. One of the newest technology is cloud computing. It is used to manage the big data produced by various applications and to build a decision support system that will make accessing the extracted data from any location. The proposed scheme is divided into seven phases. The Big Data Registration Center (BRC) plays a very important role. First, in offline mode, the BRC chooses all system parameters. Additionally, the BRC completes the registration process for a patient and a medical professional (user) in offline mode. Finally, the BRC stores the secret credentials in the memory of each wearable sensor.

To enable secure communication between smart devices, Muhal *et al.* [14] proposed PUF-based Authentication Scheme (PAS) in conjunction with session keying. The smart device initially sends a request to the gateway, which checks the validity of a registered device first. If the device is registered, the gateway exchanges a challenge to authenticate and set up a session key for future communication. When a new device request comes in, the gateway stores the device credentials before exchanging the challenge for key generation.

Privacy protection is becoming more important in edge and cloud hybrid computing-based healthcare systems because of communication channel openness and data sensitivity. Liu *et al.* [15] proposed a cooperative privacy protection scheme for wearable devices. MinHash-based and secret sharing authentication is used in the space-aware edge computing mode to improve privacy preservation without disclosing sensitive information. To compare similarities between interactive wearable devices from the associated patients without revealing any sensitive information, MinHash-based data similarity computing is established for it. The positive and negative filters are combined for secure data interactions, and the bloom filter ensures that sensitive data is stored without exposing user privacy.

Srivastava *et al.* [16] introduced a novel blockchain-based IoT model for wearable medical devices to upgrade the current IoT-based remote patient monitoring system's security and privacy features. This approach uses more powerful and lightweight cryptographic methods, such as the ARX encryption scheme, to ensure stable data transfer over the network and storage over the cloud. These algorithms support minimal encryption for small devices and are composed of the basic operations of Addition, Rotation, and XOR. Additionally, they introduce the idea of rings of signatures, which offer important privacy benefits including signature accuracy and signer anonymity. They use asymmetric and symmetric encryption techniques for different objectives. First, they adopted a double encryption approach to make the symmetric key safer over the network. They secured the blockchain-based network using the Diffie–Hellman key exchange concept to prevent unauthorized access to the public key.

Establishing a secure communication environment for wearable technology remains a challenging issue. Kumar and Grover [17] introduced an elliptic curve cryptography-based authentication protocol for wearable devices to overcome this issue. Once authentication is complete, a private session key is created for further communications between smartphones and wearables. This scheme is divided into six phases, which are the wearable device pre-deployment phase, the phase of mobile terminal registration in which the user saves the credentials needed for mutual authentication and the creation of a session key between a smartphone and wearables in the memory of the mobile terminal, Login phase, authentication and key agreement phase, password and biometric update phase, and dynamic wearable device addition in which users can add new wearables and replace any device that has been stolen or lost. IoT devices have limited resources. Hence they require a lightweight authentication system.

Gupta *et al.* [18] discussed XOR and a one-way cryptographic hash function used in a new authentication method for IoT connectivity. This scheme network comprises three entities: an authentication server, a gateway/mobile terminal, and a wearable device. The wearable technology senses the user's health information and transmits it to a gateway or mobile terminal so the user can access it. The cloud server/Trusted Authority and the mobile terminal exchange the user's health information. The authentication server facilitates mutual authentication between a wearable device and the gateway/mobile terminal, which also maintains sensitive data. The wearable technology is directly linked to the mobile terminal but is not within reach of the cloud server. As a result, they can communicate with one another through the gateway or mobile terminal. This technique is based on a five-step authentication methodology, in which a user begins an authentication phase by connecting a required wearable sensing device. Then, a session key is created for secure communication between the mobile terminal and wearable sensing device via a trusted server. It also employs current timestamps and random ones to withstand a strong replay attack. Most wearable device security solutions currently available are based on encryption to prevent unwanted parties from accessing information, but they do not address access control when done by the wearable itself.

Diez *et al.* [19] proposed a novel access control system for wearable devices to overcome this issue. It is based on applying a security policy that is enforced using a mix of hardware (Java Card) and software (secure application) solutions. The asymmetric keys are shared between the Java Card and the server. The symmetric keys are used to cipher the data, the data's security rules, the credentials of the Java Card holder, and the data encrypted and signed. The security policies and symmetric keys are encrypted in the wearable device to prevent unauthorized exposure or change, which is important to remember. The Java Card conducts all necessary tests to make sure that a program on the wearable device is a trusted application and complies with the information security policy when it wants access to some data. The program then retrieves the data and makes it available to the user's wearable device in a restricted environment that only permits completing the actions the security policy allows if the requirements are met.

Lo and Yohan [20] discussed a strong authentication mechanism based on lightweight BLE that supports wearable device-focused micropayment systems. It is divided into two stages such as user authentication and payment transaction stage. The Wearable Payment counter (WP counter), Wearable Device (WD), and Trusted Third Party server comprise the authentication protocol. Mutual Authentication is required between the WD counter and the WP counter. Physical Unclonable Function (PUF) is used in an authentication protocol to create a secure and unique session key for each communicant session. The trusted third-party service has implemented the pseudo-PUF approach to confirm the identity of the user's wearable device.

Gupta *et al.* [21] proposed novel anonymous mutual authentication and key negotiation protocol for WBAN. This scheme is based on the most fundamental symmetric cryptosystems, such as cryptographic hash functions and XOR. The WBAN centralized network model is divided into four nodes: sensor nodes, intermediate nodes, HUB nodes, and system administrative nodes. A patient's real-time health data is sensed by the sensor nodes, which are resource-constrained wearables. The hub node receives the data from the sensor nodes through an intermediary node. The linkage between the sensor node and an intermediate node represents intra-BAN communication. The intermediate node sends the data to the hub node and has greater computing and communication capabilities than the sensor nodes. Before receiving any data, an intermediary node must verify the reliability of a sensor node. Establishing a session key facilitates secure communication between the hub and sensor nodes.

Li *et al.* [22] discussed a Secure and Lightweight Authentication and Key Agreement scheme (SLAKA) based on a cryptographic hash function, bitwise exclusive or operation, and the fuzzy extractor. All devices of intelligent wearable systems are synced with their clocks used in the SLAKA scheme. Furthermore, timestamps are utilized in the message transfer between the wearable device and the wearer's Mobile Terminal (MT) to prevent replay attacks. Three authentication factors are used between wearable devices and MT, and these factors are User identity (Idi), password of the user (PWi), and Biometric information (BIOi).

Guo *et al.* [23] proposed a novel anonymous authentication and group proof protocol for wearable devices, which provides a group proof for multiple devices and achieves mutual authentication between the devices and user as well as between the user and cloud server. The user's connection with the wearable device and the cloud server is then formed via a session key. This scheme employs bitwise

XOR operations and cryptographic hash functions, which is appropriate for the limited WDs. The anonymity of the user and the WDs is ensured by having both a real identity and a pseudo-identity, as well as a temporary identity that is assigned and updated after each session. Each party stored both old and new temporary identities to resist desynchronization attacks. Timestamps are used to prevent replay attacks. The messages exchanged between the two parties involve concealing a nonce using a hash function that effectively withstands various attacks. In addition, one or more random numbers are included in every sent message to resist an adversary's offline guessing attack.

Jan *et al.* [24] discussed a lightweight and secure data-sharing method for devices in a healthcare infrastructure (LightIoT). In an offline mode, these devices are directly registered with a distant server. The lightweight authentication phase used hash algorithms and Exclusive OR (XOR) operations, which ensure that secure sessions are established between the communication devices, such as wearables, gateways, and a distant server. The privacy of transmitted biomedical data is preserved through non-reproducible pseudo-random numbers. In addition, a session key is produced for future communication between the client and gateway during the mutual authentication procedure between the two parties.

Lee *et al.* [25] discussed a mechanism for preserving medical information based on the complete data storage process in devices, including mobile devices, wearables, and servers in medical facilities. Health Insurance Portability and Accountability Act (HIPAA) privacy and security regulations are followed throughout the entire process to secure the data. This technique minimizes the work that wearable devices must perform and achieves lightness by developing ID-based key negotiation for wearable devices using extended chaotic map technology. Additionally, it uses the Blockchain's irreversibility to confirm that the data has not been altered and enhance data security. The message summary on the Blockchain is compared to the data on the medical center server to ensure that the data had not been modified.

Tanveer *et al.* [26] proposed an Elliptic curve cryptography and hash function (Esch256) based access control system and the authenticated encryption technique for wearable devices. Users could establish a session key with the cloud server and obtain authentication to the scheme. Users could securely store data in the cloud server's storage module due to the formation of session keys. The user also used a secret key created from the user's biometric data to encrypt the data before it is stored. The system also permitted users to share data without being constrained by the security measures set in place by cloud service providers.

Gupta *et al.* [27] discussed an anonymous mutual authentication system that is lightweight and secure. Only the most fundamental symmetric cryptosystem techniques, such as bitwise XOR operations and hash functions in one direction, are used in this approach to ensure its success. The network model is divided into sensor nodes (wearable devices) and gateway nodes. It safeguards against powerful replay attacks by utilizing current time stamps and random nonces. Table 5.1 shows the comparison of discussed solutions designed for wearable devices.

Table 5.1   Existing secure solutions for wearable devices

Schemes	Protocols	Security objectives	Devices
[12]	Keystroke Dynamics	Continuous Authentication	Wearables Devices
[14]	Physical Unclonable Function (PUF)	Authentication	Smart Device and Gateway
[15]	Ciphertext Policy attribute-based encryption, Bloom filter, and MinHash	Privacy Preservation	Wearable devices and Computing Units
[16]	ARX Encryption Algorithm, Digital Signature, Ring Signature, and Diffie–Hellman	Blockchain-based High Security	IoT Medical Devices
[17]	Elliptic Curve Cryptography (ECC) and Hash Function	Authentication	Mobile Terminal and Wearable devices
[18]	XOR and One-Way Hash function	Anonymous User Authentication and Key Agreement	Sensor Nodes, Gateway Nodes, and Authentication Server
[19]	Security Policy Combination of Hardware (Java Card) and software (secure application).	Access Control System	Remote Server and Wearable Devices
[20]	Physical Unclonable Function (PUF)	BLE based Authentication	Wearable devices, Wearable Payment Counter, and Trusted Third Party Server
[21]	XOR and Cryptographic Hash function	Anonymous Mutual Authentication and Key Agreement	Sensor Node, Intermediate Node, Hub Node, and System Administrator
[22]	Fuzzy Extractor, Hash function, and the Bitwise Exclusive-or Operation	Authentication and Key Agreement	Wireless Devices and Mobile Terminals (Gateway Nodes)
[23]	Hash Functions and Bitwise XOR Operations	Anonymous Authentication and Group proof protocols	Wearable Devices, Mobile Terminals, and Cloud server
[24]	Hash Functions and Exclusive OR (XOR) Operations.	Authentication	The wearable device, gateway, and Remote server
[25]	Hash Function, Chaotic function, and blockchain	Data Preserving	Sensors, Mobile devices, and Medical Center Server
[26]	ECC, a hash function (Esch256), and AEAD scheme (AEGIS-256)	Authenticated data sharing	Wearable devices, User terminal, and Cloud server
[27]	XOR and Hash Function	Anonymous Mutual Authentication	Wearable devices and Gateway nodes

5.5   Findings

After a detailed literature review, this chapter presents the main findings related to wearable device security and privacy concerns.

A. Identification: Identification of wearable devices is a significant and serious concern if explored by an adversary in the network. There is a need for a system to provide wearable device identity to other qualified devices. The users must know the wearable devices' identity to make a difference. Many researchers discussed this criterion for smart wearable devices [28].

B. Data integrity: This is another important factor for data originality during transmission. If data is altered, changed, or manipulated during transmission, the entire system is compromised. Data integrity is one of the common surveillance methods to secure data from any external interference. There is a need for a system to ensure data accuracy by using checksum or cyclic redundancy checks.

C. Trustworthiness: This factor is one of the multidisciplinary concepts and one of the complex tasks in a network. The network topologies are dynamic in nature and making devices trustworthy is difficult. There are different types of trust evaluated in the network like direct, indirect, or cumulative trust. There is a need to establish the mechanism, especially at the edge or cloud networks to make the devices trustworthy for smooth data transmission. Many studies suggested the trust mechanism for wearables devices based networks [29,30].

D. Authentication: This factor requires proper architecture and infrastructure such as servers to handle the data exchange among wearables devices, gateways, and central units. Some wearable devices are using RFID chips which are not able to exchange data with authentication servers. There is a need to design an infrastructure for wearable devices network for authentication.

E. Access control: This factor is used to give access to resources and permissions to wearable devices. This factor also focuses on the network capabilities to provide the requisite access control to wearable devices. In these networks, the access control decisions are based on context which is why a number of steps should be taken to manage the access control mechanisms.

F. Data availability and privacy: These factors are very important where users will access the network immediately and securely reach the information. There are different reasons for data unavailability such as Denial of Service (DoS) attacks to make the system unavailable for the users. On the other hand, data privacy is another challenge due to individuals' habits, location, personal information, and other interests stored for ease of system usage. These factors violate user privacy during data aggregation. There is a need to design intelligent systems to tackle data availability and privacy issues.

5.6   Conclusion

Since their first release, wearable devices have undergone significant architectural changes, and it is still difficult to identify serious security flaws in their updated functionality. However, security issues are growing quickly as wearable devices are widely used for different purposes in the IoT network. Malware is the primary tool that cybercriminals use to carry out security attacks, which significantly harm users and mostly exploit wearable devices' communication protocols, sensors, firmware vulnerabilities, and applications to steal sensitive data from consumers or break into devices. These devices have limited resources, and conventional cryptography techniques cannot be used to protect them. Recent studies on improved encryption, structured mesh architecture, various pairing algorithms, and network security solutions are discussed in detail by using different cryptography methodologies used by researchers to protect these devices' resources. Still, a highly secured mechanism is needed to improve the current security measures especially to provide, trust, privacy, access control, data integrity, and availability services. Cybersecurity methods must provide a secure mechanism for wearable technology. These devices will be more attractive in the future IoT due to their lower energy usage, increased efficiency, and enhanced security.

References

[1]   J. Yang, S. He, Y. Lin, and Z. Lv, "Multimedia cloud transmission and storage system based on internet of things," *Multimedia Tools Applications*, vol. 76, no. 17, pp. 17735–17750, 2017.

[2]   M. L. Hale, K. Lotfy, R. F. Gamble, C. Walter, and J. Lin, "Developing a platform to evaluate and assess the security of wearable devices," *Digital Communications Networks*, vol. 5, no. 3, pp. 147–159, 2019.

[3]   F. J. Dian, R. Vahidnia, and A. Rahmati, "Wearables and the Internet of Things (IoT), applications, opportunities, and challenges: A Survey," *IEEE Access*, vol. 8, pp. 69200–69211, 2020.

[4]   M. Anwar, A. H. Abdullah, A. Altameem, *et al.*, "Green communication for wireless body area networks: Energy aware link efficient routing approach," *Sensors*, vol. 18, no. 10, p. 3237, 2018.

[5]   L. Cilliers, "Wearable devices in healthcare: Privacy and information security issues," *Health Information Management Journal*, vol. 49, no. 2–3, pp. 150–156, 2020.

[6]   K. Vijayalakshmi, S. Uma, R. Bhuvanya, and A. Suresh, "A demand for wearable devices in health care," *International Journal of Engineering and Technology*, vol. 7, no. 1, pp. 1–4, 2018.

[7]   H. Tahir, R. Tahir, and K. McDonald-Maier, "On the security of consumer wearable devices in the Internet of Things," *PloS One*, vol. 13, no. 4, p. e0195487, 2018.

[8]   S. Seneviratne, Y. Hu, T. Nguyen, *et al.*, "A survey of wearable devices and challenges," *IEEE Communications Surveys Tutorials*, vol. 19, no. 4, pp. 2573–2620, 2017.

[9]   L.-H. Lee and P. Hui, "Interaction methods for smart glasses: A survey," *IEEE access*, vol. 6, pp. 28712–28732, 2018.

[10]   K. N. Qureshi, R.W. Anwar, S.N. Bhati, and G. Jeon, "Fully Integrated Data Communication Framework by Using Visualization Augmented Reality for Internet of Things Networks," *Big Data*, vol. 9, no. 4, pp. 253–264, 2021. 10.1089/big.2020.0282.

[11]   K. N. Qureshi, A. Alhudhaif, S. W. Haider, S. Majeed, and G. Jeon, "Secure Data Communication for Wireless Mobile Nodes in Intelligent Transportation Systems," *Microprocessors and Microsystems*, p. 104501, 2022/03/12/ 2022. https://doi.org/10.1016/j.micpro.2022.104501.

[12]   A. Acar, H. Aksu, A. S. Uluagac, and K. Akkaya, "WACA: Wearable-assisted continuous authentication," in *2018 IEEE Security and Privacy Workshops (SPW)*, 2018, pp. 264–269: IEEE.

[13]   J. Srinivas, A. K. Das, N. Kumar, and J. J. Rodrigues, "Cloud centric authentication for wearable healthcare monitoring system," *IEEE Transactions on Dependable Secure Computing*, vol. 17, no. 5, pp. 942–956, 2018.

[14]   M. A. Muhal, X. Luo, Z. Mahmood, and A. Ullah, "Physical unclonable function based authentication scheme for smart devices in Internet of Things," in *2018 IEEE International Conference on Smart Internet of Things (SmartIoT)*, 2018, pp. 160–165: IEEE.

[15]   H. Liu, X. Yao, T. Yang, and H. Ning, "Cooperative privacy preservation for wearable devices in hybrid computing-based smart health," *IEEE Internet of Things Journal*, vol. 6, no. 2, pp. 1352–1362, 2018.

[16]   G. Srivastava, J. Crichigno, and S. Dhar, "A light and secure healthcare blockchain for iot medical devices," in *2019 IEEE Canadian Conference of Electrical and Computer Engineering (CCECE)*, 2019, pp. 1–5: IEEE.

[17]   D. Kumar and H. S. Grover, "A secure authentication protocol for wearable devices environment using ECC," *Journal of Information Security Applications*, vol. 47, pp. 8–15, 2019.

[18]   A. Gupta, M. Tripathi, T. J. Shaikh, and A. Sharma, "A lightweight anonymous user authentication and key establishment scheme for wearable devices," *Computer Networks*, vol. 149, pp. 29–42, 2019.

[19]   F. P. Diez, D. S. Touceda, J. M. S. Cámara, and S. Zeadally, "Lightweight access control system for wearable devices," *IT Professional*, vol. 21, no. 1, pp. 50–58, 2019.

[20]   N.-W. Lo and A. Yohan, "BLE-based authentication protocol for micro-payment using wearable device," *Wireless Personal Communications*, vol. 112, no. 4, pp. 2351–2372, 2020.

[21]   A. Gupta, M. Tripathi, and A. Sharma, "A provably secure and efficient anonymous mutual authentication and key agreement protocol for wearable devices in WBAN," *Computer Communications*, vol. 160, pp. 311–325, 2020.

[22]   J. Li, N. Zhang, J. Ni, J. Chen, and R. Du, "Secure and lightweight authentication with key agreement for smart wearable systems," *IEEE Internet of Things Journal*, vol. 7, no. 8, pp. 7334–7344, 2020.

[23] Y. Guo, Z. Zhang, and Y. Guo, "Anonymous authenticated key agreement and group proof protocol for wearable computing," *IEEE Transactions on Mobile Computing*, 2021.

[24] M. A. Jan, F. Khan, S. Mastorakis, M. Adil, A. Akbar, and N. Stergiou, "LightIoT: Lightweight and secure communication for energy-efficient IoT in health informatics," *IEEE Transactions on Green Communications Networking*, vol. 5, no. 3, pp. 1202–1211, 2021.

[25] T.-F. Lee, I.-P. Chang, and T.-S. Kung, "Blockchain-based healthcare information preservation using extended chaotic maps for HIPAA privacy/ security regulations," *Applied Sciences*, vol. 11, no. 22, p. 10576, 2021.

[26] M. Tanveer, M. Ahmad, T. N. Nguyen, and A. A. Abd El-Latif, "Resource-Efficient Authenticated Data Sharing Mechanism for Smart Wearable Systems," *IEEE Transactions on Network Science*, 2022.

[27] A. Gupta, M. Tripathi, S. Muhuri, G. Singal, and N. Kumar, "A secure and lightweight anonymous mutual authentication scheme for wearable devices in Medical Internet of Things," *Journal of Information Security Applications*, vol. 68, p. 103259, 2022.

[28] J. Gubbi, R. Buyya, S. Marusic, and M. Palaniswami, "Internet of Things (IoT): A vision, architectural elements, and future directions," *Future Generation Computer Systems*, vol. 29, no. 7, pp. 1645–1660, 2013.

[29] A. R. Sfar, E. Natalizio, Y. Challal, and Z. Chtourou, "A roadmap for security challenges in the Internet of Things," *Digital Communications and Networks*, vol. 4, no. 2, pp. 118–137, 2018.

[30] M. A. Razzaq, S. H. Gill, M. A. Qureshi, and S. Ullah, "Security issues in the Internet of Things (IoT): A comprehensive study," *International Journal of Advanced Computer Science and Applications*, vol. 8, no. 6, 2017.

Chapter 6

Blockchain-envisioned arbitrable multimedia data auditing based on post quantum computing paradigm in IoT

Sunil Prajapat[1], Pankaj Kumar[1] and Ashok Kumar Das[2]

Data auditing is becoming increasingly important as numerous users want to out-source large multimedia data from the Internet of Things (IoT) devices to the cloud. This is because it allows users to confirm the accuracy of the data they are out-sourcing. However, most existing data auditing techniques fail to ensure compre-hensive data integrity, a vital prerequisite for meeting the security demands of valuable multimedia services. Moreover, when the cloud service provider (CSP) tampers with the outsourced data, users are not promptly compensated due to the lack of fair arbitration. This chapter introduces a blockchain-driven approach to enable arbitrable data auditing. In the proposed system, users often only need to perform private audits, and a smart contract is only triggered to perform a public audit when the private audit's verification is unsuccessful. The proposed hybrid auditing approach prevents users from paying audit charges and receiving immediate and rapid recovery when the CSP corrupts the outsourced data. Additionally, the presented system can ensure 100% data integrity by utilizing the deterministic checking technique based on an Number Theory Research Unit (NTRU) lattice accumulator. Furthermore, when users want compensation from the CSP, the proposed scheme can stop forged claims. We completed the prototype's implementation after assessing the security benefits. The testing outcomes of the suggested data auditing system based on blockchain demonstrate its security, effi-ciency, and advantageous characteristics.

6.1 Introduction

Intelligent multimedia and the IoT have developed quickly, which has caused vast volumes of data to rise explosively and placed a great deal of strain on the Internet

[1]Srinivasa Ramanujan Department of Mathematics, Central University of Himachal Pradesh, India
[2]Center for Security, Theory and Algorithmic Research, International Institute of Information Technology, India

as a whole. A well-known workaround to this issue is to use a CSP to store IoT and intelligent multimedia data [1–4]. To guarantee the security of outsourced data while it is being transmitted, numerous strategies have been tested and put into use [5]. Amidst the ongoing series of data breaches, concerns about data availability and integrity have arisen due to the extensive range of potential attack points [6–10]. When users outsource their confidential IoT and advanced multimedia data to a CSP, they relinquish ownership, leading to a situation where the data can be modified or deleted without their consent. To address this issue, users must periodically validate the accuracy of the data they have trusted from other sources to tackle this issue. As a result, remote data integrity verification is becoming more and more significant within the framework of cloud computing.

The majority of data integrity verification methods now in use are probabilistic [11–20]. In this respective approach, rather than analyzing the whole dataset, the verifier adopts a random selection process to choose partial data blocks for integrity verification. As a result, a 100% safeguarding of the data's integrity cannot be offered. More than a probabilistic method is necessary for large-scale IoT and intelligent multimedia data, particularly when dealing with sensitive information related to sectors such as banking, energy, transportation, and others because these systems have strict data consistency and quality requirements. Deterministic data integrity checking methods are still another type. This method provides 100% assurance of data integrity since the validator checks all data blocks rather than just a subset. Nonetheless, the deterministic approach leads to increased verification and computational demands, introducing efficiency challenges that need to be taken into account within this strategy.

A variety of data auditing systems have been developed to verify the integrity of the data that has been outsourced remotely. The present auditing may be categorized into private and public auditing approaches based on the various roles that the verifiers played [21]. In private auditing systems, the user acts as the verifier, and the user typically stores some essential information used in the verification process rather than the CSP. If a malicious user manages to gain unauthorized access to the key information utilized in the verification process, the replication from the CSP fails to pass through the verification prosperously; disagreements will occur when the validation fails. In essence, it becomes difficult to determine if the data has been altered or compromised by the CSP when the verification fails. Fair arbitration is now necessary since, if validation is unsuccessful, the CSP must reimburse the user for data corruption. A third-party auditor (TPA) is frequently employed by users in public auditing systems to confirm the accuracy of data that has been outsourced. As a result, the TPA directly impacts the audit outcomes. However, this notion is impractical, given that finding an entirely reputable TPA is only occasionally feasible.

In this study, we provide an effective hybrid auditing system based on blockchain that includes fair arbitration. Our method provides deterministic checking using lattice problem accumulators, allowing the validator to validate all data blocks respectively while minimizing computational overhead. The core idea behind an audit is that, especially for the data being outsourced $B = [b_1, b_2, b_3, ..., b_n]$, the verifier challenges the CSP by using the arbitrary index j. The CSP must calculate the associated witness wit_{bj} after receiving the challenge for all respective targeted data block b_j, and all data blocks other than b_j are considered in the witness computation. The CSP responds with (wit_{bj}, b_j), including the intended targeted data block b_j and the calculated witness. Therefore, even a small modification to the outsourced data might impact it; the subsequent response fails to satisfy the verification process. In alternative terms, if the CSP has distorted the data or is not saved, the CSP cannot produce a legitimate answer. As a result, the validator examines all data blocks rather than just some of them, safeguarding data integrity completely.

Additionally, the user uploads a copy of the data file digest acc_B to the blockchain while the data is being uploaded in addition to keeping a copy of the file, which is the essential information needed for verification. Users often only need to perform private audits since the verification may be performed by a user or through a blockchain smart contract during the audit. The utilization of public auditing by a smart contract comes into play if verification fails during private auditing. This occurs when the user fails to maintain the integrity of the data file digest, causing the response from the CSP to fail verification. Even if the CSP has not tampered with the data, disagreements may arise at this instinct. Because of the non-comparable nature of the blockchain, the data file digests acc_B stored within it remain intact and immune. Consequently, the blockchain smart contract is triggered to initiate public auditing to ensure impartial assessment in such cases. Therefore, this blockchain-based hybrid auditing system establishes fair arbitration, effectively resolving the issues that may arise between the CSP and the customer.

Quantum computer technology is entering people's horizons with its unprecedented growth and is envisioned as a new paradigm shift in the computing system. Conventional mathematical problems like discrete logarithms and prime factorization problems are easily unraveled in polynomial time with quantum computers [22]. However, abundant work cannot cope with better security against quantum attacks. Lattice cryptography supports the intractability of the mathematically hard problem with worst-case hardness assumption. Designing the schemes using cryptography based on lattice theory is recognized as the solution by the National Institute of Standards and Technology (NIST) [23]. Even on a quantum computer, there does not exist any algorithm that could compute the solution of a lattice problem in polynomial time. Lattice-based schemes proffer the appropriate security and attenuate the computational overhead. Hence becomes fruitful in several scenarios.

By leveraging this technology, it becomes possible to establish a smart contract embedded with unbiased mediation, guaranteeing that the customer will receive payment instantly and without delay if the CSP corrupts the outsourced data. As a result, this is accomplished through the execution of the smart contract's code on the blockchain. We swap out the TPA with a blockchain smart contract in our public auditing phase. A corrupt user may also submit a false claim for reimbursement to the CSP. We employ digital signature technology to prevent this.

6.1.1 Data auditing schemes

Several data auditing techniques have been developed in response to the rising need for outsourced data integrity checking [24,25]. The initial introduction of provable data possession (PDP), which became the pioneering audit technique to validate data integrity, was credited by Ateniese *et al.* [11] in 2007. However, this technique does not provide full data dynamic operation or privacy protection [12]. Next, Erway *et al.* [13] put forth a PDP system providing full dynamic data updating. Since then, extensive research has been done in this field to expand functionality and boost the effectiveness of data auditing for distant data. Finally, a public data auditing framework allowing dynamic data operations was put up by Wang *et al.* [14]. The follow-up work in Reference [15] supports numerous tasks with privacy-preserving auditing. Using doubly linked information tables, Yuan *et al.* [14] suggested a public audit mechanism for dynamic data sharing. In Liu *et al.*'s work [17], the authors developed a public auditing technique that heavily considered communication overhead and verification efficiency. They did this by using the data structure of a Merkle hash tree. In some circumstances, private auditing is also required in addition to public audits [21,26–28]. Various PDP models have also been put forth [29–31]. Using the PDP approach described earlier, a verifier can examine the integrity of remote data without the requirement to retrieve or obtain the entire dataset; instead, they need only choose a small subset of it at random and verify its accuracy. As a result, due to the inherent probabilistic nature of this process, it is impossible to safeguard the data's integrity with complete certainty.

The security of the aforementioned protocols depends on the resilience of traditional hard problems like discrete logarithms and prime factorization problems. Unfortunately, determining the solution to these problems is not strenuous with the quantum computers in the provided polynomial time [22]. Attraction toward quantum technology is heightening day by day, so the arrival of the quantum computer will make all the audit mechanisms susceptible. Therefore, these protocols cannot withstand quantum attacks. Introducing a lattice-based cryptosystem, Ajtai [32] has brought a new shift in cryptography. Algorithms employing lattice-based cryptography can withstand quantum attacks and are fruitful for various real environments. Abundant protocols are designed based on the lattice cryptosystem. Employing the hard problem of ideal lattice, a lattice-based PDP mechanism is given by Chen *et al.* [33]. Similarly, Ring Learning with Errors (RLWEs) hard problem was used by Yang *et al.* [34] to design an efficient PDP scheme. Both [35,36] are organized under the standard model, but in comparison, lattices with no special structure, ideal lattices, and RLWE lattices cannot provide better security. Therefore [33] and [34] are not efficient audit protocols for cloud-assisted environments [36], and [35] both presented efficient lattice-based audit protocols utilizing the traditional public key cryptosystem. However, both spaces cannot preclude the seepage against multiple audits on the same dataset block of the user. Additionally, the public key cryptosystem faces certificate management and storage challenges. The identity-based cryptosystem can overcome these challenges [37]. Utilizing it, Liu *et al.* and Zhang *et al.* [38,39] designed the lattice-based audit protocol that can provide privacy-preserving services. However, later it was found that both could not withstand the forgery attack.

The blockchain, the foundational technology for new cryptocurrencies, functions as a decentralized database where transactions are grouped and processed in batches. These transactions are then securely linked together using encryption, forming a continuously expanding chain of blocks. As is common knowledge, the blockchain has distributed storage, immutability, and decentralization. On the blockchain, smart contracts [40] are automatic, pre-agreed-upon executable programs. Numerous common applications, including decentralized storage [40–43], crowdsourcing systems [44–46], medical data management [40,47], and distributed ledger technologies [48,49], have been developed based on the characteristics and capabilities of the blockchain.

To replace public cloud audits with TPA's, Wang *et al.* [50] recently developed a blockchain-based fair payment mechanism by utilizing smart contracts. With the help of a smart contract, Yuan *et al.* [51] presented a blockchain-based safe deduplication and public auditing technique that provides automated user reimbursement for data tampering and automatic punishment of abusive CSPs. However, users must pay the blockchain's miners an audit fee for each verification. A blockchain-based private PDP approach that Wang *et al.* [50] suggested reduces storage space and increases efficiency significantly. However, it lacks a method for automatic retribution and reimbursement when a CSP corrupts the outsourced data. Additionally, each of these blockchain-based auditing techniques uses a probabilistic methodology. Taking into account the prior research, we employed a distinct auditing approach that combines both private and public auditing to achieve a deterministic methodology. As a result, the outcome was auditing. To encourage users and CSPs to behave honorably and to allow users to avoid paying auditing fees, we aim to guarantee the accuracy of data integrity verification and promote financial equity within the data auditing techniques.

6.1.2   Chapter contributions

The following is a summary of the contributions that contributed to our work:

- We present a robust hybrid data auditing approach leveraging blockchain technology for the IoT and intelligent multimedia. Our proposed solution solves the lattice problem of mistrust between the CSP and the user by utilizing deterministic cryptographic methods and the blockchain. Deterministic methods additionally increase the auditing system's dependability because they guarantee that all data will be present and accurate.
- To automatically punish dishonest CSPs and compensate the user for data corruption by the CSP in the intended scheme, we enforce a healthy environment.
- Our plan can simultaneously safeguard trustworthy CSPs and stop dishonest users from filing false claims.
- The proposed scheme employs a hybrid auditing design, which not only offers potential cost savings for customers in terms of audit fees and communication costs but also activates the public auditing phase exclusively when verification during the private auditing phase fails.

- By using the prototype, we experimentally validate the feasibility and effectiveness of our approach and conceptually demonstrate its correctness and soundness.

6.1.3 Chapter organization

In this section, the organization of this chapter is provided later. We initially highlight data auditing and mathematical lattices. Next, we present the preliminary materials, which include the lattices and their hard problems. After that, we demonstrate the system mode, blockchain technology, and security model. Next, we contain the proposed scheme of work model. Next, we discuss the security analysis of the intended scheme. A detailed comparative study among the state-of-the-art schemes related to auditing computational and communication costs. Finally, we conclude the work.

6.2 Mathematical preliminaries

6.2.1 Symbol

Table 6.1 lists various notations and their meanings that are used throughout this chapter

A matrix M and a vector v, respectively denoted by $||v||$ and $||\beta||_\infty = \max[||\beta_n||]$, represent the Euclidean norm of β and the norm of all columns of $\vec{\beta}$, respectively. Let's assume that $f = \sum_{n=0}^{N-1} f_n v_n$ and $g = \sum_{n=0}^{N-1} g_n v_n$ are two polynomials in R_p.

Table 6.1   Notations

Notation	Description
R	The set of the real numbers
R^+	The set of positive real numbers
Z_p	The discrete additive group
$||S||$	The norm of S
N	Dimension of the lattice
s	The Gaussian distribution's standard deviation
$D_{\mathcal{L},s,c}$	Discrete Gaussian distribution
h	Public key of cloud user
z	Public key of the cloud server
B	Private key of cloud user
$\mathbb{B}$	Private key of cloud server
H	One-way cryptographic hash function
(pk_u, sk_u)	Key pair of cloud user
(pk_s, sk_s)	Key pair of cloud server
$\mathbb{PR}$	The public parameters
m_i	File blocks
T_i	The tag of m_i
$R_p \frac{Z_p}{(X^N+1)}$	A polynomial ring with modulo $X^N + 1$.

6.2.2 Anticirculant matrices

An N-dimensional anticirculant matrix $C_N(f)$ is defined as follows:

Definition 6.1. $C_N(a)$ *is a Toeplitz matrix* [52] *that is represented by*

$$C_N(f) = \begin{bmatrix} (f) \\ (v.f) \\ \cdot \\ \cdot \\ \cdot \\ (v^{N-1}.(f)) \end{bmatrix} = \begin{bmatrix} f_0 & a_1 & \cdots & a_{N-2} & f_{N-1} \\ -f_{N-1} & f_0 & \cdots & f_{N-3} & f_{N-2} \\ \cdots & \cdots & \cdots & \cdots & \cdots \\ -f_1 & -f_{N-2} & \cdots & -f_{N-1} & f_0 \end{bmatrix}$$

where $a = \sum\limits_{n=0}^{N-1} a_n v_n \in R_p$.

For convenience, $C_N(f)$ is abbreviated as $C(f)$ in the sequence. Anticirculant matrices have a succession of respectable qualities.

Definition 6.2 (Gaussian distribution [53]). *The informal definition of Gaussian distribution is along the center $c \in R^N$ and standard deviation $s \in R_p$.*

$$\rho_{c,s}(x) = \exp\left(-\frac{||x - c||^2}{2s^2}\right)$$

Lemma 6.1 ([54]) *For $\mathcal{K} \leq 1$, it satisfies*

$$Pr[||\mathcal{Z}|| > \mathcal{K}s\sqrt{N} : z \leftarrow D_s^N] < \mathcal{K}^N \exp^{\frac{1}{2}(1-\mathcal{K}^2)}$$

and then, for any vector $v \in R^N$ and $s, t > 0$, we can get

$$Pr[|z, v| > t : z \leftarrow D_s^N] < 2\exp^{\frac{-t^2}{2||v||^2 s^2}}$$

Lemma 6.2 ([54]) *Given any $v \in Z^N$, if $s = \beta||v||$, and $\beta > 0$, then*

$$Pr[\frac{D_s^N(z)}{D_{s,v}^N(z)} < \exp^{12/\beta+1} : z \leftarrow D_s^N] = 1 - 1/2^{100}$$

6.2.3 Complexity in lattice

The *SIS* problem, a particular application of the *SVP* for integer lattices, ensures the security of our framework.

Definition 6.3 (SVP Problem). *Using the lattice $\mathcal{L} = \mathcal{L}(M)$, output the shortest nonzero vector that satisfies the condition $||v|| = \lambda_1(\mathcal{L})$. M is the basis.*

Definition 6.4 (SIS Problem). *A nonzero vector that satisfies $Mv = 0 \bmod p$ and $v \in \beta$ is determined by the SIS problem given a matrix $M \in Z_p^{N \times N}$, a prime p, and a real β.*

6.3   System model

First, the dataset is partitioned into n blocks, followed by the user generating a unique tag for each block employing their private key. After eliminating them locally, the user proceeds to transfer both the data blocks and corresponding tags to the cloud and some metadata into the blockchain. To maintain the intactness of data in the cloud, data blocks are frequently audited by TPA assigned by the user. During the auditing process, the TPA selects a subset of the data blocks at random. Then, he encapsulates a random value with the technical indicators of selected blocks and transmits it to the cloud. Upon receiving the audit challenge, the cloud reckoned the proof of intactness and sent confirmation as the challenge's output to TPA. The proof is then put through an advanced verification equation to see if it can pass. Finally, the TPA publishes the challenge and its proof into the blockchain. In Figure 6.1, we have shown a distinction between the existing auditing model and the proposed auditing model in this chapter.

6.3.1   Blockchain technology

Satoshi Nakamoto was the first to bring the blockchain concept in 2008 [55]. This decentralized, distributed ledger aids in maintaining the records in the data units. A typical structure of blockchain is shown in Figure 6.2. A chain of blocks is created by connecting these data chunks, which are referred to as blocks, with the hash values of the preceding block. Every peer end of the decentralized network keeps up this chain of blocks. These data units are divided into the block's header and data, which contain the block version, hash values, time stamps, random nonce, and transactions. The special nodes called miners add a transaction to the block after the verification protocol. Creating a block in the blockchain is referred to as mining, and miners are the peers in charge of doing so. After a new block passes the consensus protocols used for verification, it is added to the chain, and the blockchain is updated at each network peer. There are many protocols like proof of work (PoW) and proof of stake (PoS). Blockchain has many applications in the healthcare system, payment, voting, banking, etc.

6.3.2   Security model

The following are the security requirements:

- Unforgeablity: The proposed system needs to be fundamentally unbreakable against adaptive chosen message attacks.
- Public auditability: Users' confidential information should not be utilized for the auditing process so that users can relieve their burden by delegating the auditing to TPA.
- Privacy-preserving: During the audit process, TPA should not be able to determine the users' data by resolving linear equations.

6.4   Proposed scheme

The four algorithms listed later are included in the scheme. The Setup algorithm generates a few common parameters. A tag is created by the user for each file block

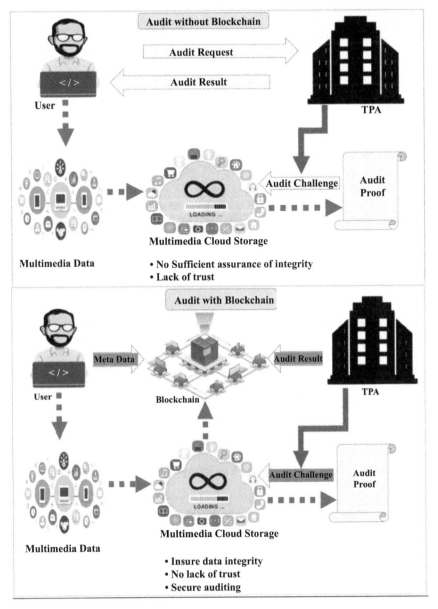

Figure 6.1   Existing auditing model versus proposed auditing model

using the Tag Sign algorithm. After that, he deletes the file blocks and tags locally before sending them to the cloud. During the Proof Gen algorithm, the TPA sends an audit request to the cloud, and in response to the request, the cloud gives proof of the intactness of data. TPA verifies the proof's accuracy in the Verify Proof algorithm. If the proof is found accurate, then TPA can be sure about the intactness of the data.

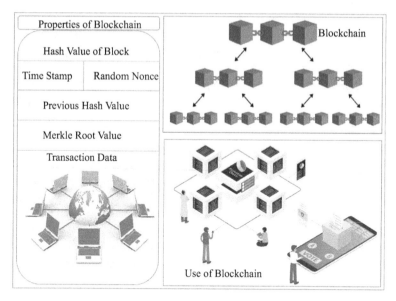

Figure 6.2   Structure of blockchain

6.4.1   Setup

This algorithm contains the following steps:

1. The KGC uses the TrapGen(P, N) algorithm to generate a $h = g * f^{-1}$, $||f|| < s\sqrt{N}$ and $||g|| < s\sqrt{N}$ with a trapdoor basis matrix $B \in Z_p^{2N \times 2N} = R_P^{2 \times 2}$ where $B = \begin{bmatrix} C(f) & C(g) \\ C(F) & C(G) \end{bmatrix}$ and h is an invertible polynomial. Here, B is the secret key (pk_u) of the cloud user and h is the corresponding public key (sk_u). Then he sends the key pair (pk_u, sk_u) to the cloud user.

2. The KGC uses the TrapGen(P, N) algorithm to create a $z = x * y^{-1}$, $||x|| < s\sqrt{N}$ and $||y|| < s\sqrt{N}$ with a trapdoor basis matrix $\mathbb{B} \in Z_p^{2N \times 2N} = R_p^{2 \times 2}$ where $\mathbb{B} = \begin{bmatrix} C(x) & C(y) \\ C(X) & C(Y) \end{bmatrix}$ and z is an invertible polynomial. Here, $\mathbb{B}$ is the secret key (pk_s) of the cloud server and z is the corresponding public key (sk_s). Then he sends the key pair (pk_u, sk_u) to the cloud server.

3. The KGC selects $2k + 2$ linearly independent vectors $a_0, a_1, ..., a_k$, $b_0, b_1, ..., b_k \in Z_p^N$, A hash function $H: \{0, 1\}^k \to Z_p^N$, where k is the bit length of a file block.

4. The public parameters $\mathbb{PR} = (h, z, a_0, a_1, ..., a_k, b_0, b_1, ..., b_k)$ are published in the blockchain.

6.4.2   Tag Sign

The message file is separated into l and $m_i \in \{0, 1\}^k$ blocks, with $i = 1, 2, ..., l$ and $i \in Z$ serving as m_j's index for every block j. This algorithm requires the following steps:

1. The cloud user determines $\alpha_i = H(j) \in \{0, 1\}^k$, $\mathbb{U}_i = a_0 + \sum_{j=1}^{k}(m_j(i) \cdot a_j) +$ $b_0 + \sum_{j=1}^{k}(\alpha_i(j) \cdot b_i) \in Z_p^N$ & $\mathbb{U}_i' = z\mathbb{U}_i \in Z_p^N$. Then, at that point, the cloud user determines $SampleD(B, h, \mathbb{U}', \beta) \rightarrow S_i$ where $\beta = s(\frac{1 + \sum_{j=1}^{k} m_i(j)}{(k+1)})$, using the Gaussian Sampler algorithm.

2. The cloud server receives (m_i, S_i), $i = 1, 2, ..., l$ as output from the cloud user.

3. The cloud server can use $h \cdot S_i = \mathbb{U}_i' \bmod p$ and $||S_i|| \leq s(\frac{1 + \sum_{j=1}^{k} m_i(j)}{(k=1)})\sqrt{N}$ to verify that these tags are accurate.

4. The user publishes $\{\mathbb{U}_i', h\}$ in the blockchain.

6.4.3   Proof Gen

The TPA chooses a subset $I = \{i_1, i_2, ..., i_d\}$ of set $1, 2, ..., l\}$ and arbitrary elements $\omega_i \in Z_p^N$, $j = i_1, i_2, ..., i_d$ to verify the integrity of the cloud-based data. This algorithm needs the following steps:

1. To the cloud server, the TPA sends $(i, \omega_i), j = i_1, i_2, ..., i_d$ and also publishes it in blockchain.

2. $u \in Z_p^N$ is chosen arbitrarily by the cloud server.

3. The cloud server determines $SampleD(z, \mathbb{B}, u, B) \rightarrow Y$

$$s = \sum_{r=j_1}^{j_d} \omega_r S_r \in Z_p^N$$

$$T = Y + \sum_{r=j_1}^{j_d} (\omega_r \sum_{j=1}^{k} (m_r(j) \cdot a_j)) \in Z_p^N.$$

4. The cloud server sends (s, T, u) it to TPA.

5. The cloud server publishes (s, T, u) in the blockchain.

6.4.4   Verify Proof

The following steps are essential for this algorithm:

1. The following equation has been verified by the TPA:

$$hs = \sum_{r=j_1}^{j_d} \omega_r z(a_0 + b_0) + zT - u + \sum_{r=j_1}^{j_d} (\omega_r z \sum_{j=1}^{k} \alpha_k(j) \cdot b_j)$$

holds true or not.

2. Finally, the TPA publishes the audit results and updates the {Chall, proof, result} into the blockchain if the above verification holds true.

6.5   Security analysis

6.5.1   Security goals

Public auditability and preserving privacy are two common design objectives:

- Public auditability: Our scheme's auditability to the public is obvious that a TPA can audit the data because our Verify Proof algorithm's verification equation does not require private information.
- Privacy-preserving: TPA should be unable to solve linear equations to deduce user data when auditing the cloud. The cloud server sends proof (s, T, u) to TPA in our Proof Gen algorithm. Take note that the initial data blocks are located in $T = Y + \sum_{r=j_1}^{j_d} (\omega_r \sum_{j=1}^{k} (m_r(j) \cdot a_j)) \in Z_p^N$. If data blocks of the same index are selected d times for audit, then TPA can obtain the d equation. However, he is unaware of Y. The number of equations is always greater than the number of mysterious variables. Therefore, he cannot solve the linear equations to reveal the user's data blocks.

6.5.2   Security features

The suggested framework is evaluated with some existing protocols on the premises of various security features in Table 6.2. The considered parameters of the comparison are the following: a) Post-quantum, b) Public verification, c) Privacy-preserving, d) Non-interactive, and e) Blockchain. Lucidly, it can be depicted from Table 6.2 that the proposed mechanism provides several advantages over the pre-existing protocols.

6.5.3   Computational and communication costs

Here, we will discuss the computational and communication cost evaluation of various schemes. We build a working version of our framework to assess its effectiveness. Our experiments use the SHA-256 hash algorithm (version 11.3.2) and the NTL Library for matrix operations and lattice reduction. An Intel(R) Core (TM) i7-1165G7 laptop running Windows 11 with 16 GB of DDR4 RAM and a 2.80 GHz processor speed was utilized for all experiments. The assessments are done with the existing lattice-based audit schemes, namely [33,34], and [59].

Table 6.2   Comparison of the features of various schemes

Scheme	[33]	[34]	[56]	[20]	[51]	[57]	[58]	Proposed
Post-quantum	✓	✓	✗	✗	✗	✗	✗	✓
Public verification	✓	✓	✓	✓	✓	✓	✓	✓
Privacy-preserving	✗	✓	✓	✗	✓	✓	✗	✓
Non-interactive	✓	✗	✓	✗	✓	✓	✓	✓
Blockchain	✗	✗	✓	✓	✓	✓	✓	✓

For the validity check matrix belongs to $Z_p^{M \times N}$ and $Z_p^{N \times N}$, the computation cost of the SampleD algorithm is equal to the cost of approximately $M^2 + 2MN$ and $N^2 + 2N$ multiplications in Z_p, respectively. The lattice used for the proposed mechanism is of $N \times N$ dimension. In comparison, $M \times N$ is the dimension of the other mechanisms. So, the computational cost and the communication costs are computed accordingly. Tables 6.3 and 6.5 show the comparisons based on the storage and communication cost and computational cost, respectively, where k is the length of the file block in a bit and d is the number of audited blocks.

We take $N = 394$, $p = 2.4e + 10$, for our scheme and $N = 256$, $q = 7.21e + 16$, $M = 2,204$ for schemes [33,34] and [59] to provide more direct comparisons. Its level of security is comparable to that of a 64-bit symmetric key cryptosystem when these parameters are adopted. Additionally, we select $k = 120$. With the adopted values, we have a comparison (Table 6.4) for the storage and communication cost and a comparison (Table 6.6) for the computational cost. Additionally, Figures 6.3 and 6.4 are obtained from Table 6.6, which represent the

Table 6.3   Storage and communication costs

Scheme	$pk + sk$	Tag length	Proof length
Chen *et al.* [33]	$MN \log p$	$MN \log p$	$2MN \log p$
Yang *et al.* [34]	$3MN \log p$	$MN \log p$	$2MN \log p$
Li *et al.* [59]	$2MN \log p$	$2MN \log p$	$MN \log p$
Proposed	$2(2N + 2k)N \log p$	$N \log p$	$3N \log p$

Note: M, N, and p mean the same as in the mechanism; also, k indicates the bit length of the file block.

Table 6.4   Storage and communication costs (in bits)

Scheme	$pk + sk$	Tag length	Proof length
Chen *et al.* [33]	3.16e7	3.16e7	6.32e7
Yang *et al.* [34]	9.48e7	3.16e6	6.32e7
Li *et al.* [59]	4.33e11	3.26e1	6.43e6
Proposed	1.79e11	2.96e6	4.93e6

Table 6.5   Computational costs

Scheme	Tag Sign	Proof Gen	Verify Proof
Chen *et al.* [33]	MN^2	$2dMN^2$	MN^2
Yang *et al.* [34]	$M^2 + 2MN + (MN)^2$	$2dM(N^2 + N)$	$N^2M + MNd$
Li *et al.* [59]	$M^2 + 2N$	$2dMN$	$2MN(1 + d)$
Proposed	$4N^2$	$2N^2 + dN$	$(d + 1)(N^2 + N) + N^2$

Note: d denotes the number of audit blocks.

Table 6.6   Computational costs (in milliseconds)

Scheme	Tag Sign	Proof Gen	Verify Proof
[33]	1.44e8	$d \times 2.88e8$	1.44e8
[34]	3.18e11	$d \times 2.9e8$	$1.44e8 + 5.6e5 \times d$
Li *et al.* [59]	2.4e11	$d \times 2.9e3$	$1.44e8 + 5.5e5 \times d$
Proposed	1.87e9	$(2+d) \times 1.4e5$	$(d+2) \times 2.18e7$

Note: *e* denotes the exponent.

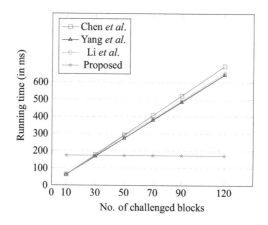

Figure 6.3   Cloud server's running time

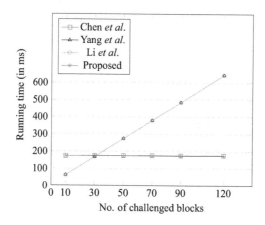

Figure 6.4   TPA's running time

running time of the cloud server and the running time of the TPA, respectively. Lucidly, we can observe from Table 6.6, Figures 6.3 and 6.4 that the computational cost of the proposed mechanism is lesser than other mechanisms. Additionally, the cloud server's operating time is less than that of the other techniques; yet, the TPA of the proposed protocol and [33] has the same running time. The proposed scheme overall computing cost, still is lower compared to protocol [33]. Therefore, the proposed mechanism offers better and more efficient computational costs than the other mechanism.

6.6 Conclusion

We developed an innovative and effective blockchain-based hybrid auditing scheme in this work. Our technology implements deterministic verifying, which offers 100% assurances of data possession and integrity, utilizing a lattice accumulator and blockchain smart contracts. This creates a positive environment between the user and the CSP. Furthermore, our system may promptly pay the customer and use a smart contract to automatically punish the dishonest CSP when the CSP loses or corrupts the outsourced data. Our scheme also safeguards the honorable CSP and stops the user from acting dishonestly. In addition, we decided against using the blockchain for public auditing in our system and instead created hybrid auditing. Since the activation of the public auditing phase using the blockchain solely occurs when verification fails in the private auditing phase, the hybrid auditing design guarantees equitable judgment while also reducing the customer's expenditure on audit fees. It was established through theoretical and experimental analysis that our approach was workable, effective, and accomplished the necessary security goals. Of course, some shortcomings in our plan still need to be fixed. For instance, the system is incapable of pinpointing the specific data blocks that may be corrupted or providing guidance on how to rectify them; it can simply verify whether the outsourced data has been compromised. In subsequent efforts, we will improve more auditing scheme features, such as finding and fixing faulty data blocks.

References

[1] Cai Z, He Z. Trading private range counting over Big IoT Data. In: 2019 IEEE 39th International Conference on Distributed Computing Systems (ICDCS); 2019. p. 144–153.

[2] Cai Z, Shi T. Distributed query processing in the edge-assisted IoT data monitoring system. *IEEE Internet of Things Journal*. 2021;8(16):12679–12693.

[3] Zheng X, Cai Z. Privacy-preserved data sharing towards multiple parties in industrial IoTs. *IEEE Journal on Selected Areas in Communications*. 2020;38(5):968–979.

[4]   Cai Z, Zheng X. A private and efficient mechanism for data uploading in smart cyber-physical systems. *IEEE Transactions on Network Science and Engineering.* 2020;7(2):766–775.

[5]   Drăgulinescu AM, Constantin F, Orza O, *et al.* Smart watering system security technologies using Blockchain. In: 2021 13th International Conference on Electronics, Computers and Artificial Intelligence (ECAI). IEEE; 2021. p. 1–4.

[6]   Cai Z, He Z, Guan X, *et al.* Collective data-sanitization for preventing sensitive information inference attacks in social networks. *IEEE Transactions on Dependable and Secure Computing.* 2016;15(4):577–590.

[7]   Miao Y, Ma J, Liu X, *et al.* Lightweight fine-grained search over encrypted data in fog computing. *IEEE Transactions on Services Computing.* 2018;12 (5):772–785.

[8]   Tong Q, Miao Y, Li H, *et al.* Privacy-preserving ranked spatial keyword query in mobile cloud-assisted fog computing. *IEEE Transactions on Mobile Computing.* 2021.

[9]   Xie H, Guo Y, Jia X. Privacy-preserving location-based data queries in fog-enhanced sensor networks. *IEEE Internet of Things Journal.* 2021;9 (14):12285–12299.

[10]   Guo Y, Xie H, Wang C, *et al.* Enabling privacy-preserving geographic range query in fog-enhanced IoT services. *IEEE Transactions on Dependable and Secure Computing.* 2021;19(5):3401–3416.

[11]   Ateniese G, Burns R, Curtmola R, *et al.* Provable data possession at untrusted stores. In: Proceedings of the 14th ACM conference on Computer and communications security; 2007. p. 598–609.

[12]   Ateniese G, Di Pietro R, Mancini LV, *et al.* Scalable and efficient provable data possession. In: Proceedings of the 4th International Conference on Security and Privacy in Communication Networks; 2008. p. 1–10.

[13]   Erway CC, Küpçü A, Papamanthou C, *et al.* Dynamic provable data possession. *ACM Transactions on Information and System Security (TISSEC).* 2015;17(4):1–29.

[14]   Fu Z, Huang F, Ren K, *et al.* Privacy-preserving smart semantic search based on conceptual graphs over encrypted outsourced data. *IEEE Transactions on Information Forensics and Security.* 2017;12(8):1874–1884.

[15]   Wang C, Chow SS, Wang Q, *et al.* Privacy-preserving public auditing for secure cloud storage. *IEEE Transactions on Computers.* 2011;62(2):362–375.

[16]   Yuan J, Yu S. Public integrity auditing for dynamic data sharing with multiuser modification. *IEEE Transactions on Information Forensics and Security.* 2015;10(8):1717–1726.

[17]   Liu C, Ranjan R, Yang C, *et al.* MuR-DPA: Top-down levelled multi-replica Merkle Hash Tree based secure public auditing for dynamic Big Data storage on cloud. *IEEE Transactions on Computers.* 2015;64(9):2609–2622.

[18]   Prajapat S, Kumar P, Sharma V. A lightweight group authentication scheme over lattices. In: 2022 4th International Conference on Advances in

Computing, Communication Control and Networking (ICAC3N). IEEE; 2022. p. 1215–1219.

[19] Prajapat S, Kumar P, Sharma V. An efficient CL-Signature scheme over NTRU lattices. In: 2022 4th International Conference on Advances in Computing, Communication Control and Networking (ICAC3N). IEEE; 2022. p. 1220–1224.

[20] Wang H, Qin H, Zhao M, *et al.* Blockchain-based fair payment smart contract for public cloud storage auditing. *Information Sciences.* 2020;519:348–362.

[21] Wang H, Wang Q, He D. Blockchain-based private provable data possession. *IEEE Transactions on Dependable and Secure Computing.* 2019;18 (5):2379–2389.

[22] Shor PW. Polynomial-time algorithms for prime factorization and discrete logarithms on a quantum computer. *SIAM Review.* 1999;41(2):303–332.

[23] Wang Q, Cheng C, Xu R, *et al.* Analysis and enhancement of a lattice-based data outsourcing scheme with public integrity verification. *IEEE Transactions on Services Computing.* 2020;15(4):2226–2231.

[24] Zafar F, Khan A, Malik SUR, *et al.* A survey of cloud computing data integrity schemes: Design challenges, taxonomy and future trends. *Computers & Security.* 2017;65:29–49.

[25] Du Y, Duan H, Zhou A, *et al.* Enabling secure and efficient decentralized storage auditing with blockchain. *IEEE Transactions on Dependable and Secure Computing.* 2021;19(5):3038–3054.

[26] Wang H, Li K, Ota K, *et al.* Remote data integrity checking and sharing in cloud-based health internet of things. *IEICE Transactions on Information and Systems.* 2016;99(8):1966–1973.

[27] Wang H, He D, Yu J, *et al.* Incentive and unconditionally anonymous identity-based public provable data possession. *IEEE Transactions on Services Computing.* 2016;12(5):824–835.

[28] Wang H. Proxy provable data possession in public clouds. *IEEE Transactions on Services Computing.* 2012;6(4):551–559.

[29] Wang H, He D, Fu A, *et al.* Provable data possession with outsourced data transfer. *IEEE Transactions on Services Computing.* 2019;14(6):1929–1939.

[30] Kuang B, Fu A, Yu S, *et al.* ESDRA: An efficient and secure distributed remote attestation scheme for IoT swarms. *IEEE Internet of Things Journal.* 2019;6(5):8372–8383.

[31] Zhang Y, Yu J, Hao R, *et al.* Enabling efficient user revocation in identity-based cloud storage auditing for shared big data. *IEEE Transactions on Dependable and Secure computing.* 2018;17(3):608–619.

[32] Ajtai M. Generating hard instances of lattice problems. In: Proceedings of the Twenty-Eighth Annual ACM Symposium on Theory of Computing; 1996. p. 99–108.

[33] Chen L, Han L, Jing J, *et al.* A post-quantum provable data possession protocol in cloud. *Security and Communication Networks.* 2013;6(5):658–667.

[34] Yang Y, Huang Q, Chen F. Secure cloud storage based on RLWE problem. *IEEE Access.* 2019;7:27604–27614.

[35] Shuang T, Li H, Zhikun C, *et al.* A method of provable data integrity based on lattice in cloud storage. *Journal of Computer Research and Development.* 2015;52(8):1862–1872.

[36] Xu W, Feng D, Liu J. Public verifiable proof of storage protocol from lattice assumption. In: 2012 IEEE International Conference on Intelligent Control, Automatic Detection and High-End Equipment. IEEE; 2012. p. 133–137.

[37] Shamir A. Identity-based cryptosystems and signature schemes. In: *Workshop on the Theory and Application of Cryptographic Techniques.* Springer; 1984. p. 47–53.

[38] Liu Z, Liao Y, Yang X, *et al.* Identity-based remote data integrity checking of cloud storage from lattices. In: 2017 3rd International Conference on Big Data Computing and Communications (BIGCOM). IEEE; 2017. p. 128–135.

[39] Zhang X, Wang H, Xu C. Identity-based key-exposure resilient cloud storage public auditing scheme from lattices. *Information Sciences.* 2019;472:223–234.

[40] Wang S, Zhang Y, Guo Y. A blockchain-empowered arbitrable multimedia data auditing scheme in IoT cloud computing. *Mathematics.* 2022;10 (6):1005.

[41] Sharma P, Jindal R, Borah MD. A comparative analysis of consensus algorithms for decentralized storage systems. *IT Professional.* 2022;24(6):59–65.

[42] Guo Y, Zhang C, Jia X. Verifiable and forward-secure encrypted search using blockchain techniques. In: ICC 2020-2020 IEEE International Conference on Communications (ICC). IEEE; 2020. p. 1–7.

[43] Tong W, Dong X, Shen Y, *et al.* A hierarchical sharding protocol for multi-domain iot blockchains. In: ICC 2019-2019 IEEE International Conference on Communications (ICC). IEEE; 2019. p. 1–6.

[44] Zhu S, Cai Z, Hu H, *et al.* zkCrowd: a hybrid blockchain-based crowdsourcing platform. *IEEE Transactions on Industrial Informatics.* 2019;16 (6):4196–4205.

[45] Guo Y, Xie H, Miao Y, *et al.* Fedcrowd: A federated and privacy-preserving crowdsourcing platform on blockchain. *IEEE Transactions on Services Computing.* 2020;15(4):2060–2073.

[46] Li C, Qu X, Guo Y. TFCrowd: A blockchain-based crowdsourcing framework with enhanced trustworthiness and fairness. *EURASIP Journal on Wireless Communications and Networking.* 2021;2021(1):1–20.

[47] Wang M, Guo Y, Zhang C, *et al.* MedShare: a privacy-preserving medical data sharing system by using blockchain. *IEEE Transactions on Services Computing.* 2021.

[48] Silvano WF, Marcelino R. Iota Tangle: A cryptocurrency to communicate Internet-of-Things data. *Future Generation Computer Systems.* 2020;112: 307–319.

[49] Nanayakkara S, Perera S, Senaratne S, *et al.* Blockchain and smart contracts: A solution for payment issues in construction supply chains. In: *Informatics.* vol. 8. MDPI; 2021. p. 36.

[50] Wang Q, Wang C, Li J, *et al.* Enabling public verifiability and data dynamics for storage security in cloud computing. In: *European Symposium on Research in Computer Security.* Springer; 2009. p. 355–370.

[51] Yuan H, Chen X, Wang J, *et al.* Blockchain-based public auditing and secure deduplication with fair arbitration. *Information Sciences.* 2020;541:409–425.

[52] Hung YH, Tseng YM, Huang SS. Lattice-based revocable certificateless signature. *Symmetry.* 2017;9(10):242.

[53] Lyubashevsky V. Lattice signatures without trapdoors. In: Annual International Conference on the Theory and Applications of Cryptographic Techniques. Springer; 2012. p. 738–755.

[54] Micciancio D, Regev O. Worst-case to average-case reductions based on Gaussian measures. *SIAM Journal on Computing.* 2007;37(1):267–302.

[55] Nakamoto S. Bitcoin: A peer-to-peer electronic cash system. 2008. https://bitcoin.org/bitcoin.pdf

[56] Zhang Y, Xu C, Lin X, *et al.* Blockchain-based public integrity verification for cloud storage against procrastinating auditors. *IEEE Transactions on Cloud Computing.* 2019;9(3):923–937.

[57] Xu Y, Zhang C, Wang G, *et al.* A blockchain-enabled deduplicatable data auditing mechanism for network storage services. *IEEE Transactions on Emerging Topics in Computing.* 2020;9(3):1421–1432.

[58] Li Z, Xin Y, Zhao D, *et al.* A noninteractive multireplica provable data possession scheme based on smart contract. Security and Communication *Networks.* 2022;2022.

[59] Li Z, Zhang T, Zhao D, *et al.* Post-quantum privacy-preserving provable data possession scheme based on smart contracts. *Wireless Communications and Mobile Computing.* 2023;2023.

Chapter 7

Trustworthy grant-free random access in an shared untrusted network: dilemma, solution, and evaluation

Xintong Ling[1,2,3], Weihang Cao[1], Jiaheng Wang[1,2,3] and Xiqi Gao[1,2,3]

The explosion of Internet of Things (IoT) applications has rendered the traditional cloud-centered network architecture insufficient. Its fragmentation by multiple non-cooperative operators hinders scalability for future IoT development. However, the lack of trust within a multi-operator network gives rise to the Rogue's Dilemma where rogue devices may skip the required backoff, gaining an unfair advantage and potentially causing network congestion. Consequently, there is an urgent need for pioneering access protocols tailored to an open network shared among multiple untrusted operators. In this chapter, we introduce Hash Access, a trustworthy grant-free random access protocol that enables a multi-operator network without shared authentication. By employing Hash Access, IoT devices can be compelled to adhere to access rules and regulate data traffic, effectively mitigating the loss of network efficiency resulting from selfish behavior among rogue devices. We further establish a comprehensive analytical model for Hash Access to thoroughly evaluate the performance in various aspects. Simulation results are presented to validate the effectiveness of Hash Access, accompanied by practical design guidelines.

7.1 Introduction

The explosive growth in the number of smart devices, services, and applications, together with the ultra-reliable low-latency communication (URLLC) and massive machine-type communication (mMTC) defined by the fifth generation (5G) technology is paving the way towards an Internet of Things (IoT) vision with massive

[1]National Mobile Communications Research Laboratory, Southeast University, China
[2]Purple Mountain Laboratories, China
[3]Frontiers Science Center for Mobile Information Communication and Security, Southeast University, China

connections, kindling huge research interests around the world. As a core technology for IoT, machine-to-machine (M2M) communications have drawn considerable attention from both industry and academia [1–3]. In M2M, a huge number of access devices transmit short data packets (typically of several bytes) sporadically in the uplink direction to report their status [1]. This feature favors grant-free random access (GFRA) without dedicated resources in IoT uplink access. GFRA not only enables efficient management of M2M access with low signaling overhead and access delay but also reduces the complexity and cost of IoT devices for massive deployment [3].

Notably, most existing grant-free access schemes are designed for the scenario where all devices either belong to or are authenticated by a common operator such that all devices can trust each other [1,2]. To achieve higher overall efficiency, each node is supposed to strictly follow the grant-free access protocol at the expense of some individual performance. For instance, random backoff in the Aloha protocol can reduce a network's collision probability but would increase the access latency for individual nodes. In practice, IoT networks usually include a massive number of devices belonging to multiple parties, which implies that IoT networks and devices are inherently untrusted. The existing IoT structure based on a dominant operator and trustworthy devices is too restrictive. Moreover, most IoT network resources are still used in an isolated manner by their owners, i.e., network operators, which hampers the scalability for future IoT evolution. Higher resource utilization efficiency can be achieved by integrating the subnetworks separated by operators into a larger inter-operative multi-operator network. Hence, in this work, we investigate the GFRA for a shared untrusted network including devices from multiple parties.

The integration of untrusted subnetworks belonging to multiple parties presents numerous new challenges to the current grant-free access structure. From the network's perspective, for resource sharing across operators, it is difficult to quantify the contributions of each node (or network operator) and provide appropriate economic payout and incentives. This has been a major hindrance to the widespread commercial success of well-known resource-sharing concepts such as cognitive radio (CR) and mobile ad hoc network (MANET) since their inception [4]. Furthermore, authentication, authorization, and accounting (AAA) control becomes highly complex and nearly intractable due to the lack of trust in an inter-host network. Once an access point (AP) reboots due to a system crash or power failure, the device registration will take a long time for a large number of IoT devices [2].

As a decentralized, secure, and efficient wireless access paradigm, blockchain radio access network (B-RAN) is emerging as a potential solution to address the above challenges [5–9]. It leverages distributed ledger technologies (DLTs) to establish a trusted foundation for the upcoming sixth-generation (6G) telecommunications. B-RAN facilitates collaboration among multiple parties and provides a unified framework for heterogeneous, distributed, and complex future IoT [10–12]. In B-RAN, the IoT devices are not constrained to specific subscribing service providers (SPs) but can receive resources and services from different subnetworks. With the help of blockchain and related critical components, B-RAN connects multiple untrusted parties including SPs and clients and further forms a multi-sided platform (MSP) that enables direct interactions among them [5].

However, B-RAN has its own problems. Establishing trust cannot be achieved solely via introducing the blockchain [5,13]. As highlighted in Reference 5, an inter-host network platform entails several fundamental trust relationships, such as SP–client, SP–SP, and client–client. Among them, the significance of the trust between client devices is often overlooked. However, the lack of trust between the client devices may lead to an interesting phenomenon named the Rogue's Dilemma [14], which can be viewed as "the tragedy of the commons" [15] in the context of wireless communications or "the tragedy of spectrum commons" [16].

Now let us show how the Rogue's Dilemma occurs in the case of GFRA, where a massive number of IoT devices share an open access spectrum without dedicated resources [17–21]. Due to the short packets with typically tens of bytes, GFRA enables efficient management with low signaling overhead and access delay and thus is favored. Traditionally, if all the devices either belong to a common operator or shared authentication, they will strictly obey the random access (RA) protocols for the entire network's performance, by, e.g., introducing random backoffs to reduce the collision probability of the whole network [1,22]. However, unlike such traditional networks, a shared network includes a massive number of devices that may belong to multiple parties [5,14]. These client devices do not trust each other and thus may ignore pre-defined protocols to acquire more than their fair share of resources for self-interest. A rogue device may aggressively skip the required backoff to shorten the waiting time in its best interest, thereby gaining an advantage while potentially causing network congestion for compliant nodes. The existing work [14] shows that even a few selfish devices may significantly compromise and undermine network efficiency and fairness. Evidently, the Rogue's Dilemma arises directly from the absence of trust among clients. It implies that despite the blockchain fostering trust in the upper layers of the shared network, coordination may still fail due to the lack of trust among clients at the foundational level.

To resolve the Rogue's Dilemma, a trustworthy grant-free access protocol named Hash Access was first proposed in Ling *et al.* [14]. Hash Access can enforce compliance with the RA rule for all devices and prevent selfish behaviors of rogue devices, ultimately establishing trust between clients at the bottom. As revealed in Reference 14, Hash Access can promote multi-party collaboration through cross-network integration and proper traffic offloading. An analytical model was proposed in Zhang *et al.* and Ling *et al.* [23,24] to show the performance of Hash Access protocol with practical design guidelines. Several variants such as non-orthogonal hash access (NOHA) [25] were subsequently developed based on Hash Access for further enhancement.

In this chapter, we formally elucidate the Rogue's Dilemma through a two-player game, aiming to illustrate the fundamental motivation why we need Hash Access in an untrusted network. Subsequently, we provide a detailed introduction to the Hash Access protocol and show how it functions as a solution to the Rogue's Dilemma. We establish an analytical model for Hash Access with a general traffic pattern and assess the characteristics of Hash Access from various perspectives. At last, we evaluate several critical aspects of Hash Access, validating our analytical model and conclusions.

The remainder of this chapter is organized as follows. Section 7.2 illustrates the Rogue's Dilemma. Section 7.3 describes the Hash Access protocol. Section 7.4 establishes an analytical model for Hash Access, and Section 7.5 analyzes the performance of Hash Access. Section 7.6 presents the simulation results, and Section 7.7 draws the conclusion.

7.2　Rogue's Dilemma

In this section, we would like to explain the Rogue's Dilemma from a game-theoretic model. We consider the simple case with two IoT devices as players that share a common spectrum but do not trust each other. In every slot, each device has two strategies: T for transmitting and W for waiting, belonging to the strategy set $S = \{T, W\}$. Denote $s_i \in \{T, W\}$ as the strategy adopted by device $i = 0, 1$. Assume that both of them always have packets to transmit. If they both attempt to transmit in a slot, i.e., $s_0 = s_1 = T$, a collision occurs, and no one successfully transmits their packets. If both of them wait, an available slot is wasted, resulting in extra access delays for both sides. One transmits and the other one waits, leading to successful transmissions. Therefore, the payoff function of device $i = 0, 1$ can be written as

$$u_i(s_i, s_{1-i}) = \begin{cases} g - c_p, & s_i = T, s_{1-i} = W, \\ -c_t, & s_i = W, \\ -c_p - c_t, & s_i = T, s_{1-i} = T. \end{cases} \tag{7.1}$$

where g is the profit of one successful transmission, c_t is the waiting cost caused by transmission delays, and c_p is the transmission cost (e.g., power consumption). Compactly, we summarize (7.1) in the payoff matrix in Table 7.1. Note that $g - c_p > -c_t$ always holds, implying one successful transmission is always better than waiting for a slot; otherwise, a successful access yields a lower payoff than wait.

Based on the above game model, we first consider a trustworthy case where two players strictly follow a given RA protocol with access probability q. The utility functions can be written as

$$u_i(T) \overset{\Delta}{=} E_{s_{1-i}}\{u_i(s_i = T, s_{1-i})\} = g - c_p - (g + c_t)q,$$

$$u_i(W) \overset{\Delta}{=} E_{s_{1-i}}\{u_i(s_i = W, s_{1-i})\} = -c_t.$$

Table 7.1　*Payoff matrix*

	T	W
T	$-c_p - c_t, -c_p - c_t$	$g - c_p, -c_t$
W	$-c_t, g - c_p$	$-c_t, -c_t$

Hence, the expected payoff of the device i is

$$
\begin{aligned}
u_i &= E_{s_i, s_{1-i}}\{u_i(s_i, s_{1-i})\} \\
&= q u_i(T) + (1 - q) u_i(W) \\
&= -(g + c_t)q^2 + (g - c_p + c_t)q - c_t.
\end{aligned} \tag{7.2}
$$

To maximize the gain, the transmit probability q of the RA protocol should be set to $q^\star = \frac{g - c_p + c_t}{2(g + c_t)}$ for both players, yielding

$$
u_{\text{trust}} \triangleq \frac{(g + c_t - c_p)^2}{4(g + c_t)} - c_t. \tag{7.3}
$$

u_{trust} represents the payoff when each player is trusted and follows the protocol honestly.

Now we consider the case that device 1 follows the RA protocol, i.e., $q_1 = q^\star$, and the rogue device 0 selfishly sets q_0 to maximize its own profit. The utility functions of device 0 are given by

$$
u_0(T) = \frac{g - c_p - c_t}{2},
$$

$$
u_0(W) = -c_t.
$$

The expected payoff of device 0 is

$$
u_0 = \frac{g - c_p + c_t}{2} q_0 - c_t. \tag{7.4}
$$

which is maximized at $q_0 = 1$. In other words, a rogue device should always skip the backoff and occupy the link. The maximum payoff of device 0 is

$$
u_{\text{selfish}} \triangleq \frac{g - c_p - c_t}{2}. \tag{7.5}
$$

As a result, the expected payoff of device 1 becomes

$$
u_{\text{honest}} \triangleq -\frac{g - c_p + c_t}{2(g + c_t)} c_p - c_t. \tag{7.6}
$$

Obviously, the selfish strategy dominates the honest one.

Now, what if both devices behave selfishly? If both devices keep transmitting, it will tragically result in collisions in every slot, with extremely low payoff $(-c_p - c_t)$. Now consider that they are smart enough to adjust their transmitting probability q_i based on the other's strategy q_{1-i} in their best interest. The network will converge to a Nash equilibrium at last in an uncoordinated manner. The utility function of device i is given by

$$
u_i(T) = g - c_p - (g + c_t)q_{1-i},
$$

$$
u_i(W) = -c_t.
$$

We calculate the mixed strategy equilibrium via the principle of indifference [26]. By letting $u_i(T) = u_i(W)$, we have

$$q_0 = q_1 = \frac{g - c_p + c_t}{g + c_t}. \tag{7.7}$$

The expected payoff is

$$u_{\text{untrust}} \overset{\Delta}{=} -c_t. \tag{7.8}$$

Hence, when two players do not trust each other, they will eventually approach the Nash equilibrium with a payoff u_{untrust}.

In Figure 7.1, we visualize the payoffs of different strategies in the game model with varying costs. Observing the above results in (7.3), (7.5), (7.6), and (7.8), we can obtain the relationship among them easily. Now we formally summarize the Rogue's Dilemma based on the two-player game in the following.

Theorem 7.1 (Rogue's Dilemma) In an open access medium shared by two devices, the payoffs of different strategies have the following relationship:

$$u_{\text{honest}} \overset{(a)}{<} u_{\text{untrust}} \overset{(b)}{<} u_{\text{trust}} \overset{(c)}{<} u_{\text{selfish}}, \tag{7.9}$$

indicating the situation where rogue behaviors for self-interests eventually result in low payoffs for everyone, even worse than the original trustworthy environment.

Proof. The inequality (a) is obvious since $g - c_p > -c_t$. The inequality (b) comes from the positivity of $\frac{(g + c_t - c_p)^2}{4(g + c_t)}$. The inequality (c) is because $u_{\text{selfish}} - u_{\text{trust}} = \frac{(g - c_p + c_t)(g + c_p + c_t)}{4(g + c_t)} > 0.$

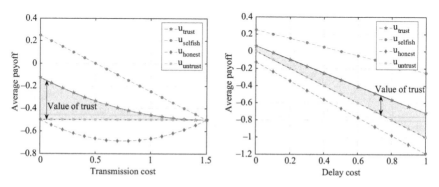

Figure 7.1   Average payoffs of different strategies in the two-player game model (The profit of a successful transmission is normalized as $g = 1$.) (a) $c_t = 0.5$. (b) $c_p = 0.5$.

Theorem 7.1 interprets how the Rogue's Dilemma occurs, and provides several interesting insights. First, if all the devices follow the access protocol honestly, the rogue behavior seems profitable to themselves due to the shorter delay, and thus results in $u_{\text{selfish}} > u_{\text{trust}}$, but affects the honest device's interests ($u_{\text{honest}} < u_{\text{trust}}$). A device can easily conclude that it is in its best interests to skip the backoff and become a rogue device. That is how the selfish nature of devices comes. However, as more devices become rogues, all of them are losing out ($u_{\text{untrust}} < u_{\text{selfish}}$). The entire network will converge to an untrusted, uncoordinated Nash equilibrium with lower payoffs than the original trusted state ($u_{\text{untrust}} < u_{\text{trust}}$). Moreover, any single device that attempts to behave honestly will suffer by a lower payoff ($u_{\text{honest}} < u_{\text{untrust}}$) and cannot change such an aggressive atmosphere. The gap between u_{trust} and u_{untrust}, i.e., $\frac{\left(g + c_t - c_p\right)^2}{4(g + c_t)}$, reflects the value of trust between clients, which is always positive. One can see the relationships in Theorem 7.1 agree with the numerical results in Figure 7.1. Essentially, the Rogue's Dilemma is the wireless communication version of "the tragedy of the commons". Even though Theorem 7.1 is based on a simplified two-player game model, the Rogue's Dilemma also holds for shared open networks with multiple devices, which is verified by the simulations in Section 7.6.

Notably, B-RAN is a typical scenario where the Rogue's Dilemma may occur. The rogue devices in B-RAN may violate the RA protocol and obtain gains in the short term; however, optimizing for the self in the short term is not optimal for all in the long term, and the cost of rogue behaviors is borne by all. The Rogue's Dilemma reveals the value of trust and stresses the necessity of establishing trust between clients in B-RAN or any other shared open networks. As suggested by the Rogue's Dilemma, if we cannot guarantee every device to obey the protocol honestly, "the tragedy of the commons" could occur in any shared untrusted networks. That explains why Hash Access is indispensable.

7.3 Hash Access protocol

Now consider such an inter-operative network of subnetworks that integrates multilateral SPs and IoT devices. These devices belong to different parties without shared authentication and could be dishonest or even selfish due to the absence of trust between them. More specifically, there are n_d untrusted and possibly selfish IoT devices attempting to access n_c shared channels. In other words, at most n_c IoT devices can access simultaneously. The value of n_c reflects the access capability of the shared open network. As illustrated in Section 7.2, the Rogue's Dilemma may occur in such a scenario. Now we would like to present the Hash Access protocol and how it prevents the Rogue's Dilemma.

According to the protocol of Hash Access, each IoT device shall perform hash queries before sending data packets until it finds a hash value below a given target value. Owing to the non-invertibility of the hash function, the AP can easily verify the validity of a solution, but it is difficult to find such a qualified solution. In this approach, an enforced backoff is automatically embedded into Hash Access, which

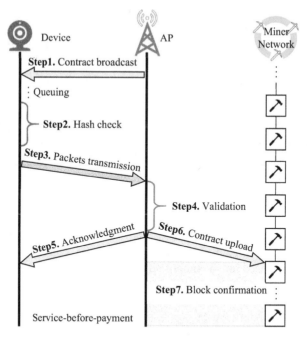

Figure 7.2   Procedure of Hash Access

can hardly be skipped. Different from the traditional RA protocol that simply assumes all the devices follow the protocol honestly, Hash Access enforces the protocol for every device and offers a feasible solution to the Rogue's Dilemma by rebuilding the trust between them.

Now we demonstrate the Hash Access procedure in Figure 7.2, with the detailed steps listed as follows. Notably, we take the example of B-RAN as a typical scenario to apply the Hash Access, but Hash Access can be applied to more general shared untrusted networks.

- **Step 1. Contract broadcast**: In B-RAN, the AP periodically broadcasts access contracts to announce the availability of GFRA services. The access contracts are digitally signed by the AP and contain the service fee, a target hash, the timestamp, and control messages.
- **Step 2. Hash check**: If a device has a packet to transmit, it starts to perform hash queries for access. The hash puzzle is formulated as

$$h = \mathrm{H}(\mathscr{T} + \mathscr{I} + \mathscr{C}), \tag{7.10}$$

where h is the hash value, $\mathrm{H}(\cdot)$ denotes a hash operation, $\mathscr{T}$ is the current timestamp, $\mathscr{I}$ is the device's unique identifier (ID),[1] and $\mathscr{C}$ is the access

---

[1]The unique identifier can rely on existing ones, e.g., the international mobile equipment identity (IMEI), and also hardware-dependent features, e.g., RF fingerprinting [27,28].

contract. This device uploads the packet, once the hash value is less than the given target hash, i.e.,

$$h = H(\mathcal{T} + \mathcal{I} + \mathcal{C}) < h_c, \tag{7.11}$$

where h_c is the target hash value. Otherwise ($h \geq h_c$), this device is denied and has to wait and perform the hash query in the next slot (The timestamp is changing for each slot to keep the hash trials fresh and independent of each other.) The device also needs to sign the smart contract $\mathcal{C}$ with its digital signature.

- **Step 3. Packets transmission**: If a device passes the hash check, it transmits the data packet, the hash value, and the access contract to the AP in the current slot, and a contention resolution (CR) timer starts simultaneously. The data packet is successfully transmitted only if there is no packet collision.
- **Step 4. Validation**: After receiving the data packets and the access contract from the IoT device, the AP verifies the hash value and the access contract.
- **Step 5. Acknowledgment**: If the hash value is below the target, the AP will accept the data packets and send the acknowledgment (ACK) messages to the device. If the hash value or the access contract is invalid, the AP will ignore the corresponding packet. If the IoT device does not receive the ACK message before the CR timer expires, it regards the transmission as a failure and repeats **Step 2** and **Step 3**.
- **Step 6. Contract upload**: As the ACK message is transmitted, the AP uploads the access contract to the miner network for the service fee.
- **Step 7. Block confirmation**: The miners check the validity of the access contract and then commit the contract to the blockchain. After the access contract is accepted by the main chain, the service fee specified in the contract will be automatically transferred from the IoT device to the AP through the blockchain.

Indeed, Hash Access requires extra computation and energy for hash operations. However, in Step 2, we design the hash query (7.10) and restrict that each device can compute the hash value once per slot, which largely saves the energy cost of Hash Access. As shown in Reference 14, the energy consumption of hash operations per second is acceptable compared with that of the data transmission.

In the process of Hash Access, the AP sets a suitable target hash value h_c to determine how hard it is for client devices to transmit data packets. More literally, we introduce a straightforward term named access difficulty to measure the difficulty of finding a hash value below the current target. Borrowed from the concept of mining difficulty in Bitcoin [29,30], the access difficulty d is defined as

$$d \triangleq \frac{h_m}{h_c}, \tag{7.12}$$

where h_m represents the maximum target hash. According to the definition of the access difficulty, the transmission probability of an IoT device in one slot, i.e., the probability that each IoT device calculates a valid hash below the target hash, can be expressed as

$$\Pr\{h < h_c\} = \frac{h_c}{h_m} = \frac{1}{d}. \tag{7.13}$$

To show it more straightforward, we give an example where the target hash is a 16-bit number. The maximum target hash is set to 0xffff in the hexadecimal version. If the current hash target is 0x1027, the access difficulty d is

$$d = \frac{0\text{xffff}}{0\text{x}1027} \approx 15.85. \tag{7.14}$$

Obviously, a larger target hash indicates less access difficulty, whereas a smaller target hash yields greater access difficulty. In principle, at a higher difficulty level, it is more difficult to pass the hash check and thus leads to a longer waiting time, whereas, at a lower difficulty level, it is easier to find a valid hash solution but results in a higher collision probability. Therefore, the value of access difficulty d should be set accordingly for traffic control in the network. An analytical model is thus called for assessing the characteristics of Hash Access and optimizing the access difficulty in the protocol.

7.4   Hash Access modeling

7.4.1   Traffic pattern

We first introduce the packet traffic model for workflow modeling. Assume that every IoT device generates new packets following an independent, identical, stationary random process with an arbitrary probability mass function (PMF):

$$\Pr\{X = k\} = \xi_k, k = 0, 1, \dots \tag{7.15}$$

where X is the random variable of newly generated packets within a slot duration τ_s for every IoT device. We define the expected value of $E[X]$ (packets/slot), or $E[X]/\tau_s$ (packets/s), as the offered load of an IoT device. We summarize the physical layer model of Hash Access in GFRA scenarios in Figure 7.3.

Based on the general traffic flow (7.15), we give several typical IoT traffic patterns as examples in the following.

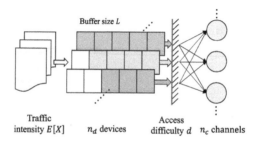

Figure 7.3   Physical layer model of Hash Access in GFRA scenarios

- Bernoulli Traffic. The arrivals of data packets follow a Bernoulli distribution [31] with a probability ξ_1 for one packet and a probability ξ_0 for none:

$$\Pr\{X = k\} = \begin{cases} \xi_0, & k = 0, \\ \xi_1, & k = 1, \\ 0, & k = 2, 3, \ldots \end{cases} \tag{7.16}$$

Bernoulli traffic implies sparse traffic where at most one packet arrives in an IoT device in a slot. Hence, in Bernoulli traffic, ξ_1 packet is expected to arrive in a slot.

- Sporadic Traffic. If each IoT device sporadically generates packets (two packets cannot arrive at the same epoch but may arrive in the same slot), we can use a Poisson process to model the IoT traffic [32,33] with the PMF:

$$\Pr\{X = k\} = \xi_k = \frac{e^{-\lambda}(\lambda)^k}{k!}, k = 0, 1, \ldots \tag{7.17}$$

where $\lambda \triangleq E[X]$ is defined as the average number of arrival packets in a slot.

7.4.2 Markov model

Now we establish a Markov model to characterize the performance of Hash Access. Let the state of the Markov chain be the length of each IoT device's packet buffer, i.e., the number of data packets awaiting their turn to transmit in each device. Since an IoT device's storage space is limited, we set the maximum buffer size to be L such that the state space Q of an IoT device is given by $Q = \{0, 1, \ldots, i, \ldots, L\}$. Define $\pi_i(t)$ as the probability that there are i packets in the buffer at time t for $i = 0, 1, \ldots, L$, and denote $\pi_i \triangleq \lim_{t \to \infty} \pi_i(t)$ as the steady state probability of state i. A state transition occurs as new packets arrive or transmissions succeed (We assume that the ACK message can always be captured successfully before the CR timer expires.). Mathematically, the state transition probability from state j to state k, denoted as $p_{j,k}$, can be represented as

$$p_{j,k} = \begin{cases} \xi_{k-j}\left(1 - \dfrac{p_s}{d}\right) + \xi_{k-j+1}\dfrac{p_s}{d}, & 1 \leq j \leq k \leq L - 1; \\[2mm] \xi_0 \dfrac{p_s}{d}, & j = 1, \ldots, L; k = j - 1; \\[2mm] \displaystyle\sum_{i=k}^{\infty}\xi_{i-j}\left(1 - \dfrac{p_s}{d}\right) \\[2mm] + \displaystyle\sum_{i=k}^{\infty}\xi_{i-j+1}\dfrac{p_s}{d}, & j = 1, \ldots, L - 1; k = L; \\[2mm] \xi_k, & j = 0; k = 0, \ldots, L - 1; \\[2mm] \displaystyle\sum_{i=k}^{\infty}\xi_i, & j = 0; k = L; \\[2mm] 1 - \xi_0\dfrac{p_s}{d}, & j = L; k = L; \\[2mm] 0, & \text{otherwise.} \end{cases} \tag{7.18}$$

where p_s is the transmission success probability. We denote the one-step state transition matrix as $\mathbf{P}$, of which the (j, k) element is given by the state transition probability $p_{j,k}$ in (7.18). Now we can characterize and express the stationary distribution $\pi = [\pi_0, \pi_1, ..., \pi_L]$ under Hash Access as

$$\pi = \pi \mathbf{P}. \tag{7.19}$$

Given the traffic model $\{\xi_k\}$ and the maximum buffer size L, π in (7.19) can be expressed by an implicit function of p_s/d, denoted by $\pi(p_s/d)$. Essentially, the term $\frac{p_s}{d}$ represents the probability that a device solves the hash puzzle and transmits the packet successfully, implying the probability of successful access. Even so, we are still far from solving the steady state distribution via (7.19), since the matrix $\mathbf{P}$ includes the transmission success probability p_s which is unknown yet. Naturally, we shall derive the transmission success probability p_s in the following section.

7.5   Performance analysis

7.5.1   *Transmission success probability*

The packet transmission success probability p_s is defined as the probability of successfully transmitting a packet to the AP with no collision. Obviously, $1-p_s$ represents the probability of packet collision. We denote π^+ as the probability that an IoT device attempts to access the AP, i.e., it has at least one data packet to transmit:

$$\pi^+ \left(\frac{p_s}{d} \right) \triangleq \sum_{i=1}^{L} \pi_i \left(\frac{p_s}{d} \right) = 1 - \pi_0 \left(\frac{p_s}{d} \right). \tag{7.20}$$

We can hardly give the closed-form expression of the stationary distribution $\mathbf{p}$. Nevertheless, by using the Cramer's rule [34], we can obtain the expression of $\pi_0 \left(\frac{p_s}{d} \right)$ from (7.19):

$$\pi_0 \left(\frac{p_s}{d} \right) = \frac{\left(\frac{\xi_0 p_s}{d} \right)^L}{\det \left([(\mathbf{I} - \mathbf{P})_{1:L-1}, \mathbf{1}] \right)}, \tag{7.21}$$

where $[(\mathbf{I} - \mathbf{P})_{1:L-1}, \mathbf{1}]$ is the matrix formed by replacing the L-th column of $\mathbf{I} - \mathbf{P}$ by an all-one column vector $\mathbf{1}$. Hence, we have

$$\pi^+ \left(\frac{p_s}{d} \right) = 1 - \frac{\left(\frac{\xi_0 p_s}{d} \right)^L}{\det \left([(\mathbf{I} - \mathbf{P})_{1:L-1}, \mathbf{1}] \right)}. \tag{7.22}$$

Consequently, the probability that only one specific device collides with the current device is $\frac{1}{d n_c} \pi^+ \left(\frac{p_s}{d} \right)$. In a network with n_d devices, the transmission success probability is

$$p_s = \left(1 - \frac{\pi^+\left(\frac{p_s}{d}\right)}{dn_c}\right)^{n_d-1} \tag{7.23}$$

$$= \left(1 - \frac{1}{dn_c}\left(1 - \frac{\left(\frac{\xi_0 p_s}{d}\right)^L}{\det\left(\left[(\mathbf{I} - \mathbf{P})_{1:L-1}, \mathbf{1}\right]\right)}\right)\right)^{n_d-1}.$$

We can calculate the value of p_s based on (23) by numerical methods. For example, we can use the fixed-point method and update p_s iteratively from an initial point until convergence.

From (7.23), we would like to discuss the impact of network parameters on p_s. Given d, p_s is increasing in the number of links n_c and decreasing in the number of devices n_d. It is straightforward because more uplink channels mean stronger access capability and massive devices cause excessive collisions. Given n_d and n_c, p_s is an implicit function of the access difficulty d determined by (7.23), and thus can be denoted by $p_s(d)$. Hence, $\pi^+\left(\frac{p_s}{d}\right)$ as a function of p_s/d, is essentially determined by d, which will be denoted as $\pi^+(d)$ in the following chapter. Meanwhile, if we simply look at (7.23), the relationship between p_s and d is unclear. In principle, a larger d means fewer devices allowed to access, implying fewer collisions and a higher successful transmission probability p_s. The monotonicity is verified by numerical and simulation results (see Figure 7.4). In Reference 24, the monotonic relationship between p_s and d is proved under a Bernoulli traffic. However, the strict proof under a general traffic model has not been obtained yet.

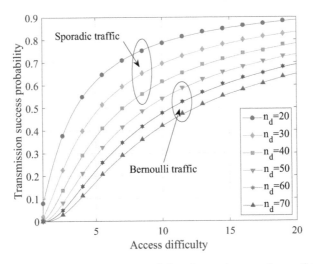

Figure 7.4   *Relationship between p_s and d with varying numbers of devices in different traffic patterns ($n_c = 8$ and $E[X]/\tau_s = 40$ packets/s).*

7.5.2 Network throughput

Now let us evaluate the network throughput of Hash Access, which is the critical performance measure in evaluating a network. We define the network throughput T as the average number of data packets successfully transmitted in a slot. The network throughput T is the product of the probability of successful transmission and the number of IoT devices that have packets to be transmitted in a slot, given by

$$T = p_s(d) \cdot \frac{n_d \pi^+(d)}{d}. \tag{7.24}$$

According to (7.22) and (7.23), $p_s(d)$ and $\pi^+(d)$ are determined by the access difficulty d. Apparently, the access difficulty d plays a critical role in affecting the network throughput T.

Naturally, the access difficulty optimization for the network throughput arises. We formulate the optimization problem as:

$$\underset{d}{\text{maximize}} \ T \ \text{in} \ (1.24) \tag{7.25}$$

$$\text{subject to} \ d \geq 1.$$

The problem in (7.25) is challenging and intractable. We even do not have the closed-form expressions of $p_s(d)$ and $\pi^+(d)$, not to mention the objective T. However, by taking advantage of the problem structure, we have the following theorem.

Theorem 7.2: Given n_c and n_d, the network throughput is upper bounded by $T_m = n_c(1 - 1/n_d)^{n_d-1}$, which can be achieved only if the optimal access difficulty $d^\star$ satisfies $p_s(d^\star) = \left(1 - \frac{1}{n_d}\right)^{n_d-1}$.

Proof. By substituting (7.23) into (7.24), the throughput can be rewritten as a function of p_s:

$$T(p_s) = n_c n_d p_s \left(1 - p_s^{\frac{1}{n_d-1}}\right). \tag{7.26}$$

The first-order derivative of this function is given by

$$T'(p_s) = n_c n_d \left(1 - \left(1 + \frac{1}{n_d - 1}\right) p_s^{\frac{1}{n_d-1}}\right). \tag{7.27}$$

Hence, $T(p_s)$ is monotonically increasing in p_s if $p_s < \left(1 - \frac{1}{n_d}\right)^{n_d-1}$ and is monotonically decreasing in p_s if $p_s > \left(1 - \frac{1}{n_d}\right)^{n_d-1}$. The maximum throughput $T_m = n_c(1 - 1/n_d)^{n_d-1}$ is achieved at the optimal access difficulty $p_s(d^\star) = \left(1 - \frac{1}{n_d}\right)^{n_d-1}$.

Theorem 7.2 indicates the optimal access difficulty $d^\star$ to maximize the network throughput T. As revealed by Theorem 7.2, the network has two states, depending on the value of $p_s(1)$. Since $p_s(d)$ is increasing in d, we have $p_s(1) \leq p_s(d) < 1.^2$ In this case $p_s(1) > \left(1 - \frac{1}{n_d}\right)^{n_d-1}$, we cannot find such a d satisfying $p_s(d) = \left(1 - \frac{1}{n_d}\right)^{n_d-1}$ to achieve the upper bound T_m. In this case, the network throughput mainly depends on the offered traffic load, and the access channel is capable of handling the current traffic intensity. The optimal access difficulty $d^\star$ should be set to 1, suggesting that packets can be transmitted immediately once they arrive. This case corresponds to the scenario that the open access resources are sufficient for all the devices with packets to transmit so that backoff is unnecessary. Meanwhile, if $p_s(1) \leq \left(1 - \frac{1}{n_d}\right)^{n_d-1}$, we can always find a proper $d^\star$ satisfying $p_s(d^\star) = \left(1 - \frac{1}{n_d}\right)^{n_d-1}$ for the upper bound T_m. Let us recall the Rogue's Dilemma in Section 7.2. In this case, the network is saturated or even congested so that Hash Access is necessary to control the aggressive traffic and prevent selfish access.

In the saturated state using $d^\star$, both the transmission success probability $p_s(d^\star)$ and the maximum throughput T_m are monotonically decreasing in n_d. It accords with our intuition that more devices result in a higher collision probability and a lower throughput. In a network with massive devices $n_d \to \infty$, one finds that $\lim_{n_d \to \infty} T_m = n_c(1 - 1/n_d)^{n_d-1} = \frac{n_c}{e}$, which only depends on the number of uplinks n_c. Actually, the uplink channels represent the available resources of the network and determine the upper bound of the system performance. From Theorem 7.2, we always have $\frac{n_c}{e} < T_m \leq \frac{n_c}{2}$ for any network with at least two devices.

7.5.3 Access delay

Now we would like to assess the delay of Hash Access based on the results of network throughput. According to Little's law [35], in a stable system, an item's waiting time equals the ratio of the average length of the waiting queue and the long-term average arrival rate (i.e., the throughput in our case). Hence, the access delay of Hash Access can be expressed as

$$D = \frac{n_d \bar{L}}{T} = \frac{d}{p_s(d)} \frac{\sum_{i=0}^{L} i\pi_i}{1 - \pi_0}, \tag{7.28}$$

where π_i is obtained from (7.19), $\bar{L} = \sum_{i=0}^{L} i\pi_i$ is the average packet number in a device's buffer, and the throughput T is given by (7.24). Equation (7.28) provides a general method to characterize the access delay of Hash Access for any traffic pattern described by (7.15). Note that the access delay was also addressed in Reference 23, where it was broken down into two components: the computation delay and the queuing delay. However, Reference 23 assumed that the distribution (say Π_i) that the device buffer has i packets just before a packet arrival epoch, i.e.,

---

$^2\lim_{d \to +\infty} \pi^+(d)/d = 0$ yields $\lim_{d \to +\infty} p_s(d) = 1$, which is the supremum of $p_s(d)$.

the distribution from the arriving packet's viewpoint, is the same as the stationary distribution π_i, which does not hold for any traffic patterns. Therefore, equation (28) provides a more accurate and general result for access delay analysis than the existing work [23].

7.6   Performance evaluation

In this section, we present the simulation results to verify our proposed analytical model. We consider the GFRA scenario using Hash Access where n_d possibly selfish IoT devices share n_c open access links. The slot duration is set to 5 ms according to the random access channel (RACH) setup in Long Term Evolution (LTE) [1]. In all the figures (except Figure 7.7), markers and lines represent the simulation and analytical results, respectively.

The monotonicity of $p_s(d)$ plays an important role in the analytical model and optimization of Hash Access. We first demonstrate the monotonic relationship between p_s and d in Figure 7.4. We consider Bernoulli and sporadic traffic patterns with different numbers of devices. As strictly proved by Ling *et al.* [24], $p_s(d)$ is monotonically increasing in d with Bernoulli traffic. Meanwhile, with sporadic traffic, one can also find the monotonic relationship for different n_d, which provides evidence for supporting the monotonicity of $p_s(d)$.

Figure 7.5 illustrates the performance of Hash Access ($n_c = 8$ and $n_d = 30$) with sporadic traffic in terms of transmission success probability, network throughput, and access delay. One can see that the analytical results (dashed lines) fit well with the simulations (markers), implying that our proposed model can characterize the performance of Hash Access accurately.

Figure 7.5(a) shows the relationship between the transmission success probability and the offered load. As the traffic intensity increases, the transmission success probability decreases because more packets compete for the limited uplink and cause more collisions. A greater access difficulty can control the number of IoT devices transmitting in a slot and reduce the collision probability. Using the optimal access difficulty, we can see that the transmission success probability is close to

$$p_s(d^\star) = \left(1 - \frac{1}{n_d}\right)^{n_d-1} \approx \frac{1}{e}.$$

Figure 7.5(b) visualizes the network throughput with varying access difficulties. In light traffic, the network is capable of supporting the offered load, and thus the network throughput depends on the traffic intensity. In heavy traffic, the network is saturated and limited by its capacity. If d is too difficult than necessary, the channels are not fully utilized; otherwise, the traffic is not effectively controlled, causing catastrophic collisions. As one can see, the optimal access difficulty $d^\star$ derived by Theorem 7.2 achieves the maximum network throughput.

We present the access delay of Hash Access at different difficulty levels in Figure 7.5(c). As the offered load increases, the access delay rises slightly initially and becomes significant once the network is congested. The delay is relatively long for a greater access difficulty since it needs more time to find a valid hash solution. Meanwhile, for a little difficulty, the access delay is short with light traffic and

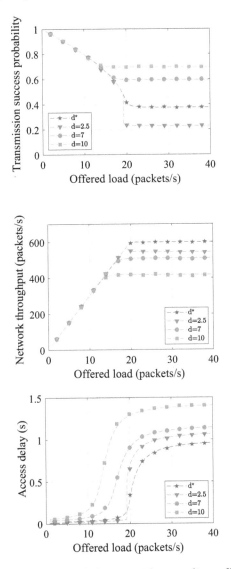

Figure 7.5   Performance of Hash Access with sporadic traffic ($n_c = 8$ and $n_d = 30$.) (a) Transmission success probability. (b) Network throughput. (c) Access delay.

increases dramatically with heavy traffic due to excessive collisions. The best access difficulty, although is not optimized for latency, still exhibits satisfactory performance in general.

Now let us look at Bernoulli traffic. Figure 7.6 verifies the optimality of $d^\star$ in networks with different numbers of devices. One can see that, the optimal access

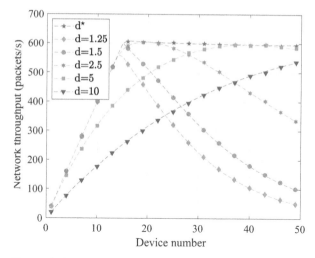

Figure 7.6 Network throughput of Hash Access versus the number of devices in Bernoulli traffic ($n_c = 8$ and $E[X]/\tau_s = 40 packets/s$).

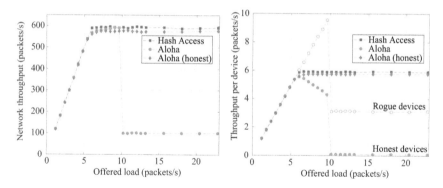

Figure 7.7 Network throughput in the presence of rogue devices with sporadic traffic ($n_c = 8$ and $n_d = 100$). (a) The point of view of the network. (b) The point of view from an individual device.

difficulty can always achieve the maximum network throughput. A greater access difficulty unduly restricts traffic flow and negatively affects the network throughput. In a network with a few devices, the transmission resources are adequate, and hence a low access difficulty can reach a close-to-optimal performance; meanwhile, with more devices, the network throughput falls rapidly due to aggressive competition.

Figure 7.7 demonstrates the throughput of Hash Access and Aloha in the presence of rogue nodes. The Aloha protocol in a trustworthy environment is shown as a benchmark. The CR based on a uniform backoff algorithm is adopted in Aloha with a maximum window of 60 slots [36]. From Figure 7.7(a), Hash Access using the optimal access difficulty achieves a slightly higher throughput than the Aloha protocol. However, in the existence of selfish devices, the network throughput of the Aloha protocol drops sharply once the shared link cannot support so many rogue devices. Hash Access enforces the backoff and thus effectively avoids such a tragic situation. Furthermore, we visualize the throughput per device in Figure 7.7(b) to show the interesting phenomenon of the Rogue's Dilemma. Now look at the performance of the Aloha protocol with 30% rogue devices. With low traffic, the network is not significantly affected, whereas, with high traffic, the rogue devices occupy the uplink for higher individual throughput, and harm the honest devices' interests. As network congestion intensifies, the throughput of rogue devices also declines rapidly. Eventually, every device's throughput is worse than the trustworthy case that everyone obeys the given RA protocol.

7.7 Conclusion

In this chapter, we demonstrated how the Rogue's Dilemma may occur in a shared untrusted network. We showed that such rogue nature of devices may congest the whole network via a simplified game model and also qualified the value of trust between clients. To address the Rogue's Dilemma, we proposed the Hash Access protocol with a detailed workflow. We further established a Markov model for general traffic patterns to quantitatively evaluate the performance of Hash Access in different aspects. Simulation results illustrate the effectiveness of the Hash Access protocol and our established model.

References

[1]   Laya A, Alonso L, Alonso-Zarate J. Is the Random Access Channel of LTE and LTE-A Suitable for M2M Communications? A Survey of Alternatives. *IEEE Commun Surv Tutorials*. 2014 firstquarter;16(1):4–16.

[2]   Shahin N, Ali R, Kim Y. Hybrid Slotted-CSMA/CA-TDMA for Efficient Massive Registration of IoT Devices. *IEEE Access*. 2018 Aug;6:18366–18382.

[3]   Hamdaoui B, Zorba N, Rayes A. Participatory IoT Networks-on-Demand for Safe, Reliable and Responsive Urban Cities. *IEEE Blockchain Technical Briefs*. 2019 Jan.

[4]   Bruno R, Conti M, Gregori E. Mesh Networks: Commodity Multihop ad hoc Networks. *IEEE Commun Mag*. 2005 Mar;43(3):123–131.

[5]   Ling X, Wang J, Le Y, *et al.* Blockchain Radio Access Network Beyond 5G. *IEEE Wireless Commun*. 2020 Dec;27(6):160–168.

[6]   Ling X, Wang J, Bouchoucha T, *et al.* Blockchain Radio Access Network (B-RAN): Towards Decentralized Secure Radio Access Paradigm. *IEEE Access*. 2019 Jan;7:9714–9723.

[7]   Wang J, Ling X, Le Y, *et al.* Blockchain Enabled Wireless Communications: A New Paradigm Towards 6G. *Natl Sci Rev*. 2021 Apr;Nwab069.

[8]   Ling X, Le Y, Wang J, *et al.* Practical Modeling and Analysis of Blockchain Radio Access Network. *IEEE Trans Commun.* 2021 Feb;69(2):1021–1037.

[9]   Xu H, Zhang L, Sun E, *et al.* BE-RAN: Blockchain-enabled Open RAN with Decentralized Identity Management and Privacy-Preserving Communication. arXiv Prepr arXiv:210110856. 2021 Jan.

[10]   Christidis K, Devetsikiotis M. Blockchains and Smart Contracts for the Internet of Things. *IEEE Access.* 2016 Jun;4:2292–2303.

[11]   Cao B, Li Y, Zhang L, *et al.* When Internet of Things Meets Blockchain: Challenges in Distributed Consensus. *IEEE Network.* 2019 Jul;33(6):133–139.

[12]   Xiong Z, Zhang Y, Luong NC, *et al.* The Best of Both Worlds: A General Architecture for Data Management in Blockchain-enabled Internet-of-Things. *IEEE Network.* 2020 Jan;34(1):166–173.

[13]   Le Y, Ling X, Wang J, *et al.* Prototype Design and Test of Blockchain Radio Access Network. In: Proc. IEEE Int. Conf. Commun. Workshops (ICC'19). Shanghai, CN; 2019.

[14]   Ling X, Le Y, Wang J, *et al.* Hash Access: Trustworthy Grant-Free IoT Access Enabled by Blockchain Radio Access Networks. *IEEE Network.* 2020 Jan;34(1):54–61.

[15]   Hardin G. The Tragedy of the Commons. *Science.* 1968 Dec;162(3859): 1243–1248.

[16]   Brito J. The Spectrum Commons in Theory and Practice. *SSRN Electr J.* 2006 May.

[17]   Berardinelli G, Huda Mahmood N, Abreu R, *et al.* Reliability Analysis of Uplink Grant-Free Transmission Over Shared Resources. *IEEE Access.* 2018 May;6:23602–23611.

[18]   Wei Y, Yu FR, Song M, *et al.* Joint Optimization of Caching, Computing, and Radio Resources for Fog-Enabled IoT Using Natural Actor-Critic Deep Reinforcement Learning. *IEEE Internet Things J.* 2019 Apr;6(2):2061–2073.

[19]   Cao B, Li M, Zhang L, *et al.* How Does CSMA/CA Affect the Performance and Security in Wireless Blockchain Networks. *IEEE Trans Ind Inf.* 2020 Jun;16(6):4270–4280.

[20]   Zhang L, Xu H, Onireti O, *et al. How Much Communication Resource is Needed to Run a Wireless Blockchain Network?* arXiv preprint arXiv:21011 0852. 2021 Jan.

[21]   Li Z, Wang W, Wu Q. Blockchain-Based Dynamic Spectrum Sharing for 5G and Beyond Wireless Communications. In: Int. Conf. Blockchain Trustworthy Syst. Dali, CN: Springer; 2020. p. 575–587.

[22]   Jiang N, Deng Y, Nallanathan A, *et al.* Analyzing Random Access Collisions in Massive IoT Networks. *IEEE Trans Wireless Commun.* 2018 Oct;17 (10):6853–6870.

[23]   Zhang B, Ling X, Le Y, *et al.* Analysis and Evaluation of Hash Access for Blockchain Radio Access Networks. In: Proc. 12th Int. Conf. Wireless Commun. Signal Process. (WCSP'20). Nanjing, CN; 2020. p. 62–67.

[24] Ling X, Zhang B, Xie H, *et al.* Hash Access in Blockchain Radio Access Networks: Characterization and Optimization. *IEEE IoT J*. 2022 Jun;9 (11):8053–8066.

[25] Farhat J, Grybosi JF, Brante G, *et al.* Non-Orthogonal Hash Access for Grant-Free IoT Blockchain Radio Access Networks. *IEEE Wireless Commun Lett*. 2021 May;10(5):1066–1070.

[26] Osborne M, Rubinstein A. *A Course in Game Theory*. Cambridge, MA: MIT Press; 1994.

[27] Li G, Yu J, Xing Y, *et al.* Location-Invariant Physical Layer Identification Approach for WiFi Devices. *IEEE Access*. 2019 Aug;7:106974–106986.

[28] Yu J, Hu A, Li G, *et al.* A Robust RF Fingerprinting Approach Using Multisampling Convolutional Neural Network. *IEEE Internet Things J*. 2019 Apr;6(4):6786–6799.

[29] Nakamoto S. Bitcoin: A Peer-to-Peer Electronic Cash System. *Tech Rep*. 2008 Oct.

[30] Tschorsch F, Scheuermann B. Bitcoin and Beyond: A Technical Survey on Decentralized Digital Currencies. *IEEE Commun Surv Tutorials*. 2016 Thirdquarter;18(3):2084–2123.

[31] Zhan W, Dai L. Massive Random Access of Machine-to-Machine Communications in LTE Networks: Modeling and Throughput Optimization. *IEEE Trans Wireless Commun*. 2018 Apr;17(4):2771–2785.

[32] Osti P, Lassila P, Aalto S, *et al.* Analysis of PDCCH Performance for M2M Traffic in LTE. *IEEE Trans Veh Technol*. 2014 Nov;63(9):4357–4371.

[33] Soltanmohammadi E, Ghavami K, Naraghi-Pour M. A Survey of Traffic Issues in Machine-to-Machine Communications Over LTE. *IEEE Internet Things J*. 2016 Dec;3(6):865–884.

[34] Horn RA, Johnson CR. *Matrix Analysis*. New York: Cambridge University Press; 1985.

[35] Kleinrock L. Theory, Volume 1, *Queueing Systems*. vol. 1. New York, NY, USA: Wiley-Interscience; 1975.

[36] Rivero-Angeles ME, Lara-Rodriguez D, Cruz-Perez FA. Gaussian Approximations for the Probability Mass Function of the Access Delay for Different Backoff Policies in S-ALOHA. *IEEE Commun Lett*. 2006 Oct;10 (10):731–733.

Chapter 8

Image compression-encryption scheme using SPIHT and 2D-BCM

Najet Elkhalil[1] and Ridha Ejbali[1]

As network technology advances, data sharing over the internet has also increased significantly. Images are the most shared data over the internet. However, certain images are sensitive and require secure storage or transmission, especially when communicated through insecure channels. Digital images typically exhibit high data correlation where compression can be done to reduce the load on transmission channels and storage memory. To address this, a proposed algorithm combines image compression and encryption techniques. The algorithm employs the Set Partitioning in Hierarchical Trees (SPIHT) technique for image compression. After compression, the algorithm proceeds to encrypt the compressed image. It achieves this by employing chaotic sequences generated using the Two dimensional Beta Chaotic Map (2D-BCM) and a permutation-diffusion architecture. Based on the experimental results and security analysis conducted, the compression-encryption algorithm exhibits a high level of sensitivity and security. As a result, the algorithm demonstrates its capability to withstand chosen plaintext attacks.

8.1 Introduction

Images are an often-used form of data that includes a lot of information and has a lot of uses in disciplines including biological research, remote sensing, military, and social media. Worldwide, millions of image data are stored and transmitted every second, making effective storage and protection of these data a crucial concern. The combination of image compression and encryption not only facilitates data reduction but also offers essential data security for image data. Researchers have integrated compression techniques with encryption algorithms to achieve dual objectives: reducing the size of data transfer and ensuring secure and efficient storage. This integration of compression and encryption techniques offers several benefits. First, it helps optimize data transfer and storage resources by reducing the overall size of the data. By compressing the data before transmission or storage, the

[1]Research Team in Intelligent Machines (RTIM), National Engineering School of Gabes, Tunisia

required bandwidth or memory capacity can be significantly reduced, resulting in more efficient utilization of network resources. Additionally, incorporating encryption into the process enhances data security. Encryption algorithms transform the compressed data into an unreadable format, making it extremely difficult for unauthorized individuals to access or decipher the information. This ensures that sensitive data remains protected, even if intercepted during transmission or compromised storage. This was confirmed by Ghadirli *et al.* [1] in their survey on color image encryption. Another image encryption scheme for color images is proposed by Wu *et al.* [2]. The scheme is based on 6D hyper-chaotic system and 2D discrete wavelet transform (DWT). The initial image is first divided into four sub-bands using the 2D DWT. Second, every sub-bands is permuted using a key stream. Third, an intermediate image was constructed from the four encrypted sub-bands using the inverse 2D DWT. To further increase the security, each pixel of the intermediate image is modified using another key stream. The proposed algorithm is resistant to different plaintext attacks.

Massood *et al.* [3] proposed a hybrid image encryption scheme based on 3D Lo-renz chaotic map. The algorithm involves shuffling and diffusion processes. Security tests validate the robustness of the scheme.

Combining image compression and encryption not only reduces data but also offers much-needed security to the image information.

With the growth of advanced technologies, new approaches, and techniques for image compression and encryption have been developed.

Embedded encryption into the compression process is proposed by Zhang *et al.* [4]. This algorithm adopts three stages of scrambling and diffusion. Several chaotic systems are used to generate the encryption key. Security tests indicate that the algorithm has high security and good compression performance.

In [5], authors propose a new compression-encryption algorithm based on the performance of chaotic sequence and the excellent proprieties of the wavelet transform. Results show the effectiveness of encryption security and the compression ratio. Drawing on the principles of Compressive Sensing (CS) and chaos theory, many scholars have proposed lossy encryption schemes combining CS and chaos [6–8]. SPIHT compressing is widely used in image compression due to its computational complexity and compression performance [9–11].

8.2 Preliminaries

8.2.1 *The two-dimensional Beta Chaotic map 2D-BCM*

The two-dimensional Beta Chaotic map (shown in Figure 8.1), introduced by the authors in [12], is a new mapping function that exhibits robust chaotic behavior and possesses a significant number of parameters. The mathematical definition of the 2D-BCM is outlined as follows:

$$x_{n+1} = k \times Beta(y_{n+1}; x1, x2, p, q) \tag{8.1}$$

$$y_{n+1} = k \times Beta(xn; y1, y2, p, q) \tag{8.2}$$

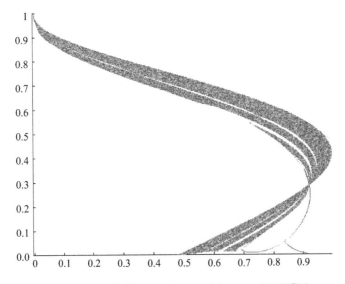

Figure 8.1   Different shapes of the new 2D-BCM

where

$$p = b_1 + c_1 \times a \tag{8.3}$$

$$q = b_2 + c_2 \times a \tag{8.4}$$

b_1, c_1, b_2 and c_2 adequately chosen constants.

   a: bifurcation parameter.
   k: amplitude control parameter.

8.2.2   2D-BCM used in the encryption process

Changing a parameter in the mathematical definition of a Chaotic map allows the generation of diverse and distinct chaotic maps and sequences, enabling researchers to study their properties, analyze their behavior, and potentially apply them in various fields such as cryptography, signal processing, or random number generation [10,11,13,14]. Using the mathematical definition of the 2D-BCM and the following parameters x1 = −1, x2 = 1, y1 = −1, y2 = 1, k = 0.93, we generated the map shown in Figure 8.2.

8.2.3   SPIHT algorithm

8.2.3.1   SPIHT tree structure

SPIHT (Set Partitioning in Hierarchical Trees) encoding is an improved version of EZW (Embedded Zero-tree Wavelet). SPIHT is based on the DWT: the image passes through DWT block to determine its wavelet coefficients. Aspatial orientation tree structure is then constructed (Figure 8.3). Each node of the spatial tree

1
0.9
0.8
0.7
0.6
0.5
0.4
0.3
0.2
0.1
0
0
0.1
0.2
0.3
0.4
0.5
0.6
0.7
0.8
0.9
1

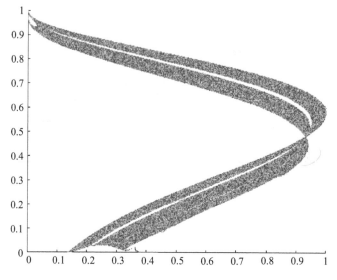

Figure 8.2 Different shapes of the new 2D-BCM

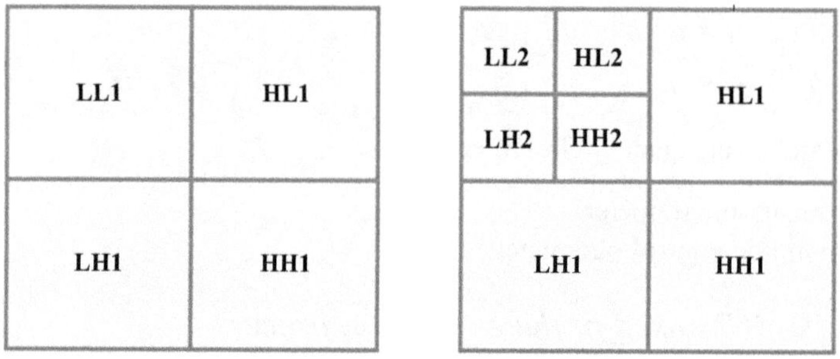

LL1
HL1
LH1
HH1
LL2
HL2
LH2
HH2
HL1
LH1
HH1

Figure 8.3 Spatial orientation tree structure

corresponds to a wavelet coefficient represented by position (i,j). Every node (i,j) have four children: (2i,2j), (2i,2j+1), (2i+1,2j), and (2i+1,2j+1), expect the lowest frequency sub-band (LL).

8.2.3.2 SPIHT encoding

The SPIHT coding technique is characterized by steps that are repeated throughout each stage and are described by a bit-plane that carries an indicator of wavelet coefficients that are quantified by the structure in a hierarchical tree. Each coefficient in the orientation tree is coded from the Most Significant Bit-plane (MSB) to the Least Significant Bit-plane (LSB), starting with the coefficients having the largest magnitudes within. SPIHT coding computes a threshold Tp in each bit-plane and assigns it to one or more of the three items listed below:

- List of insignificant sets (LIS): contains a set of wavelet coefficients that have a smaller magnitude than the threshold Tp.
- List of insignificant pixels (LIP): contains wavelet coefficients that are smaller than the threshold Tp.
- List of significant pixels (LSP): contains wavelet coefficients that are larger than the threshold Tp.

SPIHT algorithm involves three main steps defined below:

First step: initialization

Initialize the threshold $T = 2n = \lfloor \log2(\max(i,j)\{|ci,j|\}) \rfloor$, ci,j for the wavelet coefficient.

Initialize the three lists:
LSP = Ø
LIP = $all(i,j) \in LLsub - bands$
LIS = *treestructure*

Second step: Sorting Pass verify the LSP to check if the wavelet coefficients contained are significant or not.

Significant coefficients: then output 1 and the sign bit of the wavelet coefficients are represented by 1 and 0 (positive or negative), then remove the wavelet coefficient from LIP and add to the LSP.

Insignificant coefficients: keep them in the LIP and the output will be '0'. Verify all the significant sets in the LIS.

Third step: Refinement Pass refinement bit (bit) of all the coefficients in the LSP, which contains coefficients that have larger magnitudes than the Tp. LSP keeps pixels that are already evaluated and do not need to be evaluated again. Updating the threshold Tp.

8.2.4 *The 2D Beta chaotic encryption algorithm*

Step 1: resize the M*N input image into a square dimension.

Step 2: generating two different random chaotic sequences: Rseq1 and Rseq2.

The variation of one parameter of the 2D-BCM function produces a totally different map and thus different chaotic sequences.

Step 3: rearrange Rseq1 and Rseq2 into matrix forms M1 and M2 with M*N dimension. M1 and M2 are then used to shuffle the rows and columns of the input image.

Step 4: divide the resulting matrix into four blocks. Transform the blocks to a random matrix W using the equation below:

$$f_N(d) = T(d) mod G \tag{8.5}$$

$$f_R(d) = T\lfloor(\sqrt{d})\rfloor mod G \tag{8.6}$$

$$f_S(d) = T(d^2) mod G \tag{8.7}$$

$$f_D(d) = T(2d) mod G \tag{8.8}$$

And the matrix function is given below:

$$\begin{aligned} W = [ccccf_N(B_{1,1}) f_R(B_{1,2}) f_S(B_{1,3}) f_D(B_{1,4}) f_R(B_{2,1}) \\ f_S(B_{2,2}) f_D(B_{2,3}) f_N(B_{2,4}) f_S(B_{3,1}) f_D(B_{3,2}) \\ f_N(B_{3,3}) f_R(B_{3,4}) f_D(B_{4,1}) f_N(B_{4,2}) f_R(B_{4,3}) f_S(B_{4,4}) \end{aligned} \tag{8.9}$$

8.3   Compression-encryption algorithm

The encryption process is resumed in the following steps:

1. Resize the initial image in square dimensions.
2. Generate random sequences using the 2D-BCM.
3. Shuffling the rows and then the column of the input images using the generated sequences.
4. Substitute the pixel of the original image.
5. The diffusion process.

The flowchart of the proposed method is illustrated in Figure 8.4.

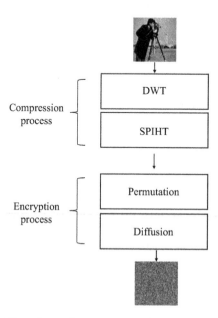

Figure 8.4   Flowchart of our compression-encryption algorithm

8.4   Results and discussion

For the purpose of experimentation, a collection of sample images was sourced from the freely available USC-SIPI database [15]. The simulation was conducted on multiple images, and the results presented in the study focus on four specific images, namely House, Airplane, Cameraman, Moon Surface Chemical Plant, Lena, Peppers, Boat, Lake, and Baboon. Figure 8.5 first row corresponds to the original, uncompressed images. Subsequently, the second row showcases the compressed ciphered images generated through the employment of SPIHT compression and the 2D-BCM chaotic map.

8.4.1   Histogram analysis

To safeguard the information contained within the original image against statistical attacks, the encrypted image must exhibit no statistical similarity to the original image. Achieving a uniform histogram for the encrypted image is crucial to ensure its resistance to such attacks. The results of the compression-encryption process are depicted in Figure 8.6. The first and second rows represent the compressed images and their corresponding histogram, respectively. On the other hand, the third and fourth rows in Figure 8.6 depict the compressed-encrypted images and their histograms, respectively. Upon examination, it is evident that the histogram of the compressed-encrypted images is uniform and significantly different from the histogram of the compressed image. This uniform distribution signifies a lack of statistical patterns or similarities to the original image, reinforcing the effectiveness of the encryption process in concealing the original image's information from statistical attacks. These results demonstrate that the encryption process successfully transforms the statistical characteristics of the original images, ensuring that the encrypted images possess a uniform histogram and are statistically dissimilar to their respective originals.

Figure 8.5   Experimental results: The first row shows the original uncompressed images and the second row shows its corresponding ciphered images

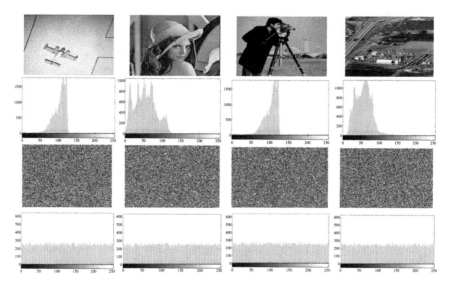

Figure 8.6   Histogram analysis

Table 8.1   Entropy of our approach and other approaches

	Lena	Peppers	Boat	Baboon
Our approach	7.9998	7.9993	7.9996	7.9993
Ref. [5]	7.9989	7.9988	7.9989	7.9987
Ref. [17]	7.9973	–	–	–

8.4.1.1   Information entropy test

The entropy value directly corresponds to the degree of randomness exhibited by the pixels. As the randomness within the pixels increases, the entropy value also rises. In the context of an 8-bit pixel value representation, where pixel values range from 0 to 255, the maximum possible entropy value is determined as 8. The computed entropy values for the test images are presented in Table 8.1.

$$H(S) = \sum_{i=1}^{2^n-1} P(S_i) \log \left(\frac{1}{P(S_i)} \right) \tag{8.10}$$

where, 2^n: the total states of the information source S_i, $P(S_i)$: the probability of the symbol S_i. By examining the values in Table 8.1, it is apparent that the entropy values obtained from the proposed cryptosystem are close to the maximum value of 8. This indicates a high degree of randomness in the cipher images generated by the algorithm. The proximity of the entropy values to the maximum value suggests that the proposed cryptosystem effectively preserves and maintains randomness during the encryption process.

Table 8.2   NPCR of our approach and other approaches

	Lena	**House**	**Boat**	**Lake**
Our approach	99.63	99.63	99.63	99.61
Ref. [5]	99.91	89.99	99.61	99.02
Ref. [17]	99.60	–	–	–

Table 8.3   UACI of our approach and other approaches

	Lena	**House**	**Boat**	**Lake**
Our approach	33.51	33.52	33.53	33.39
Ref. [5]	33.69	33.96	33.73	33.49
Ref. [17]	30.66	–	–	–

Furthermore, the comparison between the proposed algorithm and those referenced in Hamdi *et al.* [5] and [17] indicates that the proposed algorithm outperforms them in terms of randomness.

8.4.2   NPCR and UACI analysis

Differential test is another test to determine the robustness of the cryptosystem. We use Change Rate (NPCR) and Unified Average Changing Intensity (UACI) to determine this feature. NPCR is used to calculate the difference between two images by evaluating the number of pixel differences. Meanwhile, the UACI is used to obtain the difference between two images by evaluating the change of visual effect between two encrypted images. NPCR and UACI are calculated by the following formulas:

$$NPCR = \frac{\sum\limits_{i,j} D(i,j)}{M \times N} \times 100 \tag{8.11}$$

$$UACI = \frac{1}{M \times N} \left[\sum\limits_{i,j} \frac{|C_1(i,j) - C_2(i,j)|}{255} \right] \times 100 \tag{8.12}$$

where

$$D(i,j) = \{ccc0 if C_1(i,j) = C_2(i,j) 1 if C_1(i,j) = C_2(i,j)\} \tag{8.13}$$

M and N: the height and the width of the original and the cipher images, C1 and C2 are the encrypted images before and after one pixel is modified from the original image, respectively. Tables 8.2 and 8.3 represent the obtained results of NPCR and UACI of our cryptosystem compared with other algorithms. The obtained results demonstrate the robustness of the proposed cryptosystem. Thus, our cryptosystem can resist differential attacks.

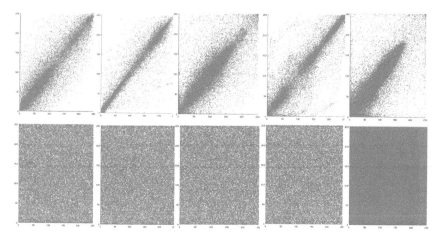

Figure 8.7   Correlation analysis

8.4.3   Correlation analysis

A correlation is a statistical measure that quantifies the relationship or dependence between two variables. When two values have a high degree of dependence, their correlation value tends to be high. In the context of encryption, it is desirable for a cipher to eliminate any dependency or relationship between the ciphertext and the plaintext. Figure 8.7 visually illustrates the distinction between the original data and the encrypted data. In this case, the original data represents an image that exhibits a substantial correlation and possesses a high correlation coefficient. However, upon encrypting the image, the resulting encrypted image demonstrates no discernible correlation. This visual contrast demonstrates the successful elimination of any dependency or relationship between the original data (plaintext) and the encrypted data (ciphertext).

8.5   Conclusion and future work

In this study, we proposed a compression-encryption scheme based on the SPIHT algorithm and 2D-BCM. The obtained results from conducting statistical and differential attacks prove that our new 2D-BCM can be employed as a reliable approach within a compression-encryption cryptosystem. These results demonstrate the robustness and strength of our proposed chaotic map in protecting data during the encryption process. Moving forward, our future aim is to explore and assess the efficiency of our 2D-BCM in conjunction with other cryptosystems. By testing its compatibility and performance alongside different cryptographic techniques, we strive to expand the scope of our research and identify potential synergies or improvements that can be achieved by integrating the 2D-BCM into various encryption frameworks.

References

[1] Ghadirli H, Nodehi A, Enayatifar R. An overview of encryption algorithms in color images. *Signal Processing*. 2019 11;164:163–185.

[2] Wu X, Wang D, Kurths J, *et al*. A novel lossless color image encryption scheme using 2D DWT and 6D hyperchaotic system. *Information Sciences*. 2016 02;349.

[3] Masood F, Ahmad J, Shah SA, *et al*. A novel hybrid secure image encryption based on Julia Set of Fractals and 3D Lorenz Chaotic map. *Entropy*. 2020 02;22:274.

[4] Zhang H, Wang Xq, Sun Yj, *et al*. A novel method for lossless image compression and encryption based on LWT, SPIHT and cellular automata. *Signal Processing: Image Communication*. 2020 03;84:115829.

[5] Hamdi M, Rhouma R, Belghith S. A selective compression-encryption of images based on SPIHT coding and Chirikov standard MAP. *Signal Processing*. 2016 09;131.

[6] Chai X, Zheng X, Gan Z, *et al*. An image encryption algorithm based on chaotic system and compressive sensing. *Signal Processing*. 2018 07;148:124–144.

[7] Lu P, Xu Z, Lu X, *et al*. Digital image information encryption based on Compressive Sensing and double random-phase encoding technique. *Optik - International Journal for Light and Electron Optics*. 2013 08;124:2514–2518.

[8] Huang R, Rhee KH, Uchida S. A parallel image encryption method based on compressive sensing. *Multimedia Tools and Applications*. 2014 09;72.

[9] Tong XJ, Chen P, Zhang M. A joint image lossless compression and encryption method based on chaotic map. *Multimedia Tools and Applications*. 2017 06;76.

[10] Zhang M, Tong X. Joint image encryption and compression scheme based on IWT and SPIHT. *Optics and Lasers in Engineering*. 2017 03;90.

[11] Elkhalil N, Zahmoul R, Ejbali R, *et al*. A joint encryption-compression technique for images based on Beta Chaotic maps and SPIHT coding. *The Fourteenth International Conference on Software Engineering Advances*. 2019;21:130–170.

[12] Najet E, Youssouf W, Ridha E. Image encryption using the new two-dimensional Beta chaotic map. *Multimedia Tools and Applications*. 2023 82;1–15.

[13] Rim Z, Ejbali R, Zaied M. Image encryption based on new Beta chaotic maps. *Optics and Lasers in Engineering*. 2017 09;96:39–49.

[14] Rim Z, Zaied M. Toward new family beta maps for chaotic image encryption; 2016. p. 004052–004057.

[15] Souden H, Ejbali R, Zaied M. A watermarking scheme based on DCT, SVD and BCM; 2019. p. 116.

[16] Vijay C, Ashish G. A 2D logistic map and Lorenz-Rossler chaotic system based RGB image encryption approach. *Multimedia Tools and Applications*. 2020.

[17] Hamid H, Mourad L, Sarah K, Tahanout M, Karim K, Sid-Ali A. A novel robust compression-encryption of images based on SPIHT coding and fractional-order discrete-time chaotic system. *Optik*. 2019;109:534–546.

Chapter 9

Security of an image utilizing modified use of DWT and SVD along with multiple watermarking

Amita Singha[1] and Muhammad Ahsan Ullah[2]

In the case of digital communication, the security of a signal is the most important factor. Security can be ensured by several techniques. In this chapter, the security of an image is developed by using digital watermarking. In the proposed technique, images as well as audio signals are used as watermarks which are the proofs of the true owner of the image being sent. To embed the watermarks into the host image, the total energy of both the host and the watermark signals are divided several times. These energy divisions are performed by using discrete wavelet transform (DWT) and singular value decomposition (SVD). The energy divisions are incorporated for utilizing the total energy distribution of the host signal for embedding the watermarks. For this, the developed technique ensures the insertion of a large piece of information into the host signal. Apart from that, the developed technique distributes the energy of the watermark signals into the entire region of the host signal which will create difficulty in removing or destroying the watermarks by the unwanted parties. The proposed technique offers a PSNR (Peak Signal to Noise Ratio) of 63.7525 dB and normalized cross-correlation (NC) close to 0.9. The robustness is tested against not only conventional attacks but also against real-life scenarios.

9.1 Introduction

Digital watermarking is a very efficient tool in providing security during digital communication between two wanted parties. By watermarking, a permanent mark that can be of any type of media can be embedded into the signal being shared. That mark acts as proof that the signal is being shared between the true owner and the true receiver. By designing a very strong embedding algorithm, the mark cannot be

[1]Institute of Energy Technology, Chittagong University of Engineering and Technology, Bangladesh
[2]Department of Electrical and Electronic Engineering, Chittagong University of Engineering and Technology, Bangladesh

erased once it is embedded into the host signal by the unwanted parties whose main objective is to create hindrance in communication. Watermarking can be classified into image watermarking [1], video watermarking [2,3], audio watermarking [4,5], or text watermarking [6]. Image watermarking is defined as the process of embedding information in an image that will act as the host image. Digital image watermarking can be visible or invisible depending on the degree of visibility of the watermark in the host image [7].

Image watermarking can be classified into several types depending on the purpose of watermarking. Watermarking can be classified into blind and non-blind watermarking depending on the necessity of the host signal to detect the watermark signal. Depending on the degree of immunity of the watermark signal against several attacks, watermarking can be fragile, semi-fragile, and robust. But, two broad classes of watermarking are spatial-domain watermarking and transform-domain watermarking. These two watermarking can be utilized to develop the other classes of watermarking. For example, spatial-domain watermarking can be used to develop fragile watermarking. The efficiency of the transform-domain water-marking is more than that of the spatial-domain watermarking as in the transform-domain watermarking the watermark is inserted by modifying some coefficients of the host signal rather than modifying the signal intensities which is the case of spatial-domain watermarking. That is why transform-domain watermarking is extensively being used.

The transform-domain watermarking can be developed by using several functions such as discrete cosine transform (DCT) [8,9], discrete wavelet transform (DWT) [10], singular value decomposition (SVD) [11–13], and many more. The combination of those functions can be used to develop watermarking algorithms [14,15]. Apart from that, some of those functions can be used with some modern techniques to develop very efficient watermarking schemes. Some examples are DWT and SVD with the firefly algorithm [16], SVD with block-based DWT [17], DCT with fractal encoding [18], DWT with Fuzzy logic [19], DWT with the neural network [20], etc.

Modifying the host image as well as the watermark before applying the watermarking technique can be very fruitful in developing a very efficient water-marking technique [21,22].

Over the past few years, several watermarking techniques have been developed that utilize multiple watermarks [23–25]. Those multiple watermarking techniques showed better performance in the case of privacy and authenticity. Multiple watermarking can also be done by inserting the same watermark signal several times into the host signal rather than using different watermarks [26]. In this chapter, DWT and SVD are used to embed multiple audio and image signals as watermarks into a single host image signal as those two techniques performed well in the case of multiple watermarking [27–29]. Besides, DWT and SVD also per-formed very well to embed hybrid signals into a single host image [30]. So, DWT and SVD are utilized in this chapter to embed different kinds of signals into a single host image. This chapter is intended to prove that conventional techniques can perform well if used differently. The sizes of the watermark signals are comparable with that of the host image. DWT and SVD are used in a way to ensure the successful embedding and extraction of the watermark signals although a large amount of energy is imposed on the host signal as comparatively bigger sizes of watermark signals are used. It is also intended to prove that, in the case of embedding different kinds of signals into a single host image, the number of watermarks also affects the successful extraction of the watermark signals in the case of several signal processing operations.

In the proposed technique, three audio signals and one image signal are used as watermarks. All those signals are of different sizes. For this, they are embedded into different levels of the host signal. To do that, the host signal should be divided to insert the watermark signals. In other words, the entire energy of the host signal should be divided to allocate the watermark signals. For that energy division, DWT is used several times to create several energy bands of the host signal. After the energy division of the host signal, the energy of the watermark signals is also divided by DWT. These divisions are done so that different parts of the energy of the watermark signals are embedded into different levels of the host signal containing frequency bands of different amounts of energy. After energy divisions, the energy of the watermarks is distributed into the host signal using SVD. The embedding of watermarks in portions has an advantage: to destroy the watermarks all the portions of energy should be destroyed. It will be difficult as it is not known which part of the energy of the watermarks is embedded into which part of the energy of the host signal. This can certainly increase the security of a signal. The utilization of energy division to embed watermarks can be considered as a contribution to the proposed technique.

The following sections will give a detailed description of the development of the proposed technique as well as the performance of that technique considering some traditional attacks as well as some real-life scenarios. A comparison with some state-of-the-art techniques will also be given which will be helpful to consider the proposed technique a strong one.

9.2 Detailed description of the proposed technique

This section is divided into three sub-sections: 'Embedding Technique', 'Embedding Procedure', and 'Extraction Procedure'. Those three sections will explain the logical structure behind the development of the proposed technique.

9.2.1 Embedding technique

In the proposed technique, the watermark audio signals are converted into two-dimensional signals so that their embedding into the host signal can be performed with ease as image and audio have different dimensions. Then, the energy of both the host and the watermark signals are divided by performing multi-level DWT. In doing so, there will be several energy levels of both the host and the watermark signals which will be utilized for embedding watermark signals. Every level of the host signal possesses a different amount of energy which will be used to embed a portion of the energy of the watermark signals. As the signal energy is divided, it will be necessary to gather all the energy back into place to create a watermarked image with no perceptual degradation as well as to extract the watermark signals. Usually, combining two signals creates energy interference. As several energy levels are available, the effects of energy interference will be severe enough to destroy both the host and the watermark signals. So, to avoid the extreme case of quality degradation, after performing DWT, SVD is applied to all the frequency bands of the signals involved. Then, the singular values of the selected bands are combined keeping in mind the energy content of the sub-bands [31] obtained after performing DWT. The higher energy content sub-band is combined with a comparatively lower energy content sub-band. This combination helps reduce energy interaction as by this combination the host signal is kept unknown to the fact that something is inserted into it. If the host signal does not feel the presence of the watermark signals in it, it will not interfere with them. In the same way, if the watermark signals are unknown to the fact that they are inserted into another signal, they will not interfere with the host signal. The embedding procedure will be clear from the next sub-section.

As mentioned earlier, the chapter intends to prove that by using conventional techniques in a modified way, a very efficient watermarking technique can be developed. In the proposed technique, DWT is used to create different energy levels to embed a large amount of data. Here DWT is used as a tool to create places in the host image so that different kinds of signals with different characteristics can be inserted into a single host image and that is the modified use of DWT. On the other hand, after performing DWT, SVD is performed to develop the algorithm by which the frequency bands of the host and the watermark signals are combined. By DWT only the locations can be created in which the watermark signals can be embedded. However, there should be a technique by which the frequency bands of the watermark signals can be embedded in particular locations. To create the technique, SVD comes into play. Utilizing SVD and considering the energy distribution of the sub-bands as outlined by Liu *et al.* [31], an embedding technique has been devised. This technique aims to efficiently manage the energy interaction introduced by minimizing the extent of energy imposed on the host image. In this way, SVD is used in a modified way. The assumptions that the modified use of DWT and SVD can be useful in developing an efficient watermarking technique can be proved through the following sections.

MATLAB® R2018a is used to develop the proposed watermarking technique.

9.2.2   Embedding procedure

In this sub-section, the 'Embedding Procedure' is discussed. The procedure is divided into several parts as the embedding of watermark signals into the host image requires some auxiliary steps in the proposed watermarking technique. The steps are as follows:

- **Decomposition of the host image**
  Step 1: A standard image of size $2,048 \times 2,048$ is used.
  Step 2: The host image is decomposed four times using DWT. In this way, four levels of decomposition are obtained. From every level of decomposition,

four non-overlapping frequency bands are obtained. Those bands are LL, LH, HL, and HH. Every level of decomposition is obtained by decomposing the HH sub-band of the previous level of decomposition.

Step 3: The 5th to 8th level decompositions will be obtained by decomposing the sub-bands obtained by the 1st level of decomposition.

Step 4: Similarly, 9th to 12th level decompositions, 13th to 16th level decompositions, and 17th to 20th level decompositions will be obtained by decomposing the sub-bands of 2nd, 3rd, and 4th level of decomposition respectively.

Step 5: Finally, SVD will be applied to the sub-bands obtained from steps 2 to 4.

- **Decomposition of the watermark image**

  Step 1: A standard test image of size 512×512 is used. That image is used as 1st watermark signal.

  Step 2: The watermark image is decomposed using DWT and four sub-bands LL, LH, HL, and HH are obtained.

  Step 3: The sub-bands obtained from step 2 are decomposed and four levels are obtained. In this way, the watermark image is decomposed to get four levels of decomposition.

  Step 4: Finally, apply SVD to the sub-bands obtained from steps 2 and 3.

- **Decomposition of the watermark audio signals**

  Step 1: Three audio files are used.

  Step 2: The sizes of the audio files are $1 \times 65,536, 1 \times 1,048,576$, and $1 \times 4,194,304$. Those audio files are converted into two-dimensional signals of sizes $256 \times 256, 1,024 \times 1,024$, and $2,048 \times 2,048$ respectively by using the 'Reshape function'. Those audio files are used as 2nd, 3rd, and 4th watermark signals respectively.

  Step 3: Steps 2 to 4 of the decomposition of the watermark image are applied to the watermark audio files.

- **Composition of host signal and watermark signals**

  Step 1: The singular values of the LL, LH, HL, and HH sub-bands of the host signal obtained by the 19th, 20th, 17th, and 18th levels of decomposition respectively will be combined with the singular values of the HL, HH, LL, and LH sub-bands respectively of the 1st watermark signal obtained by the 1st, 2nd, 3rd, and 4th levels of decomposition respectively.

  Step 2: The above step will apply to the other three watermark signals. The only difference is that for the 2nd, 3rd, and 4th watermark signals, the sub-bands obtained by 13th to 16th levels decomposition, 9th to 12th levels decomposition, and 5th to 8th level decomposition of the host signal using DWT will be applied respectively for the composition with the watermark image. The selection of the levels of decompositions obtained from decomposing the host image for the combination of the singular values depends on the size of the signals involved in the watermarking procedure. It is known that, with each level of decomposition, the size of a particular sub-band is decreased. In the proposed technique, both the host and the watermark signals are decomposed several times. For that reason, the selection of the sub-band is chosen to keep in mind the change of dimension of a signal with every level of decomposition.

Step 3: The above combinations are done by a constant k. Mathematically,

$$S_{AWM} = S_H + kS_{WM} \tag{1}$$

where S_{AWM} is the singular value of the watermarked signal; S_H is the singular value of the host signal; S_{WM} is the singular value of the watermark signal

- **Creation of the watermarked image**
  Step 1: The inverse SVD is applied to get the sub-bands of the watermarked image.
  Step 2: Then the inverse DWT (IDWT) is applied to finally get the watermarked image.

9.2.3 *Extraction procedure*

The steps of the 'Extraction Procedure' are as follows:

Step 1: The watermarked image is decomposed several times like the way the host image is decomposed using DWT.
Step 2: Then SVD is applied to the sub-bands obtained by step 1.
Step 3: The singular values of the watermark signals are obtained by the following mathematical expression:

$$S_{WM} = (S_X - S_H)/l \tag{2}$$

where S_{WM} is the singular value of the Watermark Signal. S_H is the singular value of the Host signal. S_X is the singular value of the watermarked signal.
Step 4: The watermark signals are obtained by applying inverse SVD and then applying inverse DWT.
Step 5: The audio signals are obtained in their original form by converting the two-dimensional signals into their respective audio files.

It should be noted from this sub-section that, the embedding of the watermark signals is not merely combining the singular values of the signals involved which is the case of the techniques developed in the literature. Rather, there is a complex algorithm for combining the singular values both level-wise as well as sub-band-wise (Section 9.2.1). If this algorithm is not followed properly, there will be no chance of extracting the watermark signals as well as obtaining a watermarked image with no perceptual degradation as in the proposed technique the trace of watermark signals is present in every little section of the host image. Due to this, the values of the two constants obtained k and l from equations (1) and (2) respectively will be different for different watermark signals.

9.3 Performance evaluation

The performance of the proposed watermarking technique is evaluated against several experiments.

At first, two performance criteria are considered: PSNR (Peak Signal to Noise Ratio) and NCC (Normalized Cross-Correlation). Figures 9.1 and 9.2 and Tables 9.1 to 9.5 represent the performance of the proposed technique against those two parameters.

Figures 9.1 and 9.2 indicate the efficiency of the proposed technique by the fact that there is no visible change in the host image after being watermarked.

The quality of the watermarked image is also tested by comparing the power spectral density and the power spectrum of the host image and the watermarked image. Figures 9.3 to 9.6 are referred to for those comparisons.

From Figures 9.3 and 9.4, it can be observed that there is a distribution of power along X-axis after the watermarks are embedded. So a comparatively distributed power spectrum is obtained after watermarking is done (Figure 9.4). This can be observed from Figures 9.5 and 9.6 as there is some additional power introduced to the host image indicated by the additional curves in Figure 9.6 due to the insertion of the watermarks.

From Figure 9.6, it is also observed that a significant number of frequencies are introduced which are the source of the distributed energy spectrum. Those frequencies indicate that a large amount of information is inserted into the host image. Despite this, the host image is visually unaltered which is evident in Figure 9.2.

Figure 9.1 The host image

Figure 9.2   The watermarked image

Table 9.1   Value of PSNR of the watermarked signal

Number of watermarks	PSNR (dB)
Four watermarks	63.7525

Table 9.2   Value of PSNR of watermark signals before applying attacks to the watermarked signal

Watermarks	PSNR (dB)
1st Watermark signal (audio)	175.6817
2nd Watermark signal (image)	43.0862
3rd Watermark signal (audio)	186.4285
4th Watermark signal (audio)	201.3306

Table 9.3   Value of NCC of host and watermark signals

Signals	NCC
Host signal	0.9902
1st Watermark signal (audio)	0.9828
2nd Watermark signal (image)	0.9236
3rd Watermark signal (audio)	0.9125
4th Watermark signal (audio)	0.9713

Table 9.4   Recovery of the watermark image against several attacks and filtering

Attacks	Recovered watermark image	NCC	Attacks	Recovered watermark image	NCC
No attack		0.9236	Sharpening effect		0.9082
Rotation anti-clockwise (180°)		0.9220	Gaussian low-pass filter (3 × 3)		0.9235
Rotation clockwise (180°)		0.9220	Median filter (3 × 3)		0.8645
Poisson noise		0.9126	Mean filter (3 × 3)		0.9044
Gaussian noise (0.15)		0.8733	Prewitt filter		0.7651

(Continues)

Table 9.4   (Continued)

Attacks	Recovered watermark image	NCC	Attacks	Recovered watermark image	NCC
Speckle noise (0.01)		0.9056	Sobel filter		0.7959
Salt and Pepper noise (0.01)		0.9051	Motion blurring (20,40)		0.9205
Histogram equalization		0.9170	Additive White Gaussian Noise (SNR: 0)		0.7275

To indicate the efficiency of a proposed watermarking technique, the watermark signals must be successfully extracted. Tables 9.2 and 9.3 represent the values of PSNR and NCC of the watermark signals after they are being extracted.

Another way used in this chapter to indicate the efficiency of the proposed technique is to measure the tolerance of the watermark signals against several attacks and filtering imposed on the watermarked image. In doing so, it can be easy to indicate the robustness of the proposed technique. Tables 9.4 and 9.5 indicate the quality of the extracted watermark signals against some conventional attacks and filtering.

Another aspect of deciding the efficiency of the proposed technique is considered here and that is the satisfaction of the end-users. Sometimes, the value of PSNR cannot solely indicate the quality of the watermarked image. Therefore, the HVS (Human Visual System) is needed to indicate the absence of perceptual degradation of a watermarked image. So, testing a developed watermarking technique on different images and then the visual indication of the absence of

Table 9.5 *PSNR of the extracted watermark audio signals against several operations*

Attacks	PSNR (dB)		
	1st Watermark signal (audio)	3rd Watermark signal (audio)	4th Watermark signal (audio)
Rotation anti-clockwise (180°)	176.7494	186.9687	200.6308
Rotation clockwise (180°)	176.7494	186.9687	200.6308
Poisson noise	176.0035	177.8405	176.2450
Gaussian noise (0.15)	174.2537	166.9555	161.1850
Speckle noise (0.01)	175.6205	174.7650	171.4442
Salt and Pepper noise (0.01)	175.0066	173.6220	169.9746
Histogram equalization	172.6572	183.4717	192.6917

Attacks	PSNR (dB)		
	1st Watermark signal (audio)	3rd Watermark signal (audio)	4th Watermark signal (audio)
Sharpening effect	131.1278	143.4996	153.0136
Gaussian low-pass filter (3 × 3)	187.8693	184.1055	187.1285
Median filter (3 × 3)	166.6419	174.9370	175.6801
Prewitt filter	166.1353	178.2795	158.0815
Sobel filter	168.4252	176.0555	156.4113
Motion blurring (20,40)	166.4700	174.6161	172.1711
Additive white Gaussian noise (SNR: 0)	139.9334	127.0273	119.5237

Figure 9.3   The power spectral density of the host image

Figure 9.4   The power spectral density of the watermarked image

perceptual degradation is very helpful in deciding whether a developed water-marking technique can maintain the imperceptibility criterion of digital water-marking. That is why the watermarking technique is tested on ten different standard test images. The results obtained for different standard test images are given in Table 9.6.

From the results enlisted in Table 9.6, it should be noted that, for all of the test images, there is no perceptual degradation observed after applying the proposed watermarking technique on those images which can dissatisfy the end user.

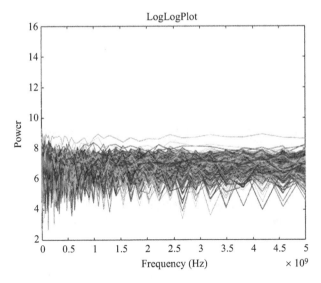

Figure 9.5   The power spectrum of the host image

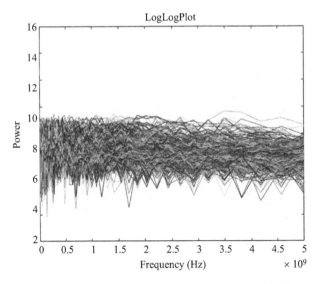

Figure 9.6   The power spectrum of the watermarked image

Therefore, the proposed technique can perform well in the case of other test images too.

Apart from the conventional attacks, the efficiency of the proposed technique is tested against two real-life scenarios. At first, the proposed technique is applied to six different test images. The watermarked images are sent via email to the end user. The end user will download those images from the email. Then the watermark

Table 9.6   Results obtained after the application of the proposed watermarking algorithm on different standard test images

Host image	Watermarked image	PSNR (dB)
		63.8303
		64.5641
		64.0017
		64.5517

(Continues)

Table 9.6   (*Continued*)

Host image	Watermarked image	PSNR (dB)
		64.1771
		64.5293
		63.7655
		63.9619

(Continues)

Table 9.6   (Continued)

Host image	Watermarked image	PSNR (dB)
		64.4591
		63.9450

signals will be extracted. This test is done to know whether after going from one device to another, the watermark signals can then exist. Tables 9.7 and 9.8 represent the quality of the extracted watermarks.

From the results obtained from Table 9.7, it should be noted that there is no rigorous quality degradation of the watermark image after being extracted from the watermarked image which is sent via email. Besides, if a comparison is done between the watermark images extracted from the watermarked images before being sent via email and the watermark images extracted from the watermarked images which are downloaded from the email sent, there is an observable sharpness in many of the watermark images which are extracted from the downloaded version of the watermarked images. That sharpness can easily improve the quality of the watermark images. In the case of watermark audio signals, there is a slight degradation in the quality which can be observed from the data listed in Tables 9.2 and 9.8. But, that degradation can minimally disturb the end user.

The next real-life scenario is to upload watermarked images to social media. The end user will download the watermarked images and then the watermark signals will be extracted. This experiment is also done on six standard test images. The results obtained are given in the Tables 9.9 and 9.10.

Table 9.7   Quality of the extracted watermark image

Watermarked image	Extracted watermark image	
	Before sending the water-marked image through an email	**After downloading the watermarked image from the email**

(Continues)

Table 9.7   (Continued)

Watermarked image	Extracted watermark image	
	Before sending the water-marked image through an email	After downloading the watermarked image from the email

Table 9.8   Quality of the extracted watermark audio signals

PSNR (dB)		
1st Watermark audio	2nd Watermark Audio	3rd Watermark Audio
182.1653	182.8180	186.4403
186.5570	186.2502	190.1565
182.6825	185.6539	190.5207
181.9860	185.7686	191.5413
179.6580	184.6599	190.0259
184.9062	185.0765	189.4439

In the second real-life scenario also, there is no disturbing perceptual change in the extracted watermark images which is evident from the data listed in Table 9.9. In fact, in some of the cases, the quality of the extracted watermark images is enhanced which is a good sign. In the case of audio watermarks, a slight quality degradation is noticed.

Table 9.9   Quality of the extracted watermark image

Watermarked image	Extracted watermark image	
	Before uploading the watermarked image to the social media	After downloading the watermarked image from the social media

(Continues)

Table 9.9   (Continued)

Watermarked image	Extracted watermark image	
	Before uploading the watermarked image to the social media	After downloading the watermarked image from the social media

Table 9.10   Quality of the extracted watermark audio signals

PSNR (dB)		
1st Watermark audio	2nd Watermark audio	3rd Watermark audio
184.5102	185.0175	188.8538
182.8120	185.9005	189.8471
182.3828	183.1920	186.4464
182.2840	181.3868	187.4200
183.4861	181.8587	186.5504
192.5725	185.6168	189.3253

9.4   Analysis of the developed technique

As mentioned earlier, four signals are used as watermarks in the proposed technique. Among them, one signal has the same size as the host signal. The ratios of the sizes of the watermark signals to that of the host signal are 0.125, 0.25, 0.5, and 1 for watermark signals one, two, three, and four, respectively. So, a large amount of data can be stored in one signal which is one of the findings of the proposed technique.

The energy of both the host and the watermark signals is divided. Every part of the energy of the host signal is utilized to embed every part of the energy of the watermark signals. The watermark signals are embedded in parts into different regions of the host signal rather than being embedded as a whole into a particular region. So, the decentralization of the watermarks over the entire region of the host signal is another finding of the developed technique.

The proposed technique works very efficiently against the real-life scenarios which is evident from the data listed in Tables 9.7 to 9.10. Apart from that, the proposed technique can be applied very efficiently to a wide range of standard test images which is evident from the results given in Tables 9.6 to 9.10.

9.5 Comparative analysis

This section will present a comparative analysis between the technique proposed in this chapter and two state-of-the-art techniques. Besides, there will be a comparison between the technique proposed in this chapter and the techniques developed in [28–30,32].

9.5.1 Comparison with [17]

In [17], the authors proposed a block-based image watermarking technique which is developed by using SVD and HVSs in the DWT domain. The watermark used is a binary logo. The authors used the lowest entropy values and edge entropy values as the best regions to insert the watermark. One level DWT is used. After that, SVD is applied to the low-low sub-band. The comparison between the technique proposed in this chapter and the technique proposed by Makbol *et al.* [17] considering some factors is given in Table 9.11.

From the data listed in Table 9.11, it should be noted that the authors of [17] utilized a portion of the host image for the insertion of the watermark so that the imperceptibility of the watermark can be maintained at a significant level. Besides, the authors of [17] used a comparatively smaller watermark. However, in the technique proposed in this chapter, the entire region of both the host and the watermark signals are utilized. Besides, the technique proposed in this chapter can embed comparatively larger watermarks maintaining the imperceptibility to a significant level which is evident from Figure 9.4 and the data listed in Table 9.6. In [17], the perceptual degradation of the extracted watermark against different attacks is severe for some of the attacks for which the watermark is not recognizable. In the technique proposed in this chapter, there is degradation in the extracted watermark against some of the attacks. But, the watermarks are recognizable for every attack. Further, the technique proposed in this chapter used four watermarks and the watermarks are inserted in parts into the host signal. So, to remove or destroy all the watermarks, every part of the energy of every watermark should be destroyed. This can inherently cause difficulty in removing all the watermarks at a time. On the other hand, the authors of [17] used only one watermark. The watermark is centralized in the case of [17] while the watermarks are distributed in the

Table 9.11   Comparison with the technique proposed in [17]

Factors	The technique proposed in this chapter	The technique proposed in [17]
Techniques used	DWT and SVD	Block-based DWT and SVD
Size of the host image	$2,048 \times 2,048$	512×512
Size of the watermark	$256 \times 256, 512 \times 512, 1,024 \times 1,024$ and $2,048 \times 2,048$	32×32
Number of levels of DWT used to decompose the host image	20	1
Number of levels of DWT used to decompose the host image	5	0
Characteristics of watermark	Image and audio	Binary logo
Number of watermarks used	4	1
Number of test images on which the proposed technique is tested	41	4
Location of the host image for the insertion of the watermark	The entire region of the host image	The lowest entropy values and edge entropy values
PSNR	Always greater than 63 dB	Lowest value: 41.39 dB; Highest value: 62.2 dB

technique proposed in this chapter. Apart from that, the proposed technique in this chapter is tested for 41 test images with the maintenance of imperceptibility to a significant level.

Considering the above comparison, it should be noted that, the technique proposed in this chapter can certainly perform better in the case of securing a signal than the one developed in [17].

9.5.2   Comparison with [18]

In [18], the authors developed an image watermarking technique using fractal encoding and DCT. The fractal encoding method is used to encode the watermark image with private scales. Then, digital watermarking is applied to the original image using DCT. The watermark image can be extracted from the original image using the private encoding scales. The fractal encoding method is used to make the watermark image immune to attacks. The comparison between the technique proposed in this chapter and the technique proposed in [18] considering some factors is given in Table 9.12.

The authors of [18] tested the robustness of their proposed technique against some attacks. From the experimental data, the perceptual degradation of the extracted image watermark in the case of the technique proposed in this chapter is less than that of the technique proposed in [18]. In the case of audio watermarks for the technique proposed in this chapter, the audible degradation is also less severe which is evident from the data listed in Table 9.5. Besides, the authors of [18] used only one watermark.

Table 9.12   Comparison with the technique proposed in [18]

Factors	The technique proposed in this chapter	The technique proposed in [18]
Techniques used	DWT and SVD	Fractal encoding and DCT
Size of the host image	2048×2048	$1,024 \times 1,024$
Size of the watermark	$256 \times 256, 512 \times 512, 1,024 \times 1,024$ and $2,048 \times 2,048$	256×256
Characteristics of watermark	Image and audio	A binary logo
Number of watermarks used	4	1
Number of test images on which the proposed technique is tested	41	1
PSNR	Always greater than 63 dB	>40 dB

Considering the above comparison, it should be noted that, the efficiency of the technique proposed in this chapter is higher than that of the technique proposed in [18].

9.5.3   Comparison with [28–30,32]

In [32], a technique of image watermarking is developed by using DWT, DCT, and SVD. In [28,29], two techniques of audio watermarking are developed by using DWT, and SVD. In [28,29,32], three images are used as watermarks. The difference between those techniques is: in [32,28], the watermark signals are concentrated into some particular regions of the host signal. However, in [29], the watermark signals are distributed over the entire energy distribution of the host signal. From the results obtained from the techniques proposed in [28,29,32], it may be noted that multiple watermarks can provide security to both image and audio signals. The image watermarking technique proposed in [30] is an updated version of the techniques proposed in [28,29,32]. In this technique, the entire portion of the host and the watermark signals are utilized. Besides, three images and one audio are used as watermark signals i.e., hybrid signals are used as watermarks. The same embedding technique that is used in [30] is utilized in the technique proposed in this chapter. But, there is a difference. In the technique proposed in this chapter, one image and three audio signals are used as watermarks. A close analysis of the results obtained reveals that, in the technique proposed in this chapter, the perceptual degradation of the image watermark occurred after imposing some attacks on the host signal is comparatively less than that of the image watermark 2 used in [30] despite being embedded in the same location as well as being same in size as the image watermark used in the technique proposed in this chapter. The results obtained in the case of image watermark 2 used in [30] after applying attacks on the host image are given in Table 9.13 for ease of analysis.

Table 9.13   Recovery of the watermark image 2 used in [30] against several attacks and filtering

Attacks	Recovered watermark image	NCC	Attacks	Recovered watermark image	NCC
No attack		0.9402	Sharpening effect		0.8952
Rotation anti-clockwise (180°)		0.9338	Gaussian low-pass filter (3 × 3)		0.9407
Rotation clockwise (180°)		0.9338	Median filter (3 × 3)		0.7937
Poisson noise		0.7866	Prewitt filter		0.7148
Gaussian noise (0.15)		0.6532	Sobel Filter		0.7695
Speckle noise (0.01)		0.7365	Motion blurring (20,40)		0.9175

(Continues)

Table 9.13 *(Continued)*

Attacks	Recovered watermark image	NCC	Attacks	Recovered watermark image	NCC
Salt and Pepper noise (0.01)		0.7335	Additive white Gaussian noise (SNR: 0)		0.5557
Histogram equalization		0.8904			

From the results listed in Tables 9.4 and 9.13, it should be noted that the audio signal has less effect on the image watermark if the number of an audio signal used as a watermark is greater than that of the image watermark. In [30], three watermark images are used which have significant effects on each other. The results obtained are the proofs of those effects. So, to get better robustness in the case of an image watermark, audio signals should also be used as a watermark as well as the number of audio watermarks should be greater than that of the image watermark to reduce the effects of mutual interference in the case of using multiple numbers of images as watermarks. In this way, the purpose of using hybrid watermark signals will be served along with the improvement of the robustness against several attacks that can be obtained. Those are the intentions of developing the proposed technique.

9.6 Conclusion

The proposed technique intends to use conventional techniques DWT and SVD differently to increase the security of a signal. The energy divisions obtained by multi-level DWT ensure a better security level as it will be not so easy to destroy all the parts of the energy of the watermark signals as they are allocated into different portions of the energy of the host signal. The use of multiple kinds, as well as multiple numbers of watermarks, increases the security level as at least one watermark can be recovered in case of very rigorous attacks imposed on a signal. Storage of a large piece of information inside a single signal can open a new window for developing new techniques of steganography. In conclusion, the proposed technique can be used to ensure the security of a signal by ensuring its true owner.

References

[1]   Das, C., Panigrahi, S., Sharma, V. and Mahapatra, K. (2014). A novel blind robust image watermarking in DCT domain using inter-block coefficient correlation. *AEU - International Journal of Electronics and Communications.* vol. 68. pp. 244–253. 10.1016/j.aeue.2013.08.018.

[2]   Thind, D. and Jindal, S. (2015). A semi blind DWT-SVD video watermarking. *Procedia Computer Science.* vol. 46. pp. 1661–1667. 10.1016/j.procs.2015.02.104.

[3]   Naved, A. and Rajesh, Y. (2013). Dual band watermarking using 2-D DWT and 2-level SVD for robust watermarking in video, *International Journal of Science and Research (IJSR)*, vol. 2 no. 9, pp. 249–252, https://www.ijsr.net/search_index_results_paperid.php?id=02013298

[4]   Berghel, H. (1997). Watermarking cyberspace, *Communications of the ACM*, vol. 40, no. 11, pp. 19–24.

[5]   Liu, Z. and Inoue, A. (2003). Audio watermarking techniques using sinusoidal patterns based on pseudorandom sequences, *IEEE Transactions on Circuits and Systems for Video Technology*, vol. 13, no. 8, pp. 801–812.

[6]   Jalil, Z. and Mirza, A. M. (2010). An invisible text watermarking algorithm using imagewatermark, In: Sobh T., Elleithy K. (eds) *Innovations in Computing Sciences and Software Engineering.* Springer, Dordrecht. https://doi.org/10.1007/978-90-481-9112-3_25

[7]   Santhi, V. and Arulmozhivarman, P. (2013). Hadamard transform based adaptive visible/invisible watermarking scheme for digital images, *Journal of Information Security and Applications.* vol. 18, *Elsevier*, (http://dx.doi.org/10.1016/j.istr.2013.01.001), pp. 167–179.

[8]   Hsu, L.-Y. and Hu, H.-T. (2015). Blind image watermarking via exploitation of inter-block prediction and visibility threshold in DCT domain, *Journal of Visual Communication and Image Representation.* vol. 32. 10.1016/j.jvcir.2015.07.017.

[9]   Maheshwari, J. P., Kumar, M., Mathur, G., Yadav, R. P. and Kakerda, R. K. (2015). Robust digital image watermarking using DCT based pyramid transform via image compression, *2015 International Conference on Communications and Signal Processing (ICCSP)*, Melmaruvathur, 2015, pp. 1059–1063, doi:10.1109/ICCSP.2015.7322663.

[10]   Rajawat, M. and Tomar, D. S. (2015). A secure watermarking and tampering detection technique on RGB image using 2 level DWT, *2015 Fifth International Conference on Communication Systems and Network Technologies*, Gwalior, 2015, pp. 638–642, doi:10.1109/CSNT.2015.245.

[11]   Zheng, P., Feng, J., Li, Z. and Zhou, M-q. (2014). A novel SVD and LS-SVM combination algorithm for blind watermarking. *Neurocomputing.* vol. 142. pp. 520–528. 10.1016/j.neucom.2014.04.005.

[12]   Jia, S-l. (2014). A novel blind color images watermarking based on SVD. *Optik - International Journal for Light and Electron Optics.* vol. 125. pp. 2868–2874. 10.1016/j.ijleo.2014.01.002.

[13]   Makbol, N. and Khoo, B. E. (2014). A new robust and secure digital image watermarking scheme based on the integer wavelet transform and singular value decomposition. *Digital Signal Processing.* 10.1016/j.dsp.2014.06.012.

[14]   Mehto, A. and Mehra, N. (2016). Adaptive lossless medical image water-marking algorithm based on DCT and DWT. *Procedia Computer Science.* vol. 78. pp. 88–94. 10.1016/j.procs.2016.02.015.

[15]   Chowdhury, A., Zaman, H. and Khan, N. N. (2014). Color image water-marking technique by featuring joint DWT-DCT domain in YIQ color space, *International Journal of Research in Computer Engineering and Electronics.* vol. 3 no. 4(July–Aug'14), pp:1–6.

[16]   Mishra, A., Agarwal, C., Sharma, A. and Bedi, P. (2014). Optimized gray-scale image watermarking using DWT–SVD and firefly algorithm. *Expert Systems with Applications.* vol. 41. pp. 7858–7867. 10.1016/j. eswa.2014.06.011.

[17]   Makbol, N. M., Khoo, B. E. and Rassem, T. H. (2016). Block-based discrete wavelet transform-singular value decomposition image watermarking scheme using human visual system characteristics. *IET Image Processing,* vol. 10 no. 1, pp. 34–52. https://doi.org/10.1049/iet-ipr.2014.0965

[18]   Liu, S., Pan, Z., and Song, H. (2017). Digital image watermarking method based on DCT and fractal encoding. *IET Image Processing,* vol. 11 no. 10, pp. 815–821. https://doi.org/10.1049/iet-ipr.2016.0862

[19]   Dhar, J. P., Islam, M. S. and Ullah, M. A. (2019). A fuzzy logic based contrast and edge sensitive digital image watermarking technique. *SN Applied Science* vol. **1**, p. 716 https://doi.org/10.1007/s42452-019-0731-x

[20]   Islam, M. S., Ahsan Ullah, M. and Prakash Dhar, J. (2019) An imperceptible and robust digital image watermarking scheme based on DWT, entropy and neural network, *Karbala International Journal of Modern Science*: vol. 5: no. 1, Article 6. Available at: https://doi.org/10.33640/2405-609X.1068

[21]   Jain, P. and Ghanekar, U. (2018). Robust watermarking technique for tex-tured images. *Procedia Computer Science.* vol. 125. pp. 179–186. 10.1016/j. procs.2017.12.025.

[22]   Andalibi, M. and Chandler, M. D. (2015). Digital image watermarking via adaptive logo texturization *IEEE Transactions on Image Processing*, vol. 24, no. 12.

[23]   Pati, M. and Chitode, J. S. (2017). Performance evaluation of digital audio watermarking based on discrete wavelet transform for ownership protection, *International Journal on Electrical Engineering and Informatics*, vol. 9, no. 1, pp. 161–172.

[24]   Thakare, R., Kakde, S., and Mani, P. (2020). Dual watermarking for colour images' copyright and authentication using DWT technique. In: Sharma D., Balas V., Son L., Sharma R., Cengiz K. (eds) *Micro-Electronics and Telecommunication Engineering. Lecture Notes in Networks and Systems,* vol. 106. Springer, Singapore. https://doi.org/10.1007/978-981-15-2329-8_49

[25]   Zhou, X., Zhang, H. and Wang, C. (2018).A robust image watermarking technique based on DWT, APDCBT, and SVD. *SS Symmetry*, vol. 10, no.3. https://doi.org/10.3390/sym10030077

[26]   Pal, K., Ghosh, G. and Bhattacharya, M. (2012). Biomedical image watermarking in wavelet domain for data integrity using bit majority algorithm and multiple copies of hidden information. *American Journal of Biomedical Engineering*. vol. 2. pp. 29–37. 10.5923/j.ajbe.20120202.06.

[27]   Singh, R., Nigam, S., Singh, A. K. and Elhoseny, M. (2020). Integration of wavelet transforms for single and multiple image watermarking. In: *Intelligent Wavelet Based Techniques for Advanced Multimedia Applications*. Springer, Cham. https://doi.org/10.1007/978-3-030-31873-4_4

[28]   Amita, S. and Ahsan Ullah, M. (2020). Audio watermarking with multiple images as watermarks, *IETE Journal of Education*, DOI: 10.1080/09747338.2020.1807418

[29]   Singha, A. and Ullah, M. A. (2020). Development of an audio watermarking with decentralization of the watermarks, *Journal of King Saud University – Computer and Information Sciences*. https://doi.org/10.1016/j.jksuci.2020.09.007

[30]   Singha, A. and Ullah, M. A. (2020). An image watermarking technique using hybrid signals as watermarks. *Multimedia Systems*. https://doi.org/10.1007/s00530-020-00708-y

[31]   Abatte, Y. Digital Image Watermarking, M.Sc. Thesis, Addis Ababa University, Ethiopia, 2005.

[32]   Singha, A. and Ullah, M. A. (2019). Transform domain digital watermarking with multiple images as watermarks. *Preprints* 2019, 2019100188. DOI:10.20944/preprints201910.0188.v1.

Chapter 10

Privacy-preserving identification for monitoring images

Bowen Zhao[1] and Xiaoguo Li[2]

Camera sensors embedded in monitor units or mobile phones make it easy to capture various personal images in daily life. Machine learning especially deep learning provides an elegant way to identify images (e.g., person re-identification, face recognition, facial expression recognition). However, a personal image usually involves an amount of sensitive data, such as identity, face, and facial expression. Accordingly, image identification poses severe challenges of privacy leakage for persons' identities, face data, facial expressions, etc. Either GDPR (General Data Protection Regulation) or EDPS (European Data Protection Supervisor) stipulates that monitoring images involve private data and are easy to intrude on the fundamental right to privacy. In this chapter, we first sort out the privacy concerns in monitoring image identification and then formalize privacy-preserving identification for monitoring images. Next, we give a general framework to achieve privacy-preserving monitoring image identification and discuss privacy-preserving person re-identification based on the proposed framework. Finally, we conclude the research challenges and attempt to foresee some new research directions in privacy-preserving monitoring image identification.

10.1 Privacy concerns in monitoring image identification

Monitoring image identification has been extensively used in many fields, such as vehicle detection and tracking via license plate recognition [1], person tracking via person re-identification [2], personal identity verification or identity authentication via face recognition [3], and affect analysis via facial expression recognition [4]. On the one hand, although monitoring image identification is useful, it triggers severe privacy concerns. Any monitoring image is captured by using cameras essentially. Practically, it is scarcely possible for monitoring cameras to capture an identification object only. In other words, monitoring images are extremely likely to involve other information, such as drivers in a vehicle image, and other persons except for the object person in a person image. Thus, monitoring image

[1]Guangzhou Institute of Technology, Xidian University, China
[2]School of Computing and Information Systems, Singapore Management University, Singapore

identification might leak the person's privacy and intrude on the right to privacy. On the other hand, monitoring image identification usually relies on a machine learning model notably a deep learning model. Technically, monitoring image identification belongs to the operation of machine learning inference [5]. Machine learning inference takes a trained machine learning model and inference data as inputs and outputs the inference result (e.g., identification result). However, the machine learning model is also regarded as private data [6]. Hence, monitoring image identification suffers from the privacy concern of model leakage. Lastly, in some scenes, the inference result is also private. For example, in terms of affect analysis, no one wants to reveal his emotions to others.

Arguably, if one can fully control monitoring cameras to capture images and perform identification operations by himself, there is likely to be no privacy leakage. Unfortunately, no one can control all monitoring cameras. Also, the majority of people usually lack a trained machine learning model used for image identification. Meanwhile, monitoring image identification based on deep learning consumes a lot of computing and storage resources. Thus, in practice, monitoring cameras capture images, and then a cloud server holding a trained model performs identification operations. If the cloud server and the owner of the monitoring camera are trustworthy, it is likely to mitigate privacy concerns. However, the cloud server is not trusted. iCloud discloses celebrity photos. Amazon Web Services (AWS) compromises the personal data of millions of Dow Jones & Company. Furthermore, it is also difficult for people to trust the owner of the monitoring camera. In a word, there are at least two reasons resulting in privacy concerns in monitoring image identification. First, monitoring images involves private information. In addition, the entity processing the monitoring image is untrustworthy. Privacy concerns in monitoring image identification are roughly divided into three types.

- **Input privacy**: Input privacy means that the input for monitoring image identification is private data and should be protected. The input for monitoring image identification consists of monitoring images and the machine learning model used to identify images. Thus, the input privacy concern includes the leakage of monitoring images and the one of the machine learning model.
- **Computation privacy**: Computation privacy indicates that the computation involved in monitoring image identification should prevent computations from leaking private data. In general, monitoring image identification extracts feature vectors from images and then performs operations over feature vectors. Feature vectors still may leak images by some attacks [7], thus, the computation privacy concern means the leakage from the intermediate result of identification.
- **Output privacy**: Output privacy denotes that the identification result in monitoring image identification is regarded as private data and should be protected. The output might be a person's identity, emotions, etc. The output privacy concern is the leakage of identification results.

Privacy-preserving technology (e.g., encryption [8], secure outsourcing computation [9]) has been widely explored to tackle privacy concerns. Privacy-preserving technology is a mechanism or solution that protects private data and avoids privacy leakage. This chapter discusses privacy-preserving monitoring image identification by using privacy-preserving technology. For simplicity, we use $[\![\cdot]\!]$ to denote a privacy-preserving technology.

10.2 Formulation of privacy-preserving monitoring image identification

In terms of privacy-preserving monitoring image identification, there are at least three parties, i.e., a data owner, a monitoring camera, and a cloud server (or say computation server). Roughly speaking, if privacy concerns are not considered, the cloud server takes as input images of the data owner captured by the monitoring camera and a trained machine learning model to execute identification operations. To tackle privacy concerns, the cloud server performs the identification operations without knowing the image information, and the monitoring camera is not allowed to transmit the data owner's images to the cloud server directly. Formally, privacy-preserving monitoring image identification can be defined as follows.

Definition 10.1: *A monitoring image identification scheme denoted by $\mathscr{F}$ is regarded as privacy-preserving if $\mathscr{F}$ can identify a monitoring image effectively and does not compromise the monitoring image. Sometimes, it also requires no leakage of a machine learning mode used to identify the monitoring image and the identification result.*

Let *Img* denotes the monitoring image, $\mathscr{M}$ denotes the trained machine learning model, and *Rel* denotes the identification result, Definition 10.1 can be formalized as

$$Rel \leftarrow \mathscr{F}(Img, \mathscr{M}). \tag{10.1}$$

Note that it requires to protect *Img*, $\mathscr{M}$, or *Rel*. Obviously, privacy-preserving technology can achieve this requirement. Formally, $\mathscr{F}$ based on privacy-preserving technology can be formalized as

$$Rel \leftarrow \mathscr{F}([\![Img]\!], \mathscr{M}), \tag{10.2}$$

$$[\![Rel]\!] \leftarrow \mathscr{F}([\![Img]\!], \mathscr{M}), \tag{10.3}$$

$$[\![Rel]\!] \leftarrow \mathscr{F}([\![Img]\!], \mathscr{M}). \tag{10.4}$$

Equation (10.2) means the privacy-preserving monitoring image identification scheme that protects monitoring images. Equation (10.3) indicates the privacy-preserving monitoring image identification scheme that protects monitoring images and the identification result. Equation (10.4) denotes the privacy-preserving monitoring image identification scheme that protects monitoring images, the identification result, and the identification model, simultaneously. According to Section 10.1, we see that Equation (10.2) only guarantees partial input privacy.

Equation (10.3) guarantees output privacy and partial input privacy. While Equation (10.4) guarantees not only input privacy but also output privacy.

Computation privacy in the above setting is distinct. In Equation (10.2), given a privacy-preserving monitoring image $[\![Img]\!]$ and an identification model $\mathcal{M}$, computation privacy requires no leakage of the monitoring image during monitoring image identification. In Equation (10.3), given a privacy-preserving monitoring image $[\![Img]\!]$ and an identification model $[\![\mathcal{M}]\!]$, computation privacy requires no leakage of the monitoring image and the identification result during monitoring image identification. In Equation (10.3), given a privacy-preserving monitoring image $[\![Img]\!]$ and a privacy-preserving identification model $\mathcal{M}$, computation privacy requires no leakage of the monitoring image, the identification model, or the identification result during monitoring image identification.

As mentioned earlier, in view of the privacy-preserving object, privacy-preserving monitoring image identification can be defined as three levels.

- *Level 1*: A privacy-preserving monitoring image identification scheme provides privacy-preserving *Level 1*, it should protect monitoring images and prevent the leakage of monitoring images during identification.
- *Level 2*: A privacy-preserving monitoring image identification scheme provides privacy-preserving *Level 2*, it should protect monitoring images and the identification result, and prevent the leakage of monitoring images and the identification result during identification.
- *Level 3*: A privacy-preserving monitoring image identification scheme provides privacy-preserving *Level 3*, it should protect monitoring images, the identification model, and the identification result, and prevent the leakage of monitoring images, the identification model, and the identification result during identification.

10.3   Framework supporting privacy-preserving monitoring image identification

This section provides a general framework supporting privacy-preserving monitoring image identification. The framework discusses entities involved in a privacy-preserving monitoring image identification scheme. Also, a general workflow for the privacy-preserving monitoring image identification scheme is illustrated.

As shown in Figure 10.1, a privacy-preserving monitoring image identification generally consists of a batch of cameras capturing images and a cloud server performing monitoring image identification in a privacy-preserving manner. Note that this section takes the privacy-preserving *Level 3* as an example as it covers all privacy concerns in privacy-preserving monitoring image identification.

- **Camera**: For the task of monitoring image identification, the camera takes charge of capturing images by the embedding camera sensor. To avoid privacy leakage, the camera adopts privacy-preserving technology to protect monitoring images.

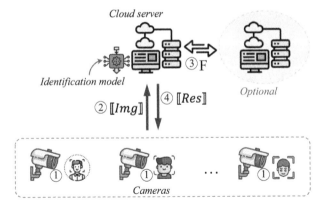

Figure 10.1   A general framework for privacy-preserving monitoring image identification

- **Cloud server**: The cloud server holding an identification model is responsible for performing monitoring image identification but learns nothing about monitoring images or the identification result. After that, the cloud server returns the identification result.

As monitoring image identification generally involves operations including addition, multiplication, comparison, etc. [3,4], $\mathscr{F}(\llbracket Img \rrbracket, \llbracket \mathscr{M} \rrbracket)$ requires privacy-preserving technology to support abundant operations over privacy-preserving data, such as addition, multiplication, and comparison [10]. Thus, homomorphic encryption (HE) is a potential privacy-preserving technology to achieve privacy-preserving monitoring image identification. On the one hand, HE as a cryptosystem provides confidence, which can protect privacy [9]. On the other hand, HE supports computations over encrypted data directly. Note that HE usually achieves addition and multiplication. In other words, HE fails to support all operations required by monitoring image identification. Secure multi-party computation (MPC) is another potential privacy-preserving technology to fulfill privacy-preserving monitoring image identification. MPC supports more diverse computations than HE over encrypted data, however, MPC usually suffers from a high communication burden, which limits its performance. In short, privacy-preserving monitoring image identification is a challenging topic and requires a careful design to balance performance and availability.

10.4   Privacy-preserving person re-identification

This section takes person re-identification, a typical monitoring image identification task, as an example and introduces a privacy-preserving person re-identification scheme [10] achieving privacy-preserving *Level 1*. Person re-identification is to check whether a person's image is the target person or not, so person re-identification takes as input including monitoring images, an identification model, and the gallery of a target person.

10.4.1   Formulation of privacy-preserving person re-identification

A privacy-preserving person re-identification scheme (PPRe-ID) achieving privacy-preserving *Level 1* can be formalized as follows

$$\{yes, no\} \leftarrow \mathscr{F}(\llbracket v \rrbracket, \llbracket \mathbf{G} \rrbracket), \tag{10.5}$$

where v means the feature vector of a monitoring image, $\mathbf{G}$ is the collection of feature vectors of a target person. $\mathscr{F}$ denotes a privacy-preserving person re-identification function that performs person re-identification operations over feature vectors in a privacy-preserving manner. If v is the feature expression of the target person, $\mathscr{F}$ outputs *yes*, otherwise, outputs *no*. Particularly, $\mathscr{F}$ can be formalized as k-reciprocal nearest neighbors operation (kRNN) based on existing work [11]. Formally, given a feature vector set $\mathbf{G} = \{\rho_1, \rho_2, \cdots, \rho_t\}$, kRNN is defined as

$$\mathscr{R}(v, \mathbf{G}, k) = \{\rho_i | \rho_i \in \mathscr{N}(v, k) \wedge v \in \mathscr{N}(\rho_i, k)\}. \tag{10.6}$$

$\mathscr{N}(v, k)$ denotes the k-nearest neighbor operation, i.e., $\mathscr{N}(v, k)$ searches for k feature vectors of $\mathbf{G}$, which are most similar to v, where the similarity metric can be measured by a distance between two feature vectors, such as Mahalanobis distance. The less the Mahalanobis distance, the more similar the two feature vectors. kRNN outputs k feature vectors of $\mathbf{G}$, where each feature vector $\rho_j \in \mathscr{R}(v, \mathbf{G}, k)$ ($k \in 1, 2, \cdots, k\}$) satisfies $\rho_i \in \mathscr{N}(v, k)$ and $v \in \mathscr{N}(\rho_i, k)$.

For a PPRe-ID solution, it is challenging to execute $\mathscr{R}(v, \mathbf{G}, k)$ without knowing $\mathbf{G}$ and v. Technically, given $\llbracket v \rrbracket$ and $\llbracket \mathbf{G} \rrbracket$, PPRe-ID requires measuring the similarity metric of feature vectors.

10.4.2   System model of privacy-preserving person re-identification

As shown in Figure. 10.2, PPRe-ID usually consists of two entities, i.e., a camera and a cloud server. To support computations required by person re-identification [11], we consider a twin-cloud server architecture to achieve operations on privacy-preserving data. The machine learning model $\mathscr{M}$ used to identify a target person is considered a public infrastructure, thus, the camera can access the identification model $\mathscr{M}$ and utilize it to extract feature vectors from monitoring images. Also, the cloud server holds the gallery of a target person.

- **Camera**: First, the camera captures the person's images, and then extracts feature vectors of the person's images by using $\mathscr{M}$. To protect the person's images, the camera adopts privacy-preserving technology $\llbracket \cdot \rrbracket$ to protect feature vectors and transmits privacy-preserving feature vectors $\llbracket v \rrbracket$ to the cloud server.

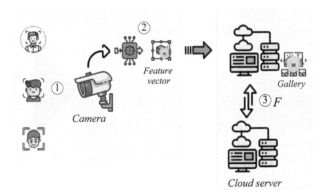

Figure 10.2   System model of privacy-preserving person re-identification

- **Cloud server**: To avoid the privacy leakage of the target person's images, the cloud server holds a privacy-preserving gallery (denoted by $[\![\mathbf{G}]\!]$) of feature vectors of the target person's images. After receiving $[\![v]\!]$, two cloud servers jointly perform k-RNN operation over $[\![v]\!]$ and $[\![\mathbf{G}]\!]$. Note that only one of the cloud servers holds $[\![\mathbf{G}]\!]$ and receives $[\![v]\!]$, while the other cloud server only provides computing servers.

In terms of the threat model, two cloud servers are considered *honest-but-curious* (or say *semi-honest*), i.e., they follow requirements to perform person re-identification operations over $[\![v]\!]$ and $[\![\mathbf{G}]\!]$, but attempt to learn the person's feature vectors or its images.

10.5   Detail of privacy-preserving person re-identification

Inspired by the work of Zhao *et al.* [10], privacy-preserving technology $[\![\,\cdot\,]\!]$ can be concretized into the Paillier cryptosystem [12], a famous public key cryptosystem. The similarity metric of feature vectors can be quantified as $v_1 \cdot v_2$, where the norm of two feature vectors v_1 and v_2 is required to be 1. Thus, given $[\![v]\!]$ and $[\![\mathbf{G}]\!]$, operations of $\mathscr{F}$ are concretized into addition, multiplication, and comparison over $[\![v]\!]$ and $[\![\mathbf{G}]\!]$ encrypted by the Paillier cryptosystem.

The Paillier cryptosystem supports additive homomorphism, i.e., it enables addition over encrypted data directly. However, the Paillier cryptosystem fails to achieve multiplication and comparison over encrypted data directly. Fortunately, the prior work of Zhao *et al.* [9] proposed a secure outsourcing computation toolkit based on a twin-cloud server architecture. Thus, multiplication and comparison over $[\![v]\!]$ and $[\![\mathbf{G}]\!]$ can be supported by the secure multiplication protocol SMUL and the secure comparison protocol SCMP proposed in secure outsourced computation toolkit on integers SOCI [9]. To facilitate the understanding, we briefly explain SMUL and SCMP first.

- **SMUL**. SMUL takes as input two ciphertexts encrypted by the Paillier crypto-system denoted by $[\![a]\!]$ and $[\![b]\!]$, and outputs $[\![ab]\!]$.
- **SCMP**. SMUL takes as input two ciphertexts encrypted by the Paillier crypto-system denoted by $[\![a]\!]$ and $[\![b]\!]$, and outputs $[\![u]\!]$. If $a \geq b$, $u = 0$, otherwise, $u = 1$.

The key idea of SMUL and SCMP is to split the private key of the Paillier crypto-system into two partial private keys. Each cloud server holds one of two partial private keys. Two cloud servers cooperate to decrypt intermediate results. To avoid privacy leakage, they adopt a mask to protect the intermediate result. After that, they take advantage of the homomorphism of the Paillier cryptosystem to generate the computation result. For example, in SMUL, to output $[\![ab]\!]$, SMUL generates intermediate results $a + r_1$ and $b + r_2$, where r_1 and r_2 are two masks and generated randomly.

According to SMUL and SCMP, we can construct SM and SC to compute $[\![v \cdot \rho_i]\!]$ and compare $[\![v \cdot \rho_i]\!]$ and $[\![v \cdot \rho_j]\!]$, where $\rho_i, \rho_j \in \mathbf{G}$.

- **SM**. SM takes as input $[\![v]\!]$ and $[\![\rho]\!]$, and output $[\![v \cdot \rho]\!]$, where v and ρ are n-dimension vector (in general, $n = 1,024$). Specifically, for each $v_i \in v$ and $g_i \in \rho$, SM calls SMUL $([\![v_i]\!], [\![g_i]\!])$ to obtain $[\![v_i g_i]\!]$, where $i \in 1, 2, \cdots, n\}$. After obtaining $\{[\![v_1 g_1]\!], [\![v_2 g_2]\!], \cdots, [\![v_n g_n]\!]\}$, SM computes and outputs $\Pi_{i=1}^{n}[\![v_i g_i]\!]$ as the result $[\![v \cdot \rho]\!]$, i.e., $[\![v \cdot \rho]\!] \leftarrow \Pi_{i=1}^{n}[\![v_i g_i]\!]$. It is easy to verify the correctness. As $v \cdot \rho = \sum_{i=1}^{n} v_i g_i$, and the Paillier cryptosystem supports additive homomorphism (i.e., $[\![a+b]\!] \leftarrow [\![a]\!] \cdot [\![b]\!]$), $\Pi_{i=1}^{n}[\![v_i g_i]\!]$ is the cipher-text of $v \cdot \rho$. Formally, $[\![v \cdot \rho]\!] \leftarrow SM([\![v]\!], [\![\rho]\!])$.
- **SC**. SC takes as input $[\![v \cdot \rho_i]\!]$ and $[\![v \cdot \rho_j]\!]$, and outputs 0 if $v \cdot \rho_i \geq v \cdot \rho_j$, otherwise, outputs 1. Given $[\![v \cdot \rho_i]\!]$ and $[\![v \cdot \rho_j]\!]$, SMUL $([\![v \cdot \rho_i]\!], [\![v \cdot \rho_j]\!])$ out-puts u, where $u = 0$ when $v \cdot \rho_i \geq v \cdot \rho_j$, otherwise $u = 1$. As SOCI supports the decryption operation through the cooperation of two cloud servers, given $[\![u]\!]$, it is easy to output u. Formally, $u \leftarrow SC([\![v \cdot \rho_i]\!], [\![v \cdot \rho]\!])$.

Now, based on SM and SC, given $[\![v]\!]$ and $[\![\mathbf{G}]\!]$, we can implement $\mathcal{R}([\![v]\!], [\![\mathbf{G}]\!], k)$ and output $\{[\![\rho_1]\!], [\![\rho_2]\!], \cdots, [\![\rho_m]\!]\}$, where m is usually less than k. There are two critical steps. The first step is to compute $\mathcal{N}([\![v]\!], k)$. The second step is to compute $\mathcal{N}([\![\rho_i]\!], k)$ and check whether $\rho_i \in \mathcal{N}(v, k) \wedge v \in \mathcal{N}(\rho_i, k)$ holds or not.

- **Step 1**: Given $[\![v]\!]$ and $[\![\mathbf{G}]\!] = \{[\![\rho_1]\!], [\![\rho_2]\!], \cdots, [\![\rho_t]\!]\}$, we compute $\{[\![v \cdot \rho_1]\!], [\![v \cdot \rho_2]\!], \cdots, [\![v \cdot \rho_t]\!]\}$ by calling SM first, and then compare them by calling SC. According to the comparison result, we can output k encrypted feature vectors as the result of $\mathcal{N}([\![v]\!], k)$. Without loss of generality, we assume $\mathcal{N}([\![v]\!], k) = \{[\![\rho_1]\!], [\![\rho_2]\!], \cdots, [\![\rho_k]\!]\}$.
- **Step 2**: Given $[\![v]\!]$ and $[\![\mathbf{G}]\!] = \{[\![\rho_1]\!], [\![\rho_2]\!], \cdots, [\![\rho_t]\!]\}$, we reconstruct $[\![\mathbf{G}']\!] \leftarrow \{[\![\mathbf{G}]\!], [\![v]\!]\}$ first. After that, for each $[\![\rho_i]\!] \in \mathcal{N}([\![v]\!], k)$, we compute $\{[\![\rho_i \cdot v]\!], [\![\rho_i \cdot \rho_1]\!], \cdots, [\![\rho_i \cdot \rho_{i-1}]\!], [\![\rho_j \cdot \rho_{i+1}]\!], \cdots, [\![\rho_i \cdot \rho_t]\!]\}$ by calling SM and compare them by calling SC. Then, we can obtain $\mathcal{N}([\![\rho]\!]_i, k)$, where $[\![\rho_i]\!] \in \mathcal{N}([\![v]\!], k)$. For each $[\![\rho_i]\!] \in \mathcal{N}([\![v]\!], k)$, if $[\![v]\!] \notin \mathcal{N}([\![\rho_i]\!], k)$, $[\![\rho_i]\!]$ is

deleted from $\{\llbracket \rho_1 \rrbracket, \llbracket \rho_2 \rrbracket, \cdots, \llbracket \rho_k \rrbracket\}$. Finally, the rest items in $\{\llbracket \rho_1 \rrbracket, \llbracket \rho_2 \rrbracket, \cdots, \llbracket \rho_k \rrbracket\}$ are the result of $\mathcal{R}(\llbracket v \rrbracket, \llbracket \mathbf{G} \rrbracket, k)$.

For a person re-identification scheme, to output *yes* and *out*, it still requires further computing. According to previous work [10,11], after obtaining $\mathcal{R}(\llbracket v \rrbracket, \llbracket \mathbf{G} \rrbracket, k)$, PPRe-ID measures the size of $\mathcal{R}(\llbracket v \rrbracket, \llbracket \mathbf{G} \rrbracket, k)$. If the size of $\mathcal{R}(\llbracket v \rrbracket, \llbracket \mathbf{G} \rrbracket, k)$ is larger than a threshold, PPRe-ID outputs *yes*, otherwise, outputs *no*.

A basic requirement for PPRe-ID is that privacy-preserving technology does not sacrifice the performance of person re-identification. Two public datasets Market-1501 and DukeMTMC-reID[*] are always used to evaluate the performance of person re-identification.

10.6   Research challenge and future research direction

This section tries to sort out research challenges suffered by privacy-preserving monitoring image identification and foresee future research directions in the field.

10.6.1   Research challenge

In terms of privacy, efficiency, and setting, there are three research challenges for privacy-preserving monitoring image identification at least.

- **Privacy-preserving Level 3**. When both input privacy and output privacy are needed to protect, privacy-preserving monitoring image identification is more complex and challenging. First, privacy-preserving *Level 3* requires extracting feature vectors without obtaining any monitoring images and an identification model. Also, output privacy stipulates for protection of intermediate results, which significantly increases the computational difficulty of privacy-preserving data.

- **Efficiency and function**. On the one hand, although privacy-preserving technologies provide a potential solution for privacy-preserving monitoring image identification, they always increase computation and communication burdens, which limits the efficiency of privacy-preserving monitoring image identification. On the other hand, privacy-preserving technologies generally support limited computations on privacy-preserving data, which restricts the type of computation of privacy-preserving monitoring image identification.

- **Heterogeneous device**. In practice, devices that capture monitoring images are heterogeneous and hold distinct power in computation and communication. Thus, not all privacy-preserving operations are supported by heterogeneous devices. In other words, it is difficult to design a privacy-preserving monitoring image identification solution to fit heterogeneous devices.

---

[*]https://paperswithcode.com/

10.6.2   Future research direction

Here, we consider three potential research directions to enrich privacy-preserving identification and make it practical.

- **Privacy-preserving affective computing**. In general, affective computing takes human images as input and takes advantage of image identification technology to recognize, process, and simulate human affects. In contrast to a person's monitoring images, a person's affects may be more sensitive. Thus, affective computing suffers from more privacy concerns. Inspired by privacy-preserving monitoring image identification, privacy-preserving affective computing is a potential research direction.
- **Privacy-preserving video identification**. Privacy-preserving monitoring image identification only focuses on privacy concerns on static images. However, video as a dynamic or stream data is highly likely to involve more private information. Thus, how to achieve privacy-privacy video identification is a future research direction to protect video privacy.
- **Practically privacy-preserving identification**. Although privacy-preserving technology is interesting and useful, its performance limits the practice. In the future, improving the performance of privacy-preserving technology and designing practically privacy-preserving identification solutions will be meaningful.

10.7   Conclusion

Privacy issues have been widely discussed, especially for monitoring image iden-tification. Privacy-preserving monitoring image identification is becoming a hot research topic. In this chapter, we first sort out privacy concerns in monitoring image identification. Then, we formalize privacy-preserving monitoring image identification and give a general framework supporting privacy-preserving mon-itoring image identification. After that, privacy-preserving person re-identification is elaborated to concretize privacy-preserving monitoring image identification. Finally, we discuss research challenges and future research directions in the privacy-preserving monitoring image identification field.

References

[1]   Hassaballah M, Kenk MA, Muhammad K, *et al.* Vehicle detection and tracking in adverse weather using a deep learning framework. *IEEE Transactions on Intelligent Transportation Systems.* 2021;22(7):4230–4242.

[2]   Ye M, Shen J, Lin G, *et al.* Deep learning for person re-identification: A survey and outlook. *IEEE Transactions on Pattern Analysis and Machine Intelligence.* 2022;44(6):2872–2893.

[3]   Wang M, Deng W. Deep face recognition: A survey. *Neurocomputing.* 2021;429:215–244.

[4]   Liu Y, Zhang X, Lin Y, *et al.* Facial expression recognition via deep action units graph network based on psychological mechanism. *IEEE Transactions on Cognitive and Developmental Systems*. 2020;12(2):311–322.

[5]   Zhang C, Yu M, Wang W, *et al.* MArk: Exploiting cloud services for cost-effective, SLO-aware machine learning inference serving. In: *USENIX Annual Technical Conference*; 2019. p. 1049–1062.

[6]   Cabrero-Holgueras J, Pastrana S. SoK: Privacy-preserving computation techniques for deep learning. *Proceedings on Privacy Enhancing Technologies*. 2021;2021(4):139–162.

[7]   Fredrikson M, Jha S, Ristenpart T. Model inversion attacks that exploit confidence information and basic countermeasures. In: *Proceedings of the 22nd ACM SIGSAC Conference on Computer and Communications Security*; 2015. p. 1322–1333.

[8]   Katz J, Lindell Y. *Introduction to Modern Cryptography*. Boca Raton, FL: CRC Press; 2020.

[9]   Zhao B, Yuan J, Liu X, *et al.* SOCI: A toolkit for secure outsourced computation on integers. *IEEE Transactions on Information Forensics and Security*. 2022;17:3637–3648.

[10] Zhao B, Li Y, Liu X, *et al.* FREED: An efficient privacy-preserving solution for person re-identification. In: *2022 IEEE Conference on Dependable and Secure Computing (DSC)*. Piscataway, NJ: IEEE; 2022. p. 1–8.

[11] Wang G, Yuan Y, Chen X, *et al.* Learning discriminative features with multiple granularities for person re-identification. In: *Proceedings of the 26th ACM International Conference on Multimedia*; 2018. p. 274–282.

[12] Paillier P. Public-key cryptosystems based on composite degree residuosity classes. In: *Advances in Cryptology–EUROCRYPT'99: International Conference on the Theory and Application of Cryptographic Techniques Prague, Czech Republic, May 2–6, 1999 Proceedings 18*. Berlin: Springer; 1999. p. 223–238.

Chapter 11

Analysis phases in multimedia data forensics for source identification, deleted data reconstruction, and perpetrator identification

Ilker Kara[1] and Emre Hasgul[2]

In the field of digital forensics, the analysis of multimedia data plays a crucial role in uncovering the truth behind criminal activities. This chapter delves into the intricate analysis phases employed in multimedia data forensics, with a primary focus on source identification, time stomping identification, and perpetrator identification. The chapter explores the methodologies and techniques utilized by digital forensics experts to extract valuable insights from multimedia data, enabling the identification of the origin of the data, and the identification of individuals responsible for cybercrimes if possible. In this chapter, the analysis of the multimedia metadata is the main focus. Therefore, the technical details on evidence acquisition are not given. However, the proper evidence acquisition is mentioned briefly. By comprehensively examining the analysis phases in multimedia data forensics, this chapter provides valuable insights into the methodologies employed to unravel the truth behind criminal activities and supports the advancement of forensic investigations in the digital age.

11.1 Evidence acquisition

The globally approved way to gather evidence acquisition in digital forensics is through the use of recognized and accepted methodologies and standards. One such widely recognized standard is the NIST (National Institute of Standards and Technology) Special Publication 800-101, "Guidelines on Mobile Device Forensics," which provides detailed guidance on the acquisition and preservation of digital evidence from mobile devices [1]. Additionally, the ISO/IEC 27037 standard, "Guidelines for Identification, Collection, Acquisition, and Preservation of Digital Evidence," offers comprehensive guidelines for evidence acquisition and preservation in digital forensics investigations [2]. These standards emphasize the

[1]Department of Medical Services and Techniques, Eldivan Medical Services Vocational School Çankırı, Karatekin University, Turkey
[2]Department of Computer Science, Hacettepe University, Turkey

importance of following proper procedures, maintaining the chain of custody, employing write-blocking mechanisms, and documenting the entire process to ensure the integrity and admissibility of the acquired evidence. Furthermore, widely recognized forensic tools, such as EnCase Forensic and Forensic Toolkit (FTK), incorporate these standards and provide functionality for acquiring digital evidence that is acceptable by the standards [3].

11.1.1   Write-blocking

Write-blocking is a critical technique used during evidence acquisition to prevent any modifications or alterations to the original storage media. Write-blocking can be achieved through hardware write-blockers, which physically block write commands, or software write-blocking tools that disable write access to the media.

11.1.2   Forensic imaging

Forensic imaging involves creating a forensic copy or image of the storage media being examined. The forensic image is a replica of the original media, including all sectors and data. Tools such as dd (disk duplicator) or specialized forensic software like EnCase or FTK Imager are commonly used to create forensic images.

11.1.3   Hashing

Hashing is the process of converting a dataset into a fixed-length string using a specific algorithm. This algorithm takes data of any size and transforms it into a string of a specific length. Hash functions typically produce the same output for the same input and even the slightest change in the input results in a significantly different hash value.

Hash values are commonly used to verify the integrity of digital evidence and detect alterations. Any change made to a file or dataset results in a completely different hash value. This method is employed to verify that data has not been altered, tampered with, or manipulated.

11.1.4   Metadata preservation

Metadata, such as file properties, timestamps, and system logs, can provide crucial information for forensic analysis. During evidence acquisition, it is important to preserve the metadata associated with the acquired files and storage media. This includes capturing metadata related to file creation, modification, and access times, as well as recording device information and other relevant metadata.

11.1.5   Documentation and chain of custody

Detailed documentation is essential during evidence acquisition. It involves recording information such as the date, time, location, individuals involved, and a description of the acquired evidence. Maintaining a proper chain of custody ensures the integrity and admissibility of the evidence in court. This involves documenting all handling, storage, and transfer of the evidence, along with the signatures of individuals involved.

11.2   Anti-forensic techniques

Anti-forensic techniques for multimedia refer to methods used to manipulate or obfuscate digital evidence in multimedia files, such as images, videos, and audio recordings, to hinder or deceive forensic analysis [4]. These techniques aim to make it more challenging for forensic investigators to extract and interpret the original data from the multimedia files. Here are some commonly used anti-forensic techniques for multimedia:

File Format Conversion: Converting a multimedia file from one format to another can alter the file's structure and metadata, making it more difficult for forensic tools to interpret and analyze the data. Attackers may convert files to less common or proprietary formats that are not well-supported by forensic software.

Data Hiding and Steganography: Steganography involves hiding data within a multimedia file without altering its perceptible characteristics. Attackers can embed sensitive information or additional files within the multimedia file using techniques like LSB (Least Significant Bit) steganography or manipulating the color channels. Forensic analysis tools may struggle to detect and extract the hidden information without prior knowledge or specialized steganalysis techniques.

Metadata Manipulation: Multimedia files often contain metadata, such as EXIF data in images or ID3 tags in audio files, which provide information about the file's origin, properties, and editing history. Attackers can manipulate or remove metadata to mislead investigators or remove traces of tampering. This includes altering time-stamps, camera details, geolocation information, or other metadata fields.

Encryption and Password Protection: Encrypting multimedia files or protecting them with passwords can make it difficult for forensic investigators to access and analyze the content. Encryption techniques can be applied to individual files or entire storage media, rendering the data unreadable without the appropriate decryption keys or passwords.

File Fragmentation and Deletion: Fragmenting multimedia files into smaller parts or deleting specific segments can make it harder for forensic tools to reconstruct the original file or recover deleted content. Attackers may overwrite file fragments with random data or employ specialized tools to securely delete specific portions of a file, making data recovery more challenging.

File Compression and Archive Formats: Compressing multimedia files or storing them within archive formats (e.g., ZIP, RAR) can make it more difficult for forensic tools to access and analyze the data. Attackers may use compression tools with strong encryption to protect the compressed files, adding an additional layer of complexity to forensic analysis.

11.3   Metadata analysis

Metadata plays a crucial role in forensic investigations, providing valuable information about the origin, history, and characteristics of digital files [5]. Metadata analysis is a powerful technique employed in digital forensics to uncover hidden information, detect tampering or manipulation, and establish the context of digital evidence. This chapter explores the significance of metadata analysis in forensic investigations, methodologies for metadata extraction, and techniques to identify anomalies or modifications in metadata.

11.4   Importance of metadata in forensic investigations

Metadata provides essential contextual information that aids forensic analysts in understanding the nature and authenticity of digital evidence. It includes various types of metadata, such as descriptive, technical, administrative, and structural metadata [6]. The analysis of metadata can reveal critical details, such as file creation and modification dates, device information, geolocation data, and software used, which can be instrumental in establishing the chain of custody and determining the integrity of digital evidence.

11.5   Analysis of metadata in forensic investigations

To conduct metadata analysis effectively, forensic investigators employ various extraction techniques to retrieve metadata from digital files. Some commonly used methods include:

Built-in File System Metadata: File systems store inherent metadata, such as file names, creation dates, modification dates, and access dates. Forensic tools leverage this built-in metadata to extract information about the files, providing valuable insights for investigations.

Embedded Metadata: Certain file formats, such as JPEG, MP3, and PDF, support embedded metadata. Forensic tools and techniques enable the extraction of this embedded metadata, including EXIF data in images, ID3 tags in audio files, and XMP metadata in documents.

File Header Analysis: Metadata can also be extracted by analyzing the file headers and footers. The structure and specific markers within these headers can provide valuable information about the file type, compression techniques, and potential alterations or manipulations.

11.6   Techniques to identify metadata tampering or modifications

Detecting tampering or modifications in metadata is a crucial aspect of forensic analysis [7]. Several techniques can be employed to identify potential anomalies:

Timestamp Analysis: Analyzing the timestamps within metadata, such as creation dates, modification dates, and DateTimeOriginal fields, can reveal inconsistencies or illogical sequences that may indicate tampering or manipulation.

Original Source Comparison: Comparing the metadata of the original, unmodified file with the file in question can help identify any discrepancies or inconsistencies, suggesting potential modifications.

Hexadecimal Analysis: By examining the hexadecimal representation of the file, investigators can search for specific markers indicating the presence or alteration of metadata. Any deviations or inconsistencies may signify tampering.

File Compression Analysis: Analyzing the compression characteristics of files, particularly in formats like JPEG, can provide insights into potential modifications. Inconsistencies in compression parameters may indicate tampering.

11.7   Tools and software for metadata analysis

Forensic investigators rely on specialized tools and software to extract, analyze, and interpret metadata effectively. These tools, such as ExifTool, Sleuth Kit, and Autopsy, provide functionalities to extract metadata from various file formats, visualize metadata relationships, and identify potential anomalies or modifications.

11.8   Time stomping

Time stomping is an anti-forensic technique used to manipulate the timestamps associated with files, to mislead investigators or hide illicit activities. This technical writing aims to provide detailed insights into identifying time stomping and understanding the methods used by attackers to alter file timestamps. By recognizing the signs of time stomping, digital forensic investigators can enhance their ability to detect and counter this technique during investigations.

Time stomping involves the deliberate modification of file timestamps, including creation, modification, and access times. Attackers employ various methods to tamper with timestamps, making it challenging for investigators to establish an accurate timeline of events. Understanding the techniques used by attackers is crucial for effective detection and analysis.

11.9   Time stomping techniques

Attackers employ several techniques to alter file timestamps and potentially cover their tracks. Some common time stomping techniques include:

Manual Timestamp Modification: Attackers directly modify the timestamps using file system utilities or programming interfaces, such as the WinAPI or POSIX API.

File Copy Timestamps: Attackers may copy the timestamps from a legitimate file and apply them to a different file, disguising the actual creation or modification time.

Timestamp Offset Modification: By altering the file system clock or manipulating system time settings, attackers can change the timestamps to arbitrary values.

File Attribute Modification: Attackers can modify file attributes, such as the Archive flag, to trigger an update in the timestamps associated with the file.

11.10   Time stomping identification

File timestamp formats: File timestamps are stored and represented in different formats depending on the file system and operating system. Understanding the specific timestamp formats is essential for accurate analysis.
   Common formats include:

(a)   FAT File Systems: FAT file systems store timestamps as 16-bit values representing the date and time in a particular format.
(b)   NTFS File Systems: NTFS uses a 64-bit file timestamp structure, which includes values for creation time, modification time, and access time, each with high-resolution precision.
(c)   HFS+ File Systems: HFS+ timestamps use a 32-bit format that represents the number of seconds since January 1, 1904.

11.10.1   Timestamp granularity

Different file systems and operating systems have varying levels of timestamp granularity. Some systems provide timestamps with high precision, such as in microseconds, while others offer timestamps with lower precision, such as in seconds. Understanding the level of granularity helps in identifying inconsistencies or discrepancies.

11.10.2   Metadata extraction

Metadata extraction tools play a crucial role in retrieving timestamp information from files. These tools can extract various metadata attributes, including timestamps, file attributes, file permissions, and file owner information. Forensic investigators rely on specialized tools to extract metadata accurately and efficiently.

11.10.3   Time zone considerations

When analyzing timestamps, it is essential to consider the time zone information associated with the file system or operating system. Time zone differences can affect the interpretation and comparison of timestamps, especially in cross-system or cross-border investigations.

11.10.4   File system journal analysis

File system journals or transaction logs maintain records of file system activities, including changes to timestamps. Analyzing these journals can help identify any modifications or inconsistencies in the timestamps. Advanced forensic tools can assist in extracting and analyzing journal entries to uncover potential time-stomping activities.

11.10.5   Hash analysis

Hashing algorithms, such as MD5, SHA-1, or SHA-256, can be used to calculate unique hash values for files. Comparing the hash values of files with their timestamps can help detect any changes made to the file's content or metadata, including timestamps. If the hash value remains the same but the timestamps have been modified, it suggests potential time stomping.

11.10.6 Operating system artifacts

Operating systems often leave behind artifacts that can provide valuable information for detecting time stomping. These artifacts may include log files, registry entries, prefetch files, or event logs. Analyzing these artifacts can reveal discrepancies between the recorded timestamps and the actual file system timestamps.

11.10.7 Anti-forensic countermeasures

Adversaries may employ anti-forensic techniques to evade detection of time stomping. These countermeasures can include the use of file system drivers or rootkits to manipulate timestamps at a lower level, making them harder to detect. Counteracting such techniques requires advanced forensic tools, kernel-level analysis, and in-depth knowledge of anti-forensic methods.

11.11 Deleted data construction

Deleted data reconstruction is a complex and technically demanding process in multimedia data forensics. It involves employing various techniques and algorithms to recover deleted files or fragments from storage media, thereby unearthing valuable evidence. In this section, we will delve into the technical details of the primary techniques used in deleted data reconstruction: file carving, slack space analysis, and unallocated space analysis.

11.11.1 File carving

File carving is a powerful technique employed in deleted data reconstruction, enabling investigators to extract files from storage media even when file system metadata is absent or corrupted. It relies on the identification of unique file signatures or patterns within the binary data of a storage device.

During the file carving process, forensic tools search for known file signatures, such as headers and footers, which define the beginning and end of specific file types. These signatures serve as markers to identify file boundaries. By scanning through the raw data, the forensic tool can extract file fragments based on these signatures and reconstruct deleted files.

Advanced file carving algorithms employ heuristics to handle fragmented files. They can analyze the interdependencies between file fragments, reconstructing the fragmented files by aligning and concatenating the identified fragments. This process involves identifying dependencies based on file system metadata or content analysis and intelligently reconstructing the original file.

File carving can be further enhanced through the use of file format-specific carving techniques. Different file formats have distinct structures, and understanding these structures can aid in more accurate and efficient file reconstruction. By incorporating knowledge about file formats into the carving process, investigators can improve the accuracy of recovered files and minimize false positives.

11.11.2   Slack space analysis

Slack space refers to the unused or unallocated space within a data cluster that remains between the end of a file and the end of the allocated space. When files are deleted, remnants of data may still exist within the slack space, providing an opportunity for recovery. To analyze slack space for deleted data reconstruction, forensic tools employ various techniques. One approach involves conducting a thorough examination of the slack space within the file system. By analyzing the file system's metadata, including file allocation tables, directory entries, and cluster bitmap information, investigators can identify the locations of deleted files and determine the extent of slack space associated with each file.

Another technique involves slack space carving, which focuses on identifying and extracting data fragments from the slack space. Similar to file carving, slack space carving searches for specific file signatures or patterns within the slack space to locate and extract deleted content. By considering the structure and character-istics of the file format, forensic tools can increase the accuracy of slack space carving.

11.11.3   Unallocated space analysis

When a file is deleted, the file system marks the corresponding disk space as unallocated, indicating that it is available for reuse. However, until the space is overwritten with new data, remnants of the deleted files may persist in this unallocated space.

To analyze unallocated space for deleted data reconstruction, forensic tools employ advanced techniques. They search for file system artifacts, such as file headers, footers, and metadata structures, within the unallocated space. By identi-fying these artifacts, investigators can determine the presence of deleted files and their associated data.

Unallocated space analysis often involves the extraction of file system meta-data and the subsequent reconstruction of deleted files based on this metadata. The forensic tools analyze the file system structures, such as the Master File Table (MFT) in NTFS or the inode table in Unix-based file systems, to recover information about deleted files. By leveraging this metadata, investigators can reconstruct the directory structure, file names, timestamps, and other crucial attri-butes associated with the deleted files.

It is worth noting that the success of deleted data reconstruction techniques depends on various factors, including the level of file fragmentation, the passage of time since deletion, and the condition of the storage media. File fragmentation can complicate the reconstruction process, as it requires identifying and assembling scattered fragments. Moreover, if a significant amount of time has elapsed since the deletion, the chances of successful recovery diminish, as the unallocated space might have been partially or entirely overwritten by new data.

11.12   Conclusion

Multimedia data forensics plays a crucial role in uncovering the truth behind criminal activities in the digital age. The analysis phases involved in this field, such as source identification, time stomping identification, and perpetrator identification, are essential for extracting valuable insights from multimedia data and supporting forensic investigations.

Proper evidence acquisition is a fundamental aspect of digital forensics, and adherence to recognized methodologies and standards ensures the integrity and admissibility of the acquired evidence. Guidelines such as NIST Special Publication 800-101 and ISO/IEC 27037 provide comprehensive guidance for evidence acquisition and preservation, emphasizing the importance of maintaining a chain of custody, employing write-blocking mechanisms, and documenting the entire process.

Anti-forensic techniques pose challenges to multimedia data forensics, as they aim to manipulate or obfuscate digital evidence. File format conversion, data hiding and steganography, metadata manipulation, encryption and password protection, file fragmentation and deletion, and file compression and archive formats are commonly used anti-forensic techniques that forensic investigators must overcome to extract and interpret the original data from multimedia files.

Metadata analysis is a powerful technique employed in digital forensics, as it provides crucial information about the origin, history, and characteristics of digital files. Metadata extraction techniques, such as built-in file system metadata, embedded metadata, and file header analysis, enable forensic investigators to retrieve valuable information for analysis. Techniques like timestamp analysis, original source comparison, hexadecimal analysis, and file compression analysis help identify anomalies or modifications in metadata, assisting in uncovering tampering or manipulation attempts.

Time stomping, as an anti-forensic technique, aims to manipulate file timestamps to mislead investigators or hide illicit activities. Understanding time stomping techniques, file timestamp formats, metadata extraction, time zone considerations, file system journal analysis, hash analysis, and operating system artifacts enables investigators to detect and counter this technique effectively.

Deleted data reconstruction is a technically demanding process that involves techniques like file carving, slack space analysis, and unallocated space analysis. File carving allows the extraction of files from storage media even when file system metadata is absent or corrupted. Slack space analysis focuses on the examination and extraction of data remnants within the unused space, while unallocated space analysis recovers deleted files from unallocated areas of the storage media.

Overall, the analysis phases in multimedia data forensics, along with proper evidence acquisition, countermeasures against anti-forensic techniques, metadata analysis, time stomping identification, and deleted data reconstruction, contribute to the advancement of forensic investigations in the digital age. By leveraging these methodologies and techniques, digital forensics experts can unravel the truth behind criminal activities, identify the source of multimedia data, and potentially identify individuals responsible for cybercrimes. This chapter provides valuable insights into the complexities of multimedia data forensics and supports the ongoing efforts to ensure justice and security in the digital realm.

References

[1] Casey, E. (2011). *Digital Evidence and Computer Crime: Forensic Science, Computers, and the Internet* (3rd ed.). New York: Academic Press.

[2] Carrier, B., and Spafford, E. H. (eds.). (2003). *Handbook of Digital Forensics and Investigation*. New York: Academic Press.

[3] Quick, D., Choo, K. K. R., and Chisnall, D. (2017). *Handbook of Digital Forensics and Investigation*. New York: Wiley.

[4] Pollitt, M. M. (2015). *Principles of Digital Forensics*. Berlin: Springer.

[5] Kessler, G. C. (2014). *Digital Forensics Explained*. Boca Raton, FL: CRC Press.

[6] Casey, E., and Iyer, R. (2004). The investigation of computer crime. *IEEE Security and Privacy*, 2(4), 30–37.

[7] Kruse II, W. G., and Heiser, J. G. (2002). *Computer Forensics: Incident Response Essentials*. Reading, MA: Addison-Wesley Professional.

Chapter 12

Violence detection in videos: a review on hand-crafted and deep-learning techniques

Tahereh Zarrat Ehsan[1], Manoochehr Nahvi[1] and Seyed Mehdi Mohtavipour[2]

Violence is a pervasive and destructive force in society, causing physical and emotional harm to victims and their families. The impact of violence is not limited to individuals but also has broader social consequences, including increased healthcare costs, loss of productivity, and decreased quality of life. To address this problem, intelligent Closed-Circuit Television (CCTV) systems have been developed to prevent violent incidents in public and private spaces. These systems use advanced technologies such as computer vision and machine learning to analyze human behavior and detect violent actions.

In recent years, there has been a growing interest in developing automatic violence recognition systems that can accurately identify violent behavior in real time. These systems use a range of techniques, from traditional handcrafted methods to state-of-the-art deep learning algorithms, to analyze video footage and detect violent actions. This book chapter aims to provide a comprehensive review of violence recognition methods, including their strengths and limitations.

In addition to discussing the technical aspects of violence recognition systems, this chapter also examines publicly available violent datasets that have been used for experiments and evaluations. These datasets are critical for training and testing violence recognition algorithms, and their availability has enabled researchers to make significant progress in this field.

Finally, this chapter discusses the challenges that remain in developing effective violence recognition systems, including issues related to real-time inference, generalization ability, and the need for more diverse datasets. Future directions for research in this area are also presented, highlighting the potential for new technologies to enhance violence recognition capabilities.

Overall, this book chapter provides a comprehensive overview of violence recognition methods and highlights the importance of continued research in this field to address the ongoing problem of violence in society.

[1]Department of Electrical Engineering, University of Guilan, Iran
[2]Department of Electrical Engineering, Iran University of Science and Technology, Iran

12.1   Introduction

Violence recognition has been a prominent research area in computer vision in recent years. It involves analyzing human behavior in consecutive video frames to detect aggressive and violent actions. With the increasing rates of violent and assault incidents in society, many CCTV cameras are installed in public and private places to monitor human behaviors. However, manual monitoring by human operators is challenging due to the numerous installed cameras. Therefore, there is a growing demand for intelligent surveillance systems to automatically monitor scenes and detect violent behaviors. As shown in Figure 12.1, the number of papers on violence recognition has increased considerably over the years, with more researchers working on designing intelligent artificial intelligence systems to monitor and detect violence in real-world environments.

In recent years, computer vision projects such as object detection and image classification have achieved great results due to improvements in computational power and deep learning. Powerful graphics processing units (GPUs) and large-scale data are two important factors in achieving robust performance. For instance, ImageNet is an image classification dataset consisting of 1,000 object classes with millions of training data. Deep models that are trained on this huge dataset can achieve remarkable results due to the millions of training images. However, violence recognition faces challenges such as the absence of large-scale datasets for training, which affects model robustness considerably. As the existing dataset is not large enough, the model cannot learn the pattern comprehensively, and model generalizability is limited. Another challenge of violence detection systems is real-time on-the-edge applications. Automatic surveillance systems consist of low-power embedded systems that should process and analyze video frames in real time. Therefore, designing a violence detection system that considers real-world deployment constraints is crucial.

Violence detection methods are developed using HandCrafted (HC) and Deep Learning (DL) techniques. In HC techniques, the main steps for analyzing human

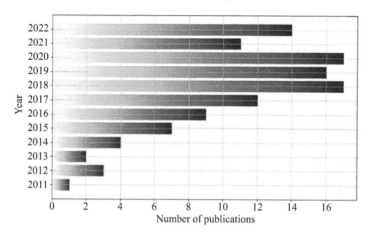

Figure 12.1   Number of violence recognition publications from 2011 to 2022

behaviors are behavior representation and classification. Behavior representation involves finding valuable features to describe human actions. Diverse features such as motion, acceleration, and appearance are used to represent human actions. In the behavior classification step, a two-class machine learning model is used to learn the features and categorize human actions as normal or violent. HC features are time-consuming because they require feature engineering to consider different properties of the image and video and consequently, find discriminative feature descriptors. Previous HC works have designed various descriptors by using image histograms, Bag of Words (BoW), and dictionary learning to capture important information from video sequences. On the other hand, Deep Neural Network (DNN) extracts and learns the features automatically. Samples of violent and normal datasets with corresponding labels are given to DNN, and high-level features are learned in the deep layers. Different techniques such as Convolutional Neural Networks (CNN), Long Short Term Memory (LSTM) are used in this category.

While there have been numerous surveys on human action recognition or activity recognition in the literature [1–3], there are only a few surveys on violence recognition. In [4,5], CNN-based violence recognition techniques are discussed, where variants of CNNs such as tiled convolution [6], dilated convolution [7], network in network convolution [8], and inception convolution [9] are explained. More recent reviews of violence recognition techniques are proposed in [10,11], which cover a wider range of violence detection techniques, including traditional machine learning as well as deep learning approaches. The main goal of this chapter is to present a more comprehensive literature review of violence recognition methods, discuss more papers, and present future directions. Current achievements and existing challenges are discussed in detail, including not only theoretical methods but also challenges in deployment to real-world applications. Our main contributions are summarized as follows:

1. Detailed analysis of violence recognition techniques and categorization based on behavior representation techniques and classification methods.
2. Comprehensive discussion of existing violence recognition datasets.
3. Complete evaluation and comparison of existing violence recognition techniques.
4. Presenting challenges and future directions.

The rest of the chapter is organized as follows: Section 12.2 covers traditional handcrafted methods for violence recognition. In Section 12.3, DNN models for violence recognition are reviewed. Section 12.4 explains datasets and their details. We cover challenges and future directions in Section 12.5, and finally, in Section 12.6, we provide our conclusion.

12.2   Traditional handcrafted methods

Figure 12.2 illustrates the flowchart of traditional violent recognition methods using HC techniques, which consists of three main parts: feature extraction, feature

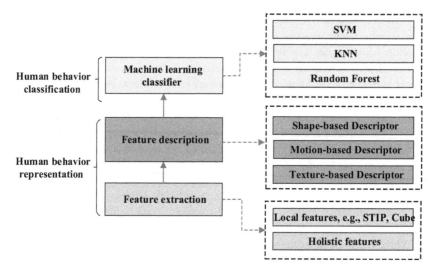

Figure 12.2   Categorization of traditional Handcrafted violence recognition methods

description, and classification. Feature extraction is a crucial step as it significantly affects the subsequent processing. This step involves selecting interest pixels or important regions of the frames from the video. The feature extractor should detect the critical part of human regions and remove irrelevant background details. Extracted features should provide discriminative information for the classification between normal and violent actions. For instance, if the detector identifies only people's heads, it will not be helpful in the classification as people's heads are similar for normal and violent actions and do not contain important discriminative information. A good detector should identify discriminative pixels such as hands or legs, whose shapes and motions are significantly different between violent and normal actions.

After identifying the interest regions, descriptors describe the extracted points using motion, texture, and appearance information. Finally, a machine learning model such as SVM, KNN, or random forest with two output classes is trained on the descriptor to categorize actions into normal and violent classes. In the following subsections, we explore the feature detection and description techniques proposed in the literature for violence detection applications.

12.2.1   Feature extraction

The techniques used for feature extraction in violence recognition applications can be classified into two categories: local and holistic. In the local technique, key points in the video frames are selected based on low-level image analysis such as image intensity comparison, image motion analysis, and gradients. The local extractor aims to detect local representative parts of each image that provide useful information for classifying human actions. The advantage of the local descriptor is

Table 12.1   Feature extraction for handcrafted violence recognition

Feature extraction	Description	References
3D Harris [12]	Key points with high-intensity variations in both spatial and temporal domain	[13]
3D TRoF [14]	Thresholding the determinants of spatiotemporal Hessian matrix	[15,16]
3D Cuboid trajectory	Consecutive bounding boxes of moving objects obtained by tracking	[17–20]
3D Movement filtering	Remove motionless pixels of each frame, and select pixels with high velocity	[21–25]
2D SIFT [26]	Difference of Gaussians function applied in scale space to a series of smoothed and resampled images	[27,28]
2D WLD [29]	Intensity difference between the current pixel and its neighbors	[30,31]
2D FAST [32]	Pixels that are sufficiently brighter or darker than the central pixel	[33,34]

its focus on people's regions and the ability to discard irrelevant information, which can improve model performance. However, a disadvantage of this method is its significant impact on the final classification. For example, if the detectors fail to find humans in the frame or the extraction is incomplete, subsequent processes such as description and classification will be incorrectly estimated. In real-world applications, where the environment is not controlled and can be affected by noise and illumination changes, designing a robust extractor is challenging. On the other hand, the holistic approach considers the entire frame for representation. Table 12.1 provides an overview of the local and global extractor techniques presented in the literature for violence recognition which are discussed in the next section.

12.2.1.1   Local extractor

Local feature extractors have been widely utilized in computer vision applications, including image and video classification, action recognition, and image and video analysis [35,36]. These extractors select a subset of pixels from the entire frame or video to estimate the characteristics of the whole frame or video. Local extractors can be categorized into 2D and 3D detectors. The 2D detector processes the individual frame to find informative pixels, while the 3D detector processes consecutive frames to find representative regions. The 2D detector considers only the spatial properties of the image, such as edges or contours, to detect interest points, while the 3D detector considers both the spatial and temporal dimensions to capture both temporal and spatial information. Since violence recognition involves analyzing human action over time, the 3D detector can find a better representative subset of pixels. However, the computational time required for 3D methods is higher than that of 2D methods. The goal of a local extractor is to find invariant features that resist changes, such as rotation, scale variations, and viewpoint changes. In this review, we will discuss popular 2D and 3D local detectors that have appeared in the violence detection literature.

The 3D Harris detector [12] is a technique that finds key points with high-intensity variations in both the spatial and temporal domains. It is robust to different variations of the video, such as translation, transformation, and illumination changes. As 3D Harris is applied directly to the video, it does not need any pre-processing, such as foreground detection, background subtraction, or moving object detection. Temporal Robust Features (TRoF) is another 3D detector that is an extended version of the 2D Speeded-Up Robust Features (SURF) [37] method to the temporal dimension. It finds local blobs by thresholding the determinants of spatio-temporal Hessian matrices centered at candidate pixels. This technique is fast and scale-invariant. Features from Accelerated Segment Test (FAST) [32] is a 2D technique that finds interest pixels in each frame that are sufficiently brighter or darker than the central pixel. The advantage of this method is its lower computational time compared to other techniques, such as 3D Harris and SURF. V-FAST [38] and 3D FAST [39] extend FAST to the temporal dimension to identify local interest regions. 2D Scale-invariant feature transform (SIFT) [26] detects points by maximizing and minimizing the difference of Gaussian images. SIFT is robust to local affine distortion, scale, rotation, illumination, and viewpoint changes. 3D SIFT [40] extended SIFT to the temporal dimension. Another spatiotemporal SIFT technique is proposed in [41] which is specialized for human action recognition problems. 2D Weber Local Detector (WLD) [29] finds key points with intensity differences between the current pixel and its neighbors. The advantage of this method is its robustness to noise. Mesh saliency [42] is another 3D detector based on Gaussian-weighted mean curvatures. The salient point method [43] decomposed 3D input in multiscale images and selects interest points by computing the difference between Gaussian of scaled images. SD corners [44] also decomposed 3D input in multiscale images but they analyzed each scale independently to find salient points in each scale. HKS [45] is another 3D technique that is robust to various transformations. This method computes Laplace–Beltrami operator on the 3D images to find interest points. Authors in [46], evaluated different 3D detectors via human-generated ground-truth data. A comparison of different local point detectors with ground truth images is shown in Figure 12.3. The first left column depicts human-generated ground truth, and the other algorithms from left to right are as follows: mesh saliency, salient points, 3D Harris, 3D-SIFT, SD-corners, and HKS. As can be seen, mesh saliency and SD corners detect many false positive points while 3D Harris and 3D SIFT are more efficient.

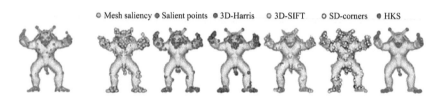

Figure 12.3   *Comparison of different interest points detected by the algorithms [46]*

Another way of identifying regions of interest is through the use of cuboid trajectories, which involve the accumulation of consecutive human bounding boxes. This method involves an object detector and tracker that obtains human bounding boxes and trajectories over multiple frames [17]. Another type of feature extractor is movement filtering, which identifies interest regions in the frame based on their motion intensities. This technique removes motionless pixels in each frame and selects pixels with high velocity. Various approaches have been proposed in the literature to remove motionless pixels, such as using optical flow analysis to identify high-motion regions [21,22], subtracting consecutive frames, or using background subtraction to extract moving pixels [23–25,47]. However, these techniques may not always be suitable as they may also detect non-human moving pixels such as cars, clouds, tree movements, and other irrelevant pixels. Table 12.1 provides a review of 2D and 3D local feature detectors that have appeared in violence recognition literature. As can be seen, most approaches use 3D detectors as they can identify the most significant parts of the video and provide more informative results for video analysis tasks. The best method can be selected based on application constraints such as memory resources and real-time performance.

12.2.1.2 Holistic extractor

Holistic techniques consider entire 2D frames or 3D consecutive frames for video analysis. The disadvantage of the Holistic method is that it is not human-centric and all irrelevant information such as background, non-human objects, and environments are selected in this stage.

12.2.2 Feature descriptor

After feature extraction, the selected points must be described by shape, motion, or texture information. In the following subsections, the feature descriptors that have appeared in violence recognition literature are explored.

12.2.2.1 Shape-based

Shape-based techniques use spatial and appearance information such as image gradients and shape form to obtain a representative feature. Image gradient was widely used in violence recognition papers to describe the human body, edge, and contour information [13]. It is calculated by computing the directional change in the intensity of the image. In the literature, mostly Histogram of Oriented gradient (HOG) descriptors were used to represent the videos [33]. Another shape-based descriptor is based on blob analysis [17] and [25] where blob shape, and distances between detected blobs and blob areas are used for feature representation. The Binary Robust Invariant Scalable Key-points (BRISK) descriptor performs intensity comparison to obtain a binary scale and rotation invariance descriptor [18].

12.2.2.2 Motion-based

As violence recognition involves rapid movements, many descriptors use motion information to discriminate between violence and normal action [33]. Optical flow-based descriptors use magnitude and orientation information to represent human

Table 12.2   Feature descriptor for handcrafted violence recognition

Descriptor	Techniques	References
Shape	Gradient	[13,22–24,33,54]
	Blob analysis	[17,25]
	Brisk	[18]
Motion	Optical flow-based	[19,21,23,33,50,51,54–67]
	Trajectory-based	[34,68]
	Distribution-based	[48,52]
Texture	GLCM	[53]
	LBP	[63]

actions. Approaches in this category include Differential Histogram of Optical Flow (DHOF) [48], Orientation Histogram of Optical Flow (OHOF) [21], Violent Flow (ViF) [49], Oriented Violent Flow (OViF) [50], and Statistical Characteristic of the Optical Flow (SCOF) [51]. The authors of [34] proposed a motion-based descriptor by tracking the pixels in consecutive frames using Kanade–Lucas–Tomasi (KLT) tracker. The spatial proximity of the trajectories was used to define a descriptor. Descriptors in [48,52] modeled chaotic motion distributions of human trajectory to learn human behavior. Motion-based feature descriptors are effective in capturing the dynamic nature of violent actions. However, they may suffer from issues such as motion blur and noise. Also, optical flow-based techniques can be computationally expensive, particularly when dealing with high-resolution video data. This can limit their usefulness in real-time applications.

12.2.2.3   Texture-based

Texture-based techniques use information about the spatial arrangement of color or intensities to describe an image. For instance, the Gray-Level Co-Occurrence Matrix (GLCM) descriptor [53] represents violent actions in crowded scenes. It models crowd dynamics by encoding changes in crowd texture using temporal summaries of gray-level intensities.

Overall, the selection of feature descriptors depends on the nature of the video data and the specific task at hand. Shape-based descriptors are effective in capturing human body structure, while motion-based descriptors are useful for capturing dynamic motion movements. Texture-based descriptors are suitable for crowded scenes where human actions may not be clearly visible. Table 12.2 summarizes the different methods of feature description.

12.3   Deep neural networks

This section provides a brief overview of the state-of-the-art DL-based frameworks for violence recognition. Common deep architectures for violence recognition include 2D CNNs, 3D CNNs, LSTMs, and combinations of these networks. With their ability to learn complex patterns, DLs are expected to continue playing a

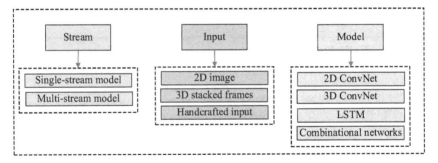

Figure 12.4   Deep learning-based violence recognition framework

significant role in violence recognition research. Figure 12.4 illustrates that DL-based frameworks differ in terms of the number of streams, input types, and architectures. Single and multi-stream frameworks are presented in the stream part, using different types of information such as motion, appearance, and human-centric (HC) features as network inputs. DL-based architectures can be categorized into end-to-end and hybrid models. End-to-end models take the entire 2D image or 3D stacked frames without specific preprocessing or feature extraction as input to the network, with feature extraction and classification computed inside the deep layers of the network. In contrast, hybrid approaches utilize a combination of traditional HC and DL-based methods.

12.3.1   End-to-end

In the following subsections, we review the end-to-end violence recognition DL frameworks. These networks take raw input data and learn to directly produce the desired output, without relying on any pre-processing or feature engineering steps.

12.3.1.1   2D and 3D CNNs

lCNNs are deep learning models that consist of an input layer, hidden layers, and an output layer. In each convolutional layer, filters are applied to the image to extract local features. CNNs have two variations based on the input dimension. In 2D CNNs, the input is a 2D image, while in 3D CNNs, the input is stacked with consecutive frames. 2D CNNs describe spatial information of the image, while 3D CNNs represent spatiotemporal relationships along the spatial and temporal domains. Recent studies have shown the effectiveness of CNNs in violence recognition. For instance, in [69,70], raw stacked frames were given to 3D CNN to classify video samples. They only differ in architecture layers and hyperparameters. In [71], a triple-staged end-to-end deep learning violence detection framework was proposed. A 2D-CNN is trained to detect a person, and a 3D-CNN is designed on human shape information to classify actions. Another framework containing person detection is presented in [72]. The person's optical flow was obtained with the FlowNet network, and actions were classified with a 2D-CNN. In Table 12.3, CNN-based violence recognition techniques are summarized.

Table 12.3   Deep-based violence recognition frameworks

	Method		Description	References
End-to-End	CNNs	3D CNNs	Accumulation of raw consecutive frames as input	[69–71,104,105,132–137]
		2D CNNs	Individual raw frame as input	[52,71,72,74,75,78]
	LSTMs		Accumulation of raw consecutive frames as input	[14,73–75]
Hybrid	HC	Trajectory	Consecutive bounding boxes of moving objects obtained by tracking	[76]
		Shape	Spatial-based feature to represent the appearance of people	[20, 78–84,106,118,138]
		Motion	Optical flow techniques	[20,47,52,77–80,83,85, 103,106,138–141]
		Skeleton	Key points of the human body, such as the top of the head, neck, shoulders, elbows, wrists, hips, knees, and ankles	[86,142]
	Pre-trained DNN	Transfer Learning	Pre-trained DNN fine-tuned on the violent dataset	[92,93,107,108,120,136, 143–145]
		Deep Feature extraction	Pre-trained models are used for feature extraction while machine learning or DNN techniques are used for classification	[15,20,27,30,31,83,93–95,98–100,102,103,109, 139,146–150]

12.3.1.2   LSTMs

LSTM model is specifically designed for time series data and is capable of capturing long-term temporal dependencies among frames. In a recent study by Halder and Chatterjee [73], a combination of CNN and bidirectional LSTM was used for violence recognition. The CNN was used to extract features from consecutive frames, and the extracted features were given to the bidirectional LSTM for action classification. Different frameworks have been proposed in [74] for classifying violent actions using stacked frames. Both 3D CNN and convolutional LSTM were used for feature learning and classification, with the results showing that convolutional LSTM outperformed 3D CNN due to its better modeling of temporal dependencies among actions. In another study by Ullah *et al.* [75], a hybrid model was proposed that combined person detection using a lightweight 2D CNN with Convolutional LSTM and Gated Recurrent Unit (GRU) for learning and detecting violent actions.

12.3.2   Hybrid frameworks

Hybrid frameworks for violence recognition can be broadly categorized into two groups. The first group utilizes an HC feature extractor that combines traditional low-level image processing techniques with DNNs. Specifically, the HC feature extractor detects interest regions using low-level image processing techniques, and the extracted features are then used to train a DNN for the final classification task. In contrast, the second group of hybrid frameworks employs pre-trained DNNs either as a feature extractor or as a baseline for transfer learning. In the following subsections, we provide a comprehensive review of the violence recognition methods in both groups.

12.3.2.1 Neural networks with handcrafted features

Hybrid frameworks for violence recognition have been developed using a variety of techniques. One approach involves extracting HC features based on trajectory, motion, and skeleton information, and training DL models on these features. In Table 12.3, we summarize the HC features that have been learned and classified with DNNs. For example, trajectory-based features were extracted in [76] to capture spatiotemporal information, and a CNN was trained on these features. Similarly, Baba *et al.* [77] utilized CNNs to compute motion information through optical flow as the input of the network. In [52], motion information was obtained for each video frame, and the difference of consecutive motion was given to the CNN. Another multi-stream CNN was designed in [78] to learn spatial, motion, and spatiotemporal information. In this model, a novel motion energy feature was proposed that adds human bounding boxes in consecutive frames to represent human actions. In [79], another multi-stream CNN was proposed that models spatial, temporal, and acceleration information. In [80], a multi-stream 2D and 3D-CNN including an attention-based spatial RGB stream, temporal stream, and local spatial stream was presented for violence recognition application. An attention mechanism was added to the spatial stream to highlight important parts of the frame and discard irrelevant regions such as the background or other objects in the scene. In [81], another multi-stream 3D-CNN was presented which used RGB frames and temporal information as input. In [47], motion saliency maps (MSMs) were presented to capture salient regions of feature maps derived from the motion boundaries. These features were combined with 2D CNN for final classification. Other approaches include using HOG descriptors in [82] to represent human behavior and designing an LSTM network for behavior modeling, as well as utilizing pre-trained person detectors in [83] to find people in each frame and training a CNN on 3D human tubes to classify actions. In [84], several HC features such as HOG and Local Binary Patterns (LBP) were utilized to describe human actions, and a simple feed-forward neural network was used for classification. Similarly, Freire-Obregón *et al.* [85] proposed a CNN-based model that tracks humans using You Only Look Once (YOLO) and a visual tracking Siamese network, where human bounding boxes in consecutive frames are given to the inflated 3D CNN for classification. Finally, Omarov *et al.* [86] obtained skeleton data by PoseNet model and designed a simple feed-forward neural network for classification.

12.3.2.2   Pre-trained DLs

As pre-trained architectures such as visual geometry group (VGG) [87], MobileNet [88], Inception [89], ResNet [90], and EfficientNet [91] have been trained on millions of images, they can capture informative spatial features. Therefore, they are widely used in violence detection papers to represent human shapes and actions. Violence detection using pre-trained DL is divided into two groups, transfer learning and deep feature extraction which are discussed in the following text below.

In transfer learning techniques, the weights of the first few layers of the pre-trained models remain frozen, and only a few final layers of the network are retrained on violence datasets. Transfer learning has the advantage of reducing overfitting and improving model performance. In [92], the authors compared the results of training CNN and LSTM models from scratch and with transfer learning. The results demonstrated that a combination of CNN and LSTM with transfer learning obtains better performance than training networks from scratch. This is because existing violence datasets are small, and the model overfits the training dataset, making it unable to learn the patterns in data comprehensively. A deep architecture pre-trained on Kinetics-400 action recognition dataset is used in the study by Huszár *et al.* [93] to fine-tune violence scenarios. Using transfer learning allows designing lightweight neural networks that can be trained with low-power GPU and it also reduces the training time compared to training the whole network from scratch.

Pre-trained networks can also be utilized as feature extractors in violence detection papers. For instance, the VGG network has been used in [15,94,95] to extract spatial features, which are then classified with LSTM architecture. Similarly, Xia *et al.* [96] and Accattoli *et al.* [97] employed VGG for feature extraction, but they designed an SVM to learn the extracted features. A similar VGG-based network was designed in the study by Hanson *et al.* [30], but instead of raw frames, the result of frame differencing was given to the VGG for feature extraction, and LSTM was trained for classification. Spatial information was extracted with a pre-trained ResNet model in [98], which was learned with Convolutional LSTM for classification. In Sumon *et al.* [31], different pre-trained networks including VGG and ResNet were used for feature extraction, and the features were learned with various networks such as CNN, LSTM, and fully con-nected networks. Experimental results showed that ResNet features, in combination with LSTM, provided better accuracy compared to the other models. Another LSTM-based network was proposed in [99], where deep features were extracted with a pre-trained ResNet and classified with Convolutional LSTM. A pre-trained model named X3D-M was used in [93] to extract dynamic features from the video. As this model was pre-trained on an action recognition dataset, it could provide more accurate results compared to other pre-trained models such as VGG or ResNet. In Pang *et al.* [100], a multi-modal method based on the fusion of audio and visual information was proposed. Audio and visual features were extracted from pre-trained VGGish [101] and Inflated 3D ConvNet (I3D) [16] models, respectively. Three modules including attention, fusion, and mutual learning were designed to detect violent actions. A multi-stream network was proposed in the work by Islam *et al.* [102], where background suppressed frames and the difference of consecutive frames was fed to a pre-trained MobileNet, analyzed in separate streams, and finally concatenated to detect violence. In the work by Tian *et al.* [27], several pre-trained models were used to extract features from video frames, and dilated convolution and attention mechanisms were utilized to capture long- and short-term temporal dependencies. Another hybrid model was proposed in the work by Ullah *et al.* [103], where important shots were extracted using CNN. Optical flow motion and visual information were obtained by using pre-trained residential CNN and DarkNet models, respectively. These features were learned with an LSTM model. The advantage of using pre-trained models is reducing training time compared to training from scratch. However, the generalization ability of these models depends on the dataset that pre-trained models are trained on. If the dataset is considerably different from the violence recognition dataset, the generalizability will be low [28]. Overall, pre-trained networks have been widely used in violence detection research, with VGG and ResNet being the most commonly used models for feature extraction.

12.4 Datasets

In this section, we provide an overview of the existing violence recognition datasets, and the details of these datasets are presented in Table 12.4. Some samples of publicly available datasets are also shown in Figure 12.5, where the red square indicates violent actions and the blue squares represent normal samples. One widely used dataset is the Hockey [33] dataset, which consists of two classes: normal and violent, gathered from real-world hockey games. The normal class includes playing hockey in the stadium, while the violent class consists of fights between players. However, this dataset lacks sufficient variations in terms of scene, background, lighting, and people's appearance. Another commonly used dataset is the Movies [33] dataset, which consists of video clips mostly gathered from Hollywood movies. The normal class includes walking, running, and playing football at the stadium, while the violent class is composed of violent actions such as kicking and wrestling. The Violent Flow [49] dataset is also collected from football stadiums but includes a crowded environment where groups of people are involved in fights. The Behave [111] dataset consists of groups of people where the group size is lower than that in the Violent Flow dataset. In normal actions, people walk and run in the street, while violent actions are performed with a group of six or seven people fighting with each other. The Caviar [112] dataset is captured in public places with different scenarios such as fighting and passing out, people walking alone, people walking together, meeting with others, entering and exiting the scene, and leaving a package. The University of Central Florida (UCF) Crime [113] dataset contains real-world surveillance systems with 13 abnormalities, including abuse, arrest, arson, assault, burglary, explosion, fighting, robbery, shooting, stealing, shoplifting, and vandalism. This dataset is not specialized for violence detection and contains other abnormal behaviors as well. The AIRTLab

Table 12.4 Details of violence recognition datasets

Dataset	#Number of clips	Description	#Max AUC score	Year	#Ref. number
Hockey [33]	1,000 clips of 50 frame-length	Actions of players in hockey game	100% which was achieved by [78]	2011	70
Movies [33]	200 clips	Gathered from action movies	100% which was achieved by [14,30,47,69,73,80,95,104–109]	2011	35
Violent Flows [49]	246 clips of 1–7 s	Gathered from YouTube and football stadium	Maximum AUC is 99.5% which was achieved by [73,97], and [110]	2012	47
Behave [111]	200,000 frames	Group normal and violent actions in the street	Maximum AUC is 100% which was achieved by [23]	2010	14
Caviar [112]	26,500 frames	Indoor violent and action sequences	Maximum AUC is 93% which was achieved by [48], and [59]	2004	5
UCF [113]	–13,320 clips	101 action categories collected from YouTube	Maximum AUC is 96% which was achieved by [72]	2012	9
AIRTLab [114]	350 clips	Indoor challenging violent and normal actions	Maximum AUC is 99.6% which was achieved by [74]	2020	2
RWF [115]	2,000 clips of	Surveillance cameras in real-world scenes	Maximum AUC is 92% which was achieved by [47]	2020	6
VID [104]	– 3,391 clips	Combination of Hockey, Movies, UCF, and HMDB [86] datasets	Maximum AUC is 98.5% which was achieved by [80]	2017	2
EsV [80]	– 3,416 clips	Adds 25 real elevator surveillance video clips to the VID	– Maximum AUC is 98.6% which was achieved by [80]	2020	1
Surv [116]	–150 violent and 150 non-violent videos	Gathered mostly from YouTube and some surveillance camera	Maximum AUC is 92% which was achieved by [47]	2020	6
RLVS [15]	1,000 violent and 1000 normal clips	Different environments such as streets, prisons, and schools	Maximum AUC is 98% which was achieved by [47]	2019	4
MediaEval [117]	10,000 clips	Violent actions including blood, gun, and death	Maximum AUC is 99% which was achieved by [118]	2014	7
VSD [119]	32 movies	Hollywood movies with diverse genres, from extremely violent to musical	Maximum AUC is 97% which was achieved by [120]	2015	1
CCTV-Fights [121]	– 1,000 clips of	Real-world fights, recordedfrom CCTVs or mobile cameras	Maximum AUC is 76% which was achieved by [121]	2019	1
XD-Violence [122]	–217 h, containing 4,754 clips	–video and audio modalities	Maximum AUC is 93.59% which was achieved by [110]	2020	2

Figure 12.5   Samples of violence recognition datasets including violent (red) and normal (blue) behaviors

[114] dataset includes non-violent clips with fast movements and similarity with some violent behaviors such as hugging, giving high fives and clapping, exulting, and gesticulating. The violent class consists of aggressive and fighting behaviors such as pushing and kicking between several people. The Real World Fighting (RWF) [115] is a large-scale violent dataset consisting of 2,000 surveillance camera videos, which is good for training DNNs. The Violent Interaction Detection (VID) [104] dataset is a combination of the Hockey, Movies, UCF, and HMDB [123] datasets. The Elevator Surveillance Video (EsV) [80] added 25 new clips of elevators to the VID dataset. The Surveillance Cameras (Surv) [116] dataset consists of real-world human actions gathered from YouTube and other surveillance datasets like CamNet [124] and Synopsis dataset [125,126]. The Real-Life Violence Situations (RLVS) [15] dataset is composed of violent videos gathered

from different environments such as streets, prisons, and schools, and non-violent videos captured normal human actions such as playing football, basketball, tennis, swimming, and eating. The MediaEval [117] dataset contains violent actions including blood, gun, and death, and it is a completed version of an earlier dataset [127]. The VSD [119] contains violent actions from Hollywood movies and short web videos downloaded from YouTube. CCTV-Fights [121] includes 1,000 clips of real fights with a total duration of more than 8 h, captured from CCTV cameras. Finally, XD-violence [122] is the only multi-modal video audio large-scale dataset that consists of 217 h of violent actions, making it a good source for training DNNs.

Table 12.4 reports the highest Area Under ROC Curve (AUC) score for each dataset, which is one of the most important metrics for evaluating classification tasks. A maximum value of 100 indicates that the two classes are completely separated by the model, while a minimum value of zero represents the worst performance. State-of-the-art AUC for Movies, Hockey, and Behave datasets are 100 and proposed methods could classify samples with the highest accuracy. However, the performance on some datasets such as CCTV-Fights and XD-violence is still lower than other datasets. State-of-the-art results have been achieved with multi-stream CNNs [80] that incorporate attention mechanisms to focus on important regions in the frame. Also, for each dataset, the number of references that use the dataset for evaluation is written. As can be seen in the table, most methods evaluated their works in hockey datasets. On the contrary, some datasets such as EsV, VSD, and CCTV-Fights were used by only a few papers.

12.5 Challenges and future directions

Although violence recognition has been a hot topic in recent years, an accurate method has yet to be introduced. The challenges in violence recognition significantly affect the potential applicability of violence recognition methods in real-world problems. Some of these challenges are discussed below:

- Generalization ability: In order to be deployed and commercialized, violence detection models must provide accurate performance in every environment. However, existing techniques lack comprehensive evaluation of different environments. As methods mostly train and test on the same dataset, their generalizability in new scenes is not known. Authors should evaluate the model's generalizability by training in one environment and testing in another to provide comprehensive results.
- Small size of violent datasets: Due to human rights, collecting real-world violent samples is very difficult, and actual fighting videos are mostly not published publicly. As a result, there are only a few violent datasets containing a small range of actions. Since machine learning and deep learning techniques require millions of datasets for training, small datasets degrade the model's performance. For instance, the size of the largest violence recognition dataset is approximately 10,000 clips, which is significantly lower than famous image classification datasets such as ImageNet. As some violent actions are very

similar to non-violent ones, it is very difficult for the machine to discriminate between them by training on a small dataset. Therefore, due to the complex nature of violent actions, a large-scale dataset capturing various scenes by different actors is strongly needed in this field.

- Edge-based constraint: Real-time violence recognition and edge computing are crucial for many applications such as surveillance systems and security cameras. Surveillance cameras are equipped with a low-power on-the-edge device near the sensor to process and detect human actions. Therefore, an on-the-edge device is a challenging constraint that affects the processing speed of the model. DNNs should be optimized to be able to run on lightweight and inexpensive devices such as Nvidia Jetson Nano and Nvidia Xavier NX. However, most of the existing methods are not designed for real-time applications and have high computational costs. Developing real-time violence recognition models with low computational costs is a challenge that needs to be addressed in future works.

- Multi-modal violence recognition: Most of the existing violence recognition methods rely on visual information only, but violence can also be detected by audio and other sensory cues such as infrared sensors. Incorporating infrared sensors into machine learning algorithms, the accuracy and reliability of violence detection systems can be greatly improved, leading to more effective and efficient monitoring of individuals and environments. Additionally, infrared sensors can be used in low-light or nighttime settings where visual detection may not be possible, further increasing the usefulness of these sensors in behavior analysis [128]. However, multi-modal datasets are rare and require more effort in data collection and annotation.

- Video-based annotation: Violent datasets are gathered from various scenes with multiple objects and people in the environments. However, the available datasets are video-based annotated, and there is no information about the location of violent actions in the frames. For example, as shown in Figure 12.5, the whole video is annotated as violent and there is no information about the location of abnormality. To train more robust models, preparing frame-based annotation with a human location in each frame would be helpful.

- Modeling temporal dependency among frames: As described in Section 3, CNNs and LSTMs have mostly been used among DNN networks for violence recognition. However, 3D CNNs cannot accurately model temporal dependency among video frames [129]. Although LSTMs better model temporal relationships in videos, they cannot efficiently model long-term dependency and require powerful computational resources for training [130]. They are also sensitive to vanishing gradients. On the other hand, transformers [131] solve these problems by using self-attention mechanisms in the layers. They also can be parallelized across multiple GPUs, making them faster and more efficient than LSTMs and RNNs. Moreover, transformers generalize better to new data than LSTMs and RNNs because they learn global patterns in the data rather than relying on local correlations. As transformers can be easily fine-tuned on new datasets, they can be a useful tool for transfer learning in violence recognition tasks.

12.6   Conclusion

Violence recognition is a highly discussed topic in the computer vision community. In this chapter, we have discussed various solutions for this topic, including both traditional handcrafted methods and recent deep learning frameworks. We have categorized and analyzed handcrafted features and descriptors based on shape, motion, and texture information. Moreover, we have compared and reviewed different deep learning networks for violence recognition and incorporated details of available violent datasets and state-of-the-art AUC scores for each dataset. In future works, a large-scale dataset that includes high intra-class similarities and inter-class variations is strongly needed. Also, methods should comprehensively evaluate the generalizability of their frameworks in different environments. Applicability in real-world, cheap on-the-edge devices is another problem that must be considered in future works.

References

[1]   Kong Y, Fu Y. Human action recognition and prediction: A survey. *International Journal of Computer Vision.* 2022;130:1366–401.

[2]   Sarkar A, Banerjee A, Singh PK, Sarkar R. 3D human action recognition: Through the eyes of researchers. *Expert Systems with Applications.* 2022:116424.

[3]   Sun Z, Ke Q, Rahmani H, Bennamoun M, Wang G, Liu J. Human action recognition from various data modalities: A review. *IEEE Transactions on Pattern Analysis and Machine Intelligence.* 2022.

[4]   Tripathi G, Singh K, Vishwakarma DK. Violence recognition using convolutional neural network: A survey. *Journal of Intelligent & Fuzzy Systems.* 2020;39:7931–52.

[5]   Ali A, Senan N. A review on violence video classification using convolutional neural networks. Recent advances on soft computing and data mining: The Second International Conference on Soft Computing and Data Mining (SCDM-2016), Bandung, Indonesia, August 18-20, 2016 Proceedings Second: Berlin: Springer; 2017. p. 130–40.

[6]   Ngiam J, Chen Z, Chia D, Koh P, Le Q, Ng A. Tiled convolutional neural networks. *Advances in Neural Information Processing Systems.* 2010;23.

[7]   Yu F, Koltun V. Multi-scale context aggregation by dilated convolutions. *arXiv preprint arXiv:*151107122. 2015.

[8]   Lin M, Chen Q, Yan S. Network in network. *arXiv preprint arXiv:*13124400. 2013.

[9]   Szegedy C, Liu W, Jia Y, Sermanet P, Reed S, Anguelov D, *et al.* Going deeper with convolutions. Proceedings of the IEEE Conference on Computer Vision and Pattern Recognition 2015. p. 1–9.

[10] Ramzan M, Abid A, Khan HU, Awan SM, Ismail A, Ahmed M, *et al.* A review on state-of-the-art violence detection techniques. *IEEE Access.* 2019;7:107560–75.

[11] Ullah FUM, Obaidat MS, Ullah A, Muhammad K, Hijji M, Baik SW. A comprehensive review on vision-based violence detection in surveillance videos. *ACM Computing Surveys.* 2023;55:1–44.

[12] Laptev I. On space-time interest points. *International Journal of Computer Vision.* 2005;64:107–23.

[13] Yu J, Song W, Zhou G, Hou J-j. Violent scene detection algorithm based on kernel extreme learning machine and three-dimensional histograms of gradient orientation. *Multimedia Tools and Applications.* 2019;78:8497–512.

[14] Jahlan HMB, Elrefaei LA. Detecting violence in video based on deep features fusion technique. *arXiv preprint arXiv*:220407443. 2022.

[15] Soliman MM, Kamal MH, Nashed MAE-M, Mostafa YM, Chawky BS, Khattab D. Violence recognition from videos using deep learning techniques. 2019 Ninth International Conference on Intelligent Computing and Information Systems (ICICIS): Piscataway, NJ: IEEE; 2019. p. 80–5.

[16] Carreira J, Zisserman A. Quo vadis, action recognition? A new model and the kinetics dataset. Proceedings of the IEEE Conference on Computer Vision and Pattern Recognition 2017. p. 6299–308.

[17] Serrano I, Deniz O, Bueno G, Garcia-Hernando G, Kim T-K. Spatio-temporal elastic cuboid trajectories for efficient fight recognition using Hough forests. *Machine Vision and Applications.* 2018;29:207–17.

[18] Serrano I, Deniz O, Espinosa-Aranda JL, Bueno G. Fight recognition in video using hough forests and 2D convolutional neural network. *IEEE Transactions on Image Processing.* 2018;27:4787–97.

[19] Xu L, Gong C, Yang J, Wu Q, Yao L. Violent video detection based on MoSIFT feature and sparse coding. 2014 IEEE International Conference on Acoustics, Speech and Signal Processing (ICASSP): Piscataway, NJ: IEEE; 2014. p. 3538–42.

[20] Traoré A, Akhloufi MA. Violence detection in videos using deep recurrent and convolutional neural networks. 2020 IEEE International Conference on Systems, Man, and Cybernetics (SMC): Piscataway, NJ: IEEE; 2020. p. 154–9.

[21] Zhang T, Yang Z, Jia W, Yang B, Yang J, He X. A new method for violence detection in surveillance scenes. *Multimedia Tools and Applications.* 2016;75:7327–49.

[22] Febin I, Jayasree K, Joy PT. Violence detection in videos for an intelligent surveillance system using MoBSIFT and movement filtering algorithm. *Pattern Analysis and Applications.* 2020;23:611–23.

[23] Zhou P, Ding Q, Luo H, Hou X. Violence detection in surveillance video using low-level features. *PLoS One.* 2018;13:e0203668.

[24] Deepak K, Vignesh L, Srivathsan G, Roshan S, Chandrakala S. Statistical features-based violence detection in surveillance videos. *Cognitive Informatics and Soft Computing: Proceeding of CISC 2019*: Berlin: Springer; 2020. p. 197–203.

[25] Serrano Gracia I, Deniz Suarez O, Bueno Garcia G, Kim T-K. Fast fight detection. *PLoS One.* 2015;10:e0120448.

[26]   Lowe DG. Object recognition from local scale-invariant features. Proceedings of the Seventh IEEE International Conference on Computer Vision: Piscataway, NJ: IEEE; 1999. p. 1150–7.

[27]   Tian Y, Pang G, Chen Y, Singh R, Verjans JW, Carneiro G. Weakly-supervised video anomaly detection with robust temporal feature magnitude learning. Proceedings of the IEEE/CVF International Conference on Computer Vision 2021. p. 4975–86.

[28]   Tendle A, Hasan MR. A study of the generalizability of self-supervised representations. *Machine Learning with Applications.* 2021;6:100124.

[29]   Chen J, Shan S, He C, Zhao G, Pietikäinen M, Chen X, *et al.* WLD: A robust local image descriptor. *IEEE Transactions on Pattern Analysis and Machine Intelligence.* 2009;32:1705–20.

[30]   Hanson A, Pnvr K, Krishnagopal S, Davis L. Bidirectional convolutional LSTM for the detection of violence in videos. Proceedings of the European Conference on Computer Vision (ECCV) Workshops 2018. 280–295.

[31]   Sumon SA, Goni R, Hashem NB, Shahria T, Rahman RM. Violence detection by pretrained modules with different deep learning approaches. *Vietnam Journal of Computer Science.* 2020;7:19–40.

[32]   Viswanathan DG. Features from accelerated segment test (fast). *Proceedings of the 10th Workshop on Image Analysis for Multimedia Interactive Services,* London, UK2009. p. 6–8.

[33]   Bermejo Nievas E, Deniz Suarez O, Bueno García G, Sukthankar R. Violence detection in video using computer vision techniques. Computer Analysis of Images and Patterns: 14th International Conference, CAIP 2011, Seville, Spain, August 29–31, 2011, Proceedings, Part II 14: Berlin: Springer; 2011. p. 332–9.

[34]   Fradi H, Luvison B, Pham QC. Crowd behavior analysis using local mid-level visual descriptors. *IEEE Transactions on Circuits and Systems for Video Technology.* 2016;27:589–602.

[35]   Berlin SJ, John M. Spiking neural network based on joint entropy of optical flow features for human action recognition. *The Visual Computer.* 2022;38:223–37.

[36]   Mubarak AS, Serte S, Al-Turjman F, Ameen ZSi, Ozsoz M. Local binary pattern and deep learning feature extraction fusion for COVID-19 detection on computed tomography images. *Expert Systems.* 2022;39:e12842.

[37]   Bay H, Ess A, Tuytelaars T, Van Gool L. Speeded-up robust features (SURF). *Computer Vision and Image Understanding.* 2008;110:346–59.

[38]   Yu T-H, Kim T-K, Cipolla R. Real-time Action Recognition by Spatiotemporal Semantic and Structural Forests. *BMVC* 2010. p. 6.

[39]   Koelstra S, Patras I. The fast-3D spatio-temporal interest region detector. *2009 10th Workshop on Image Analysis for Multimedia Interactive Services*: Piscataway, NJ: IEEE; 2009. p. 242–5.

[40]   Godil A, Wagan AI. Salient local 3D features for 3D shape retrieval. *Three-Dimensional Imaging, Interaction, and Measurement*: Bellingham, WA: SPIE; 2011. p. 275–82.

[41] Scovanner P, Ali S, Shah M. A 3-dimensional sift descriptor and its application to action recognition. Proceedings of the 15th ACM International Conference on Multimedia 2007. p. 357–60.

[42] Lee CH, Varshney A, Jacobs DW. Mesh saliency. ACM SIGGRAPH2005 Papers; 2005. p. 659–66.

[43] Castellani U, Cristani M, Fantoni S, Murino V. Sparse points matching by combining 3D mesh saliency with statistical descriptors. *Computer Graphics Forum: Wiley Online Library*; 2008. p. 643–52.

[44] Novatnack J, Nishino K. Scale-dependent 3D geometric features. 2007 IEEE 11th International Conference on Computer Vision: Piscataway, NJ: IEEE; 2007. p. 1–8.

[45] Sun J, Ovsjanikov M, Guibas L. A concise and provably informative multi-scale signature based on heat diffusion. *Computer Graphics Forum: Wiley Online Library*; 2009. p. 1383–92.

[46] Dutagaci H, Cheung CP, Godil A. Evaluation of 3D interest point detection techniques via human-generated ground truth. *The Visual Computer.* 2012;28:901–17.

[47] Kang M-s, Park R-H, Park H-M. Efficient spatio-temporal modeling methods for real-time violence recognition. *IEEE Access.* 2021;9:76270–85.

[48] Ehsan TZ, Nahvi M. Violence detection in indoor surveillance cameras using motion trajectory and differential histogram of optical flow. 2018 8th International Conference on Computer and Knowledge Engineering (ICCKE): Piscataway, NJ: IEEE; 2018. p. 153–8.

[49] Hassner T, Itcher Y, Kliper-Gross O. Violent flows: Real-time detection of violent crowd behavior. 2012 IEEE Computer Society Conference on Computer Vision and Pattern Recognition Workshops: Piscataway, NJ: IEEE; 2012. p. 1–6.

[50] Gao Y, Liu H, Sun X, Wang C, Liu Y. Violence detection using oriented violent flows. *Image and Vision Computing.* 2016;48:37–41.

[51] Huang J-F, Chen S-L. Detection of violent crowd behavior based on statistical characteristics of the optical flow. 2014 11th International Conference on Fuzzy Systems and Knowledge Discovery (FSKD): Piscataway, NJ: IEEE; 2014. p. 565–9.

[52] Ehsan TZ, Mohtavipour SM. Vi-Net: a deep violent flow network for violence detection in video sequences. 2020 11th International Conference on Information and Knowledge Technology (IKT): Piscataway, NJ: IEEE; 2020. p. 88–92.

[53] Lloyd K, Marshall D, Moore SC, Rosin PL. Detecting violent crowds using temporal analysis of GLCM texture. arXiv preprint arXiv:160505106. 2016.

[54] Khokher MR, Bouzerdoum A, Phung SL. Violent scene detection using a super descriptor tensor decomposition. 2015 International Conference on Digital Image Computing: Techniques and Applications (DICTA): Piscataway, NJ: IEEE; 2015. p. 1–8.

[55] Zhang T, Jia W, He X, Yang J. Discriminative dictionary learning with motion weber local descriptor for violence detection. *IEEE Transactions on Circuits and Systems for Video Technology.* 2016;27:696–709.

[56]   Zhang T, Jia W, Yang B, Yang J, He X, Zheng Z. MoWLD: a robust motion image descriptor for violence detection. *Multimedia Tools and Applications.* 2017;76:1419–38.

[57]   Senst T, Eiselein V, Sikora T. A local feature based on Lagrangian measures for violent video classification. 6th International Conference on Imaging for Crime Prevention and Detection (ICDP-15): IET; 2015. p. 1–6.

[58]   Mohammadi S, Kiani H, Perina A, Murino V. Violence detection in crowded scenes using substantial derivative. 2015 12th IEEE International Conference on Advanced Video and Signal Based Surveillance (AVSS): Piscataway, NJ: IEEE; 2015. p. 1–6.

[59]   Esen E, Arabaci MA, Soysal M. Fight detection in surveillance videos. 2013 11th International Workshop on Content-Based Multimedia Indexing (CBMI): Piscataway, NJ: IEEE; 2013. p. 131–5.

[60]   Fu EY, Leong HV, Ngai G, Chan S. Automatic fight detection based on motion analysis. 2015 IEEE International Symposium on Multimedia (ISM): Piscataway, NJ: IEEE; 2015. p. 57–60.

[61]   Mohammadi S, Perina A, Kiani H, Murino V. Angry crowds: detecting violent events in videos. Computer Vision–ECCV 2016: 14th European Conference, Amsterdam, The Netherlands, October 11–14, 2016, Proceedings, Part VII 14: Berlin: Springer; 2016. p. 3–18.

[62]   Mabrouk AB, Zagrouba E. Spatio-temporal feature using optical flow based distribution for violence detection. *Pattern Recognition Letters.* 2017;92:62–7.

[63]   Vashistha P, Bhatnagar C, Khan MA. An architecture to identify violence in video surveillance system using ViF and LBP. 2018 4th International Conference on Recent Advances in Information Technology (RAIT): Piscataway, NJ: IEEE; 2018. p. 1–6.

[64]   Yang Z, Zhang T, Yang J, Wu Q, Bai L, Yao L. Violence detection based on histogram of optical flow orientation. Sixth International Conference on Machine Vision (ICMV 2013): Bellingham, WA: SPIE; 2013. p. 236–9.

[65]   Senst T, Eiselein V, Kuhn A, Sikora T. Crowd violence detection using global motion-compensated Lagrangian features and scale-sensitive video-level representation. *IEEE Transactions on Information Forensics and Security.* 2017;12:2945–56.

[66]   Singh K, Preethi KY, Sai KV, Modi CN. Designing an efficient framework for violence detection in sensitive areas using computer vision and machine learning techniques. 2018 Tenth International Conference on Advanced Computing (ICoAC): Piscataway, NJ: IEEE; 2018. p. 74–9.

[67]   Fu EY, Huang MX, Leong HV, Ngai G. Cross-species learning: A low-cost approach to learning human fight from animal fight. Proceedings of the 26th ACM International Conference on Multimedia; 2018. p. 320–7.

[68]   Lloyd K, Rosin PL, Marshall AD, Moore SC. Violent behaviour detection using local trajectory response. 7th International Conference on Imaging for Crime Detection and Prevention (ICDP 2016): IET; 2016. p. 1–6.

[69]   Li J, Jiang X, Sun T, Xu K. Efficient violence detection using 3d convolutional neural networks. 2019 16th IEEE International Conference on

Advanced Video and Signal Based Surveillance (AVSS): Piscataway, NJ: IEEE; 2019. p. 1–8.

[70] Ye L, Liu T, Han T, Ferdinando H, Seppänen T, Alasaarela E. Campus violence detection based on artificial intelligent interpretation of surveillance video sequences. *Remote Sensing*. 2021;13:628.

[71] Ullah FUM, Ullah A, Muhammad K, Haq IU, Baik SW. Violence detection using spatiotemporal features with 3D convolutional neural network. *Sensors*. 2019;19:2472.

[72] Xu Q, See J, Lin W. Localization guided fight action detection in surveillance videos. 2019 IEEE International Conference on Multimedia and Expo (ICME): Piscataway, NJ: IEEE; 2019. p. 568–73.

[73] Halder R, Chatterjee R. CNN-BiLSTM model for violence detection in smart surveillance. *SN Computer Science*. 2020;1:201.

[74] Sernani P, Falcionelli N, Tomassini S, Contardo P, Dragoni AF. Deep learning for automatic violence detection: Tests on the AIRTLab dataset. *IEEE Access*. 2021;9:160580–95.

[75] Ullah FUM, Muhammad K, Haq IU, Khan N, Heidari AA, Baik SW, *et al.* AI-assisted edge vision for violence detection in IoT-based industrial surveillance networks. *IEEE Transactions on Industrial Informatics*. 2021;18:5359–70.

[76] Meng Z, Yuan J, Li Z. Trajectory-pooled deep convolutional networks for violence detection in videos. Computer Vision Systems: 11th International Conference, ICVS 2017, Shenzhen, China, July 10-13, 2017, Revised Selected Papers 11: Berlin: Springer; 2017. p. 437–47.

[77] Baba M, Gui V, Cernazanu C, Pescaru D. A sensor network approach for violence detection in smart cities using deep learning. *Sensors*. 2019;19:1676.

[78] Mohtavipour SM, Saeidi M, Arabsorkhi A. A multi-stream CNN for deep violence detection in video sequences using handcrafted features. *The Visual Computer*. 2022:1–16.

[79] Dong Z, Qin J, Wang Y. Multi-stream deep networks for person to person violence detection in videos. Pattern Recognition: 7th Chinese Conference, CCPR 2016, Chengdu, China, November 5–7, 2016, Proceedings, Part I 7: Berlin: Springer; 2016. p. 517–31.

[80] Li H, Wang J, Han J, Zhang J, Yang Y, Zhao Y. A novel multi-stream method for violent interaction detection using deep learning. *Measurement and Control*. 2020;53:796–806.

[81] Li C, Zhu L, Zhu D, *et al.* End-to-end multiplayer violence detection based on deep 3D CNN. Proceedings of the 2018 VII International Conference on Network, Communication and Computing 2018. p. 227–30.

[82] Fenil E, Manogaran G, Vivekananda G, Thanjaivadivel T, Jeeva S, Ahilan A. Real time violence detection framework for football stadium comprising of big data analysis and deep learning through bidirectional LSTM. *Computer Networks*. 2019;151:191–200.

[83] Choqueluque-Roman D, Camara-Chavez G. Weakly supervised violence detection in surveillance video. *Sensors*. 2022;22:4502.

[84] Ali A, Senan N. Violence video classification performance using deep neural networks. Recent Advances on Soft Computing and Data Mining: Proceedings of the Third International Conference on Soft Computing and Data Mining (SCDM 2018), Johor, Malaysia, February 6–7, 2018: Berlin: Springer; 2018. p. 225–33.

[85] Freire-Obregón D, Barra P, Castrillón-Santana M, Marsico MD. Inflated 3D ConvNet context analysis for violence detection. *Machine Vision and Applications.* 2022;33:1–13.

[86] Omarov B, Narynov S, Zhumanov Z, Gumar A, Khassanova M. A skeleton-based approach for campus violence detection. *CMC Computers Materials & Continua.* 2022;72:315–31.

[87] Simonyan K, Zisserman A. Very deep convolutional networks for large-scale image recognition. arXiv preprint arXiv:14091556. 2014.

[88] Howard AG, Zhu M, Chen B, Kalenichenko D, Wang W, Weyand T, *et al.* Mobilenets: Efficient convolutional neural networks for mobile vision applications. *arXiv preprint arXiv*:170404861. 2017.

[89] Szegedy C, Vanhoucke V, Ioffe S, Shlens J, Wojna Z. Rethinking the inception architecture for computer vision. Proceedings of the IEEE Conference on Computer Vision and Pattern Recognition; 2016. p. 2818–26.

[90] He K, Zhang X, Ren S, Sun J. Deep residual learning for image recognition. Proceedings of the IEEE Conference on Computer Vision and Pattern Recognition; 2016. p. 770–8.

[91] Tan M, Le Q. Efficientnet: Rethinking model scaling for convolutional neural networks. International Conference on Machine Learning: PMLR; 2019. p. 6105–14.

[92] Sumon SA, Shahria MT, Goni MR, Hasan N, Almarufuzzaman A, Rahman RM. Violent crowd flow detection using deep learning. Intelligent Information and Database Systems: 11th Asian Conference, ACIIDS 2019, Yogyakarta, Indonesia, April 8–11, 2019, Proceedings, Part I 11: Berlin: Springer; 2019. p. 613–25.

[93] Huszár VD, Adhikarla VK, Négyesi I, Krasznay C. Toward fast and accurate violence detection for automated video surveillance applications. *IEEE Access.* 2023;11:18772–93.

[94] Asad M, Yang J, He J, Shamsolmoali P, He X. Multi-frame feature-fusion-based model for violence detection. *The Visual Computer.* 2021;37:1415–31.

[95] Abdali A-MR, Al-Tuma RF. Robust real-time violence detection in video using CNN and LSTM. 2019 2nd Scientific Conference of Computer Sciences (SCCS): Piscataway, NJ: IEEE; 2019. p. 104–8.

[96] Xia Q, Zhang P, Wang J, Tian M, Fei C. Real time violence detection based on deep spatio-temporal features. Biometric Recognition: 13th Chinese Conference, CCBR 2018, Urumqi, China, August 11-12, 2018, Proceedings 13: Berlin: Springer; 2018. p. 157–65.

[97] Accattoli S, Sernani P, Falcionelli N, Mekuria DN, Dragoni AF. Violence detection in videos by combining 3D convolutional neural networks and support vector machines. *Applied Artificial Intelligence.* 2020;34:329–44.

[98]   Vosta S, Yow K-C. A cnn-rnn combined structure for real-world violence detection in surveillance cameras. *Applied Sciences.* 2022;12:1021.

[99]   Sharma M, Baghel R. Video surveillance for violence detection using deep learning. *Advances in Data Science and Management: Proceedings of ICDSM 2019*: Berlin: Springer; 2020. p. 411–20.

[100] Pang W-F, He Q-H, Hu Y-j, Li Y-X. Violence detection in videos based on fusing visual and audio information. ICASSP 2021-2021 IEEE International Conference on Acoustics, Speech and Signal Processing (ICASSP): Piscataway, NJ: IEEE; 2021. p. 2260–4.

[101] Hershey S, Chaudhuri S, Ellis DP, Gemmeke JF, Jansen A, Moore RC, *et al.* CNN architectures for large-scale audio classification. 2017 IEEE International Conference on Acoustics, Speech and Signal Processing (ICASSP): Piscataway, NJ: IEEE; 2017. p. 131–5.

[102] Islam Z, Rukonuzzaman M, Ahmed R, Kabir MH, Farazi M. Efficient two-stream network for violence detection using separable convolutional LSTM. 2021 International Joint Conference on Neural Networks (IJCNN): Piscataway, NJ: IEEE; 2021. p. 1–8.

[103] Ullah FUM, Obaidat MS, Muhammad K, *et al.* An intelligent system for complex violence pattern analysis and detection. *International Journal of Intelligent Systems.* 2022;37:10400–22.

[104] Zhou P, Ding Q, Luo H, Hou X. Violent interaction detection in video based on deep learning. *Journal of Physics: Conference Series*: 2017. p. 012044.

[105] Sudhakaran S, Lanz O. Learning to detect violent videos using convolutional long short-term memory. 2017 14th IEEE International Conference on Advanced Video and Signal-based Surveillance (AVSS): Piscataway, NJ: IEEE; 2017. p. 1–6.

[106] Carneiro SA, da Silva GP, Guimaraes SJF, Pedrini H. Fight detection in video sequences based on multi-stream convolutional neural networks. 2019 32nd SIBGRAPI Conference on Graphics, Patterns and Images (SIBGRAPI): Piscataway, NJ: IEEE; 2019. p. 8–15.

[107] Mumtaz A, Bux Sargano A, Habib Z. Fast learning through deep multi-net CNN model for violence recognition in video surveillance. *The Computer Journal.* 2022;65:457–72.

[108] Jain A, Vishwakarma DK. Deep NeuralNet for violence detection using motion features from dynamic images. 2020 Third International Conference on Smart Systems and Inventive Technology (ICSSIT): Piscataway, NJ: IEEE; 2020. p. 826–31.

[109] Rendón-Segador FJ, Álvarez-García JA, Enríquez F, Deniz O. Violencenet: Dense multi-head self-attention with bidirectional convolutional lstm for detecting violence. *Electronics.* 2021;10:1601.

[110] Huszár, V.D., Adhikarla, V.K., Négyesi, I. and Krasznay, C. Towards fast and accurate violence detection for automated video surveillance applications. *IEEE Access*, 2023.

[111] Blunsden S, Fisher R. The BEHAVE video dataset: ground truthed video for multi-person behavior classification. *Annals of the BMVA.* 2010;4:4.

[112] Fisher RB. The PETS04 surveillance ground-truth data sets. Proc 6th IEEE International Workshop on Performance Evaluation of Tracking and Surveillance 2004. p. 1–5.

[113] Soomro K, Zamir AR, Shah M. UCF101: A dataset of 101 human actions classes from videos in the wild. *arXiv preprint arXiv*:12120402. 2012.

[114] Bianculli M, Falcionelli N, Sernani P, *et al.* A dataset for automatic violence detection in videos. *Data in Brief.* 2020;33:106587.

[115] Cheng M, Cai K, Li M. RWF-2000: an open large scale video database for violence detection. 2020 25th International Conference on Pattern Recognition (ICPR): Piscataway, NJ: IEEE; 2021. p. 4183–90.

[116] Aktı Ş, Tataroğlu GA, Ekenel HK. Vision-based fight detection from surveillance cameras. 2019 Ninth International Conference on Image Processing Theory, Tools and Applications (IPTA): Piscataway, NJ: IEEE; 2019. p. 1–6.

[117] Demarty C-H, Ionescu B, Jiang Y-G, Quang VL, Schedl M, Penet C. Benchmarking violent scenes detection in movies. 2014 12th International Workshop on Content-based Multimedia Indexing (CBMI): Piscataway, NJ: IEEE; 2014. p. 1–6.

[118] Penet C, Demarty C-H, Gravier G, Gros P. Multimodal information fusion and temporal integration for violence detection in movies. 2012 IEEE International Conference on Acoustics, Speech and Signal Processing (ICASSP): Piscataway, NJ: IEEE; 2012. p. 2393–6.

[119] Demarty C-H, Penet C, Soleymani M, Gravier G.VSD, a public dataset for the detection of violent scenes in movies: Design, annotation, analysis and evaluation. *Multimedia Tools and Applications.* 2015;74:7379–404.

[120] Khan SU, Haq IU, Rho S, Baik SW, Lee MY. Cover the violence: A novel deep-learning-based approach towards violence-detection in movies. *Applied Sciences.* 2019;9:4963.

[121] Perez M, Kot AC, Rocha A. Detection of real-world fights in surveillance videos. ICASSP 2019-2019 IEEE International Conference on Acoustics, Speech and Signal Processing (ICASSP): Piscataway, NJ: IEEE; 2019. p. 2662–6.

[122] Wu P, Liu J, Shi Y, *et al.* Not only look, but also listen: Learning multimodal violence detection under weak supervision. Computer Vision–ECCV 2020: 16th European Conference, Glasgow, UK, August 23–28, 2020, Proceedings, Part XXX 16: Berlin: Springer; 2020. p. 322–39.

[123] Kuehne H, Jhuang H, Garrote E, Poggio T, Serre T. HMDB: a large video database for human motion recognition. 2011 International Conference on Computer Vision: Piscataway, NJ: IEEE; 2011. p. 2556–63.

[124] Zhang S, Staudt E, Faltemier T, Roy-Chowdhury AK. A camera network tracking (CamNeT) dataset and performance baseline. 2015 IEEE Winter Conference on Applications of Computer Vision: Piscataway, NJ: IEEE; 2015. p. 365–72.

[125] Wang W-C, Chung P-C, Huang C-R, Huang W-Y. Event based surveillance video synopsis using trajectory kinematics descriptors. 2017 15th IAPR International Conference on Machine Vision Applications (MVA): Piscataway, NJ: IEEE; 2017. p. 250–3.

[126] Huang C-R, Chung P-CJ, Yang D-K, Chen H-C, Huang G-J. Maximum a posteriori probability estimation for online surveillance video synopsis. *IEEE Transactions on Circuits and Systems for Video Technology.* 2014;24:1417–29.

[127] Demarty C-H, Penet C, Gravier G, Soleymani M. The mediaeval 2012 affect task: violent scenes detection. *Working Notes Proceedings of the MediaEval* 2012 Workshop; 2012.

[128] Pourmomtaz N, Nahvi M. Multispectral particle filter tracking using adaptive decision-based fusion of visible and thermal sequences. *Multimedia Tools and Applications.* 2020;79(25–26):18405–34.

[129] Dosovitskiy, A., Beyer, L., Kolesnikov, A., *et al.*, 2020. An image is worth 16×16 words: Transformers for image recognition at scale. *arXiv preprint arXiv:2010.11929.*

[130] Manttari J, Broomé S, Folkesson J, Kjellstrom H. Interpreting video features: a comparison of 3D convolutional networks and convolutional LSTM networks. Proceedings of the Asian Conference on Computer Vision 2020.

[131] Vaswani A, Shazeer N, Parmar N, *et al.* Attention is all you need. *Advances in Neural Information Processing Systems.* 2017;30.

[132] Ding C, Fan S, Zhu M, Feng W, Jia B. Violence detection in video by using 3D convolutional neural networks. Advances in Visual Computing: 10th International Symposium, ISVC 2014, Las Vegas, NV, USA, December 8–10, 2014, Proceedings, Part II 10: Berlin: Springer; 2014. p. 551–8.

[133] Naik AJ, Gopalakrishna M. Deep-violence: individual person violent activity detection in video. *Multimedia Tools and Applications.* 2021;80:18365–80.

[134] Zhenhua T, Zhenche X, Pengfei W, Chang D, Weichao Z. FTCF: Full temporal cross fusion network for violence detection in videos. *Applied Intelligence.* 2023;53:4218–30.

[135] Song W, Zhang D, Zhao X, Yu J, Zheng R, Wang A. A novel violent video detection scheme based on modified 3D convolutional neural networks. *IEEE Access.* 2019;7:39172–9.

[136] Haque M, Afsha S, Nyeem H. Developing BrutNet: A new deep CNN model with GRU for realtime violence detection. 2022 International Conference on Innovations in Science, Engineering and Technology (ICISET): Piscataway, NJ: IEEE; 2022. p. 390–5.

[137] Jiang B, Xu F, Tu W, Yang C. Channel-wise attention in 3D convolutional networks for violence detection. 2019 International Conference on Intelligent Computing and its Emerging Applications (ICEA): Piscataway, NJ: IEEE; 2019. p. 59–64.

[138] Mondal S, Pal S, Saha SK, Chanda B. *Violent/non-violent video classification based on deep neural network.* 2017 Ninth International Conference on Advances in Pattern Recognition (ICAPR): Piscataway, NJ: IEEE; 2017. p. 1–6.

[139] Biradar K, Dube S, Vipparthi SK. DEARESt: Deep convolutional aberrant behavior detection in real-world scenarios. 2018 IEEE 13th international conference on industrial and information systems (ICIIS): Piscataway, NJ: IEEE; 2018. p. 163–7.

[140]   Ehsan TZ, Nahvi M, Mohtavipour SM. Learning deep latent space for unsupervised violence detection. *Multimedia Tools and Applications.* 2023;82:12493–512.

[141]   Ehsan TZ, Nahvi M, Mohtavipour SM. DABA-net: Deep acceleration-based AutoEncoder network for violence detection in surveillance cameras. 2022 International Conference on Machine Vision and Image Processing (MVIP): Piscataway, NJ: IEEE; 2022. p. 1–6.

[142]   Su Y, Lin G, Zhu J, Wu Q. Human interaction learning on 3D skeleton point clouds for video violence recognition. Computer Vision–ECCV 2020: 16th European Conference, Glasgow, UK, August 23–28, 2020, Proceedings, Part IV 16: Berlin: Springer; 2020. p. 74–90.

[143]   Mumtaz A, Sargano AB, Habib Z. Violence detection in surveillance videos with deep network using transfer learning. 2018 Second European Conference on Electrical Engineering and Computer Science (EECS): Piscataway, NJ: IEEE; 2018. p. 558–63.

[144]   Irfanullah, Hussain T, Iqbal A, Yang B, Hussain A. Real time violence detection in surveillance videos using convolutional neural networks. *Multimedia Tools and Applications.* 2022;81:38151–73.

[145]   Keçeli A, Kaya A. Violent activity detection with transfer learning method. *Electronics Letters.* 2017;53:1047–8.

[146]   Peixoto BM, Lavi B, Dias Z, Rocha A. Harnessing high-level concepts, visual, and auditory features for violence detection in videos. *Journal of Visual Communication and Image Representation.* 2021;78:103174.

[147]   Peixoto B, Lavi B, Martin JPP, Avila S, Dias Z, Rocha A. Toward subjective violence detection in videos. ICASSP 2019-2019 IEEE International Conference on Acoustics, Speech and Signal Processing (ICASSP): Piscataway, NJ: IEEE; 2019. p. 8276–80.

[148]   Peixoto B, Lavi B, Bestagini P, Dias Z, Rocha A. Multimodal violence detection in videos. ICASSP 2020-2020 IEEE International Conference on Acoustics, Speech and Signal Processing (ICASSP): Piscataway, NJ: IEEE; 2020. p. 2957–61.

[149]   Roman DGC, Chávez GC. Violence detection and localization in surveillance video. 2020 33rd SIBGRAPI Conference on Graphics, Patterns and Images (SIBGRAPI): Piscataway, NJ: IEEE; 2020. p. 248–55.

[150]   Asad M, Yang Z, Khan Z, Yang J, He X. Feature fusion based deep spatiotemporal model for violence detection in videos. Neural Information Processing: 26th International Conference, ICONIP 2019, Sydney, NSW, Australia, December 12–15, 2019, Proceedings, Part I 26: Berlin: Springer; 2019. p. 405–17.

Chapter 13

Enhancing medical image security: a look into crypto-watermarking method via LabVIEW

Rim Amdouni[1] and Mohamed Ali Hajjaji[2]

This chapter presents a novel method for watermarking and encryption of medical images using the Haar Discrete Wavelet Transform (DWT). The proposed system aims to securely embed patients' private information into medical images followed by encrypting the watermarked images using a chaos-based cryptosystem to enhance robustness. Our approach utilizes standard grayscale images for embedding patients' private data, with the insertion block placed immediately after the Haar DWT process. The encryption phase incorporates the SHA-2 hash function and the Rossler chaotic system for key generation, ensuring both confusion and diffusion for enhanced security. The system includes the transmission of watermarked encrypted data to the cloud, enabling authorized parties to securely access and retrieve the watermarked data. The successful implementation of the proposed system using LabVIEW on the MyRIO board demonstrates its practicality and functionality. Performance evaluation was conducted by subjecting the system to various attacks, including compression, noise, filtering, and geometric transformation. Experimental results showcased low distortion, high robustness in the watermarking process, and enhanced security in the encryption phase.

13.1 Introduction

In today's interconnected world, the Internet and widely used communication systems have made our lives more convenient than ever before. However, along with the benefits, technology also brings forth various challenges. While easy access to vast amounts of information is desirable, it is crucial to address the issues related to the protection and security of multimedia data.

Ensuring the security and privacy of sensitive information, especially in domains such as medical imaging, is of utmost importance. Medical data, including Electronic Health Records (EHRs), often contain patients' private information that needs to be kept confidential. Additionally, medical images used for diagnosis must

[1]National Engineering School of Monastir, University of Monastir, Tunisia
[2]Higher Institute of Applied Sciences and Technology, University of Sousse, Tunisia

be safeguarded against unauthorized modifications or tampering. In response to these challenges, different techniques have been developed in the medical field, including watermarking and cryptography [1,2]. Watermarking methods involve the addition of copyright data or unique identifiers into the original information, typically embedded within the original image. By incorporating digital signatures diagnostic documents, patient records, or other relevant information, watermarking techniques enhance the confidentiality and authenticity of patient data [3]. These advancements enable the integration of additional files with the original image, preserving the confidentiality and integrity of the accompanying medical documents.

Cryptography, as a complementary mechanism, has been proposed to further enhance the security of medical images. It provides additional layers of protection to ensure the confidentiality and integrity of the data. By employing cryptographic techniques, the information can be securely encrypted, making it more resistant to unauthorized access or tampering [4].

Various techniques of cryptographic watermarking have emerged and are being applied in different domains. Among these domains, the field of medicine greatly benefits from these techniques, as they play a crucial role in securing patient data encapsulation and processing of files and diagnostic images [5,6]. In particular, these techniques aid in authenticating and exchanging information efficiently through the use of Patient Electronic Records (PER), thereby expediting treatment procedures.

These algorithms aim to embed imperceptible yet robust marks within the multimedia content, enabling subsequent verification and identification. Additionally, the integration of watermarking and cryptography techniques in a comprehensive framework offers several advantages in terms of data protection. By combining these methods, a multi-layered defense mechanism can be established to address potential vulnerabilities associated with each method individually [7]. However, when it comes to copyright protection in this context, conventional encryption techniques face certain limitations. While encryption is generally considered the ideal solution for securing broadcasted information, classical encryption methods like Advanced Encryption Standard (AES) [8], Data Encryption Standard (DES) [8], and others are not well-suited for real-time embedded applications.

In the given context, we present a novel approach that combines watermarking and encryption techniques for medical images, specifically using the Haar Discrete Wavelet Transform (DWT). This chapter emphasizes the theoretical foundations and the practical aspects of the proposed methodology. It sheds light on the advantages of the combined watermarking and cryptography approach and demonstrates the real-world viability and effectiveness of the implementation using LabVIEW. To evaluate the security and robustness of the proposed approach, extensive experiments are conducted. These experiments involve the secure transmission of watermarked encrypted images from LabVIEW to the Cloud, where the images are securely stored. Authorized parties equipped with the program can then retrieve and decrypt the images while preserving the embedded watermark. The results of these experiments showcase the enhanced security and reliability achieved through the fusion of watermarking, cryptography, and LabVIEW implementation.

In summary, this chapter presents a comprehensive framework that combines watermarking and cryptography techniques, implemented through LabVIEW, to bolster multimedia data security, with a specific focus on medical images. The integration of these methodologies aims to provide data confidentiality, integrity, and authenticity, ensuring protection against unauthorized access and manipulation. Through the exploration of theoretical foundations, practical implementation, and experimental validation, this article offers valuable insights for researchers and practitioners in the field of multimedia data protection.

13.2 Related works

Huang *et al.* [9] explored the application of HDWT (Hilbert curve-based Discrete Wavelet Transform) in lossless embedding techniques. The authors begin by introducing the importance of lossless data hiding and the motivation for using HDWT in this context. They provide an overview of the DWT and the Hilbert curve, explaining the concepts of multi-resolution analysis and the ordering of wavelet coefficients. The paper reviews existing lossless embedding techniques, highlighting their limitations and the gap that the proposed technique aims to address. The authors then present their novel technique, describing the steps involved in embedding additional data without introducing distortion. Experimental results are provided, demonstrating the effectiveness and performance of the proposed method through quantitative metrics and visual comparisons.

Hamidi *et al.* [10] presented a hybrid watermarking method that combines the DWT, Discrete Cosine Transform (DCT), and Scale-Invariant Feature Transformation (SIFT). Their objective is to develop a feature-based image watermarking scheme that can withstand image processing attacks and geometric distortions while maintaining good imperceptibility. The proposed method embeds a robust watermark in the DWT-DCT domain to handle image processing manipulations and utilizes SIFT to protect the watermark from geometric attacks. Specifically, the watermark is embedded in the middle band of DCT coefficients in the HL1 band of the DWT. SIFT feature points are registered for use in the extraction process, enabling the correction of geometric transformations.

Şahin *et al.* [11] focused on the practical implementation of chaotic systems using Multisim and LabVIEW software. They highlighted the growing interest in chaotic systems due to their nonlinear behavior, sensitivity to initial conditions, and unpredictable features. The authors specifically focus on the Sprott case. A chaotic system and design the corresponding circuit using operational amplifiers (OP-AMPS) and other appropriate components in the Multisim environment. By simulating the chaotic differential equations mathematically, they observe the desired chaotic behavior. The authors further conduct co-simulation between Multisim and LabVIEW to simulate the circuit behavior. The obtained simulation results demonstrate similar behavior compared to the theoretical chaotic system.

Şahin [2] explored the utilization of a memristor-based hyperchaotic system for image encryption, with DNA encoding implemented on LabVIEW. The author introduced the concept of memristors, a type of electronic component with memory properties, and their potential for chaotic system design. The paper focused on a specific hyperchaotic system constructed using memristors. Additionally, the author proposed an image encryption technique based on DNA encoding, which uses the characteristics of DNA molecules for encryption purposes. The implementation of this technique was carried out using LabVIEW software. The paper likely presented the design and simulation process, highlighting the steps involved in encoding and decoding images. Experimental results and performance analysis were provided to demonstrate the effectiveness of the proposed approach.

Yadav *et al.* [12] presented a system for attendance management using fingerprints, microcontrollers, and LabVIEW. The authors aimed to develop a reliable and efficient attendance system by utilizing biometric fingerprint recognition technology. The paper introduced the concept of fingerprint recognition as a secure and accurate method for attendance tracking. The authors described the system architecture, which includes a microcontroller for interfacing with fingerprint sensors and LabVIEW for data processing and management. They explained the design and implementation of the system, including fingerprint image acquisition, feature extraction, and matching algorithms. The paper discussed the integration of the microcontroller with LabVIEW and the communication protocols used.

Hosam and Nadhir Ben [13] explored the generation of random numbers from biological signals using the LabVIEW environment and subsequent statistical analysis. The authors investigate the utilization of biological signals as a source of random numbers, considering their inherent variability and complexity. They discussed the importance of random number generation in various fields and highlighted the potential benefits of using biological signals in this context. The paper focuses on the implementation of the random number generation process using LabVIEW, describing the methodology and techniques employed. The authors explained the acquisition and preprocessing of biological signals, followed by the extraction of random numbers using specific algorithms or statistical methods. The generated random numbers are then subjected to statistical analysis, which may include tests for randomness, distribution analysis, and other relevant statistical measures. The paper presented the experimental results, discussing the statistical properties and performance of the generated random numbers.

Levický and Peter [5] focused on the hardware implementation of the Haar DWT and its application to image watermarking. By developing a dedicated hardware architecture, the authors aim to achieve efficient and real-time processing capabilities. The paper highlighted the advantages of hardware implementations for image processing tasks and showcased the practical utility of the proposed implementation through image watermarking. Through experimental evaluation, the authors demonstrate the performance and effectiveness of their hardware implementation for the Haar DWT.

13.3   Proposed algorithm

The proposed algorithm integrates watermarking and cryptography techniques to enhance the security of medical data. This algorithm, implemented using

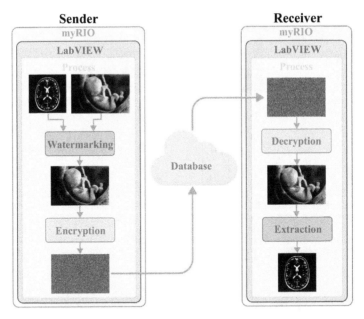

Figure 13.1   The architecture of the proposed approach

LabVIEW, follows a step-by-step process to embed watermarks, encrypt the data, and securely transmit it to the cloud for storage. The algorithm can later retrieve the encrypted data from the cloud, decrypt it, and recover the embedded watermark. Figure 13.1 outlines the key steps of the proposed algorithm. Indeed, the proposed algorithm combines watermarking and cryptography techniques to provide a robust and comprehensive security solution for multimedia data. By seamlessly integrating LabVIEW for implementation and utilizing the cloud for secure storage and retrieval, the algorithm ensures the confidentiality, integrity, and authenticity of the multimedia data, enabling authorized parties to securely access and recover the watermarked content while preserving its embedded information.

13.3.1   Watermarking algorithm

In the watermarking process, an original image is utilized as input to insert a binary image that is one-fourth the size of the original image. This insertion is achieved through the use of the Haar DWT in two dimensions (2D) as shown in Figure 13.2. The Haar DWT-2D is a widely employed technique for image decomposition and analysis.

13.3.1.1   The Haar DWT

The DWT is a widely utilized technique in the field of image processing and its various applications [14]. It involves the decomposition of an image into four sub-bands: a low pass band (LL) and three high pass bands corresponding to horizontal (HL), vertical (LH), and diagonal (HH) frequencies. This decomposition allows for

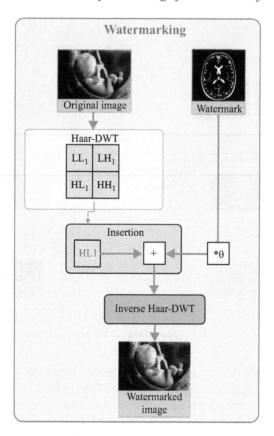

Figure 13.2   Flow chart of the watermarking process

capturing both coarse and fine details within the image. Moreover, the DWT can be iteratively applied to further decompose the low pass band, enabling a multi-level decomposition.

In image watermarking, the DWT has gained significant popularity due to its advantageous features such as excellent spatiotemporal localization and its correlation with the human visual system (HVS) [15]. By utilizing the DWT, watermark information can be precisely localized in both space and time domains, ensuring robustness against signal processing operations while minimizing visual distortion. The DWT's ability to exploit the characteristics of the HVS makes it an effective choice for embedding watermarks imperceptibly to human observers.

Figure 13.3 illustrates a one-level decomposition of the DWT, showcasing the separation of the image into the aforementioned sub-bands. This depiction visually represents the process of the DWT, highlighting the decomposition of the image into different frequency components for subsequent watermarking or analysis purposes.

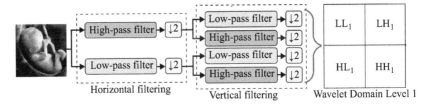

Figure 13.3 One-level decomposition of the DWT

13.3.1.2 Insertion process

The watermark insertion process in our system involves three essential data inputs: the Original Image (I), the Watermark (W), and the Visibility factor (θ).

$$W_{image} = I_{HL} + (\theta * Watermark)$$
$$with\{\theta : The\_Visibility\_Factor$$

(13.1)

These inputs play specific roles in preserving and protecting the data within the host document. First, The Original Image (I) serves as the host document, containing the data that needs to be safeguarded and retained. It forms the foundation for embedding the watermark and ensuring its seamless integration. Then, the Watermark (W) represents the information to be inserted into the image. In our case, the watermark is a binary mark. Finally, the Visibility factor (θ) determines the strength of the watermark's visibility in the image. This coefficient is carefully chosen to strike a balance between the watermark's robustness and its perceptibility. By adjusting the visibility factor, the system can maintain an optimal level of robustness while ensuring the watermark remains inconspicuous to the human eye.

By considering these three data inputs—the Original Image, the Watermark, and the Visibility factor—our system enables the effective insertion of binary watermarks, ensuring data preservation and protection in a manner that maintains both robustness and perceptual quality. The LabVIEW architecture of the insertion process is shown in Figure 13.4.

13.3.1.3 Extraction process

Similarly, the extraction process involves retrieving the watermark from the watermarked-decrypted image obtained during the embedding process in the DWT domain as shown in Figure 13.5.

This process entails subtracting the two obtained images and dividing the result by a common factor to obtain the extracted watermark. The extraction process utilizes three key functions:

• Decryption function: This function is used to decrypt the ciphered watermarked image, ensuring its accessibility and integrity.
• DWT/IDWT functions: These functions are applied to both the host image and the watermarked image obtained from the decryption process.

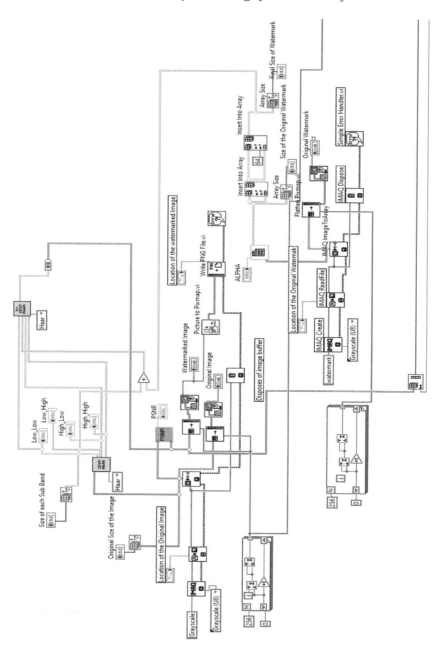

Figure 13.4   LabVIEW implementation of the insertion process

Figure 13.6 despite the front panel demonstrates the extraction results while Figure 13.7 details the different components used for the implementation of the extraction phase on the block diagram.

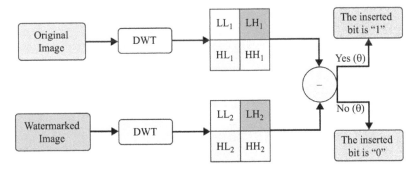

Figure 13.5   Extraction of i*th bit of watermark*

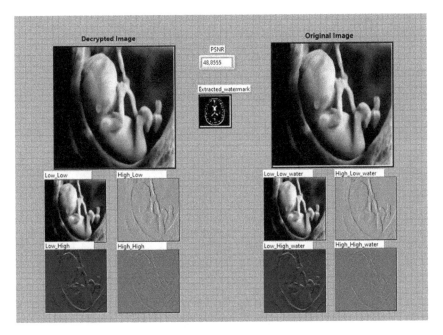

Figure 13.6   LabVIEW interface for extraction

13.3.2   Encryption algorithm

The encryption process in the proposed algorithm combines chaos-based key generation and confusion-diffusion properties to enhance the robustness and security of the algorithm as shown in Figure 13.8. By leveraging chaos theory, the algorithm achieves a high level of randomness and unpredictability in key generation, making it resistant to cryptographic attacks. Additionally, the confusion-diffusion technique further strengthens the encryption process by spreading the influence of each key bit throughout the entire encrypted data, providing a higher level of security.

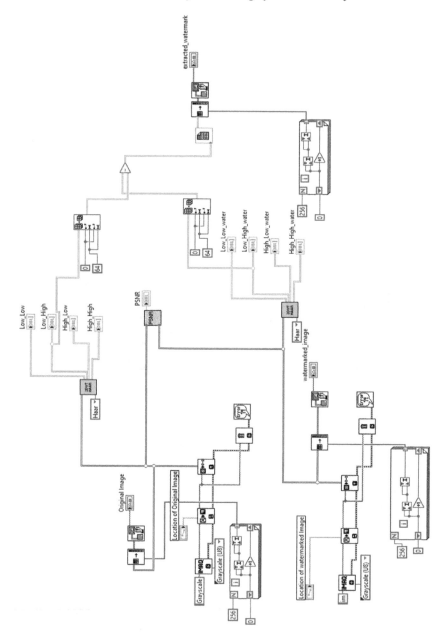

Figure 13.7   LabVIEW implementation of the extraction process

13.3.2.1   Key generation

Rossler chaotic system

The encryption process in the proposed algorithm incorporates the Rossler Chaotic System for key generation [16]. The Rossler system is a three-dimensional chaotic

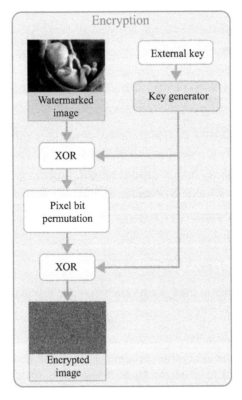

Figure 13.8   Flow chart of the encryption process

dynamical system first proposed by Otto E. Rossler in 1976 [17]. It is characterized by a set of nonlinear differential equations that describe the evolution of its state variables as in (13.2).

$$\begin{cases} \dot{x} = -x - z \\ \dot{y} = x + a * y \\ \dot{z} = z * x - z * c + b \end{cases} \tag{13.2}$$

With x, y, and z are the state variables, while a, b, and c are parameters that determine the behavior of the system. The Rossler system exhibits chaotic behavior for certain parameter values ($a = b = 0.2$ and $c = 5.7$), and initial conditions ($x_0 = y_0 = 1$ and $z_0 = 0$) leading to complex and irregular dynamics.

By utilizing the Rossler Chaotic System, the algorithm benefits from its unique properties, such as sensitivity to initial conditions and a wide range of chaotic behaviors, to enhance the security and robustness of the encryption process (Figure 13.9).

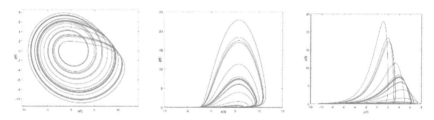

Figure 13.9   Chaotic attractors (x,y),(x,z),(y,z)

Euler's numerical resolution method is designated to solve these ODEs and discretize the Rossler Chaotic System for a 0.005 step size value:

$$x_{i+1} = x_i + \alpha \times f(x)$$
$$y_{i+1} = y_i + \alpha \times f(y) \quad\quad\quad\quad (13.3)$$
$$z_{i+1} = z_i + \alpha \times f(z)$$

Where x_i, y_i, and z_i present the system variables of the Rossler chaotic attractor and α is the discretization step.

13.3.2.2   Key sequences

In the proposed image encryption scheme, a pseudo-random number generator (PRNG) is employed to generate random sequences for cryptographic operations. The PRNG relies on an initial state obtained through an Initial State Generator module. In this study, the initial state is derived from the original image by applying the SHA-256 Hash function, resulting in a 256-bit external key. The chaotic dynamics of the Rossler attractor are then harnessed to generate a sequence of chaotic values [18]. Subsequently, these chaotic values are subjected to modulation using a modulation block, yielding the desired output. This process ensures the encryption of the image with a key derived from the original image's characteristics, enhancing the security and robustness of the encryption scheme.

13.4   Confusion

In the proposed image encryption scheme, the confusion step is implemented using the XOR (exclusive OR) operation. After generating the key sequence from the Rossler system and obtaining the watermarked image data, the XOR operation is applied between the key sequence and the image data. The XOR operation introduces confusion by combining the bits of the key sequence with the corresponding bits of the image data, resulting in a modified ciphertext. This bitwise operation ensures that each bit of the encrypted image is influenced by the corresponding bit of the key sequence, increasing the complexity and non-linearity of the encrypted data.

13.5 Diffusion

To further enhance the security of the image encryption scheme, a diffusion step involving pixel bit permutation is incorporated. This step aims to disperse the information across the image, reducing any correlations between neighboring pixels and spreading the influence of each bit throughout the entire image. The diffusion step involves rearranging the bits of each pixel in a controlled and systematic manner. In fact, the bit positions within each pixel are permuted according to a specific permutation algorithm. By shuffling the bit positions within the pixels, the diffusion step ensures that changes in one bit affect multiple pixels and vice versa, increasing the complexity and mixing of the encrypted image data.

Figure 13.10 shows the different blocks implemented using LabVIEW of the encryption process starting with the Initial Key, The Rossler Chaotic System, The Modulation Block, and finally the Encryption Sub.VI.

13.6 LabVIEW implementation

13.6.1 Programmation LabVIEW

LabVIEW is a powerful programming language and development environment that offers a seamless platform for implementing the crypto-watermarking system on MyRIO [19]. With LabVIEW's graphical programming approach, the development and integration of the system's cryptographic and watermarking functionalities become more intuitive and efficient. Using LabVIEW, the cryptographic algorithms can be implemented through a combination of built-in functions and custom-designed modules. LabVIEW provides a comprehensive set of cryptographic functions and libraries, allowing for the secure encryption and decryption of multimedia data. Furthermore, its graphical nature simplifies the implementation of watermarking techniques. Watermarking algorithms can be designed and implemented using the extensive library of image-processing functions [20]. The graphical programming paradigm allows for a visual representation of the watermarking process, making it easier to understand and modify the algorithm as needed. Figure 13.11 describes the design flow using LabVIEW.

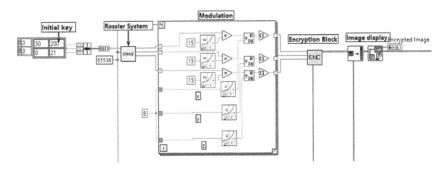

Figure 13.10   LabVIEW implementation of the encryption process

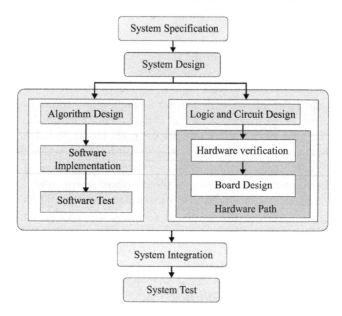

Figure 13.11   LabVIEW design flow showing separate software and hardware design flows

On the other hand, MyRIO, a versatile embedded system platform, can be seamlessly integrated with LabVIEW for real-time execution of the crypto-watermarking system. LabVIEW provides dedicated modules for MyRIO that enable seamless communication between the software and hardware components. This integration ensures the efficient execution of the system on the MyRIO plat-form, enabling real-time processing and secure data transmission (Figure 13.12).

13.6.2   Data storage

Cloud storage for medical data has emerged as a reliable and efficient solution for healthcare organizations to manage their vast volumes of patient information [21]. By leveraging cloud technology, medical facilities can securely store, access, and share medical records, images, and other critical data. One of the key advantages of using the cloud for medical data storage is its scalability. Healthcare providers deal with ever-increasing amounts of patient data, including EHRs, medical images, and diagnostic reports. Cloud storage offers the flexibility to expand storage capacity as needed, eliminating the constraints of physical infrastructure limitations. This scalability ensures that healthcare organizations can accommodate the growing volume of medical data without compromising performance or incurring significant upfront costs. Cloud storage also enhances data accessibility and availability. Authorized healthcare professionals can securely access patient records and medi-cal images from anywhere, at any time, using internet-connected devices [3]. This enables seamless collaboration among healthcare providers, improving care

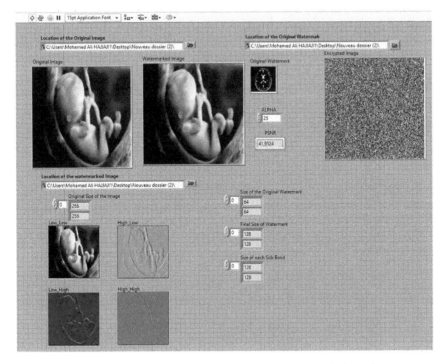

Figure 13.12   LabVIEW interface of the proposed algorithm

coordination and facilitating remote consultations. Figure 13.13 explains the Cloud Exchange process, while Figures 13.14 and 13.15 show the LabVIEW blocks for send and receive respectively.

13.6.3   Proposed system implementation on MyRIO

NI MyRIO is an innovative tool that enables users to leverage the capabilities of the LabVIEW RIO architecture, a widely accepted and industry-proven hardware/ software design approach while providing a gradual learning curve for advanced embedded and FPGA programming concepts. With NI MyRIO, users gain access to powerful hardware and software technologies necessary for their projects.

The implementation of the crypto-watermarking system involves utilizing LabVIEW to develop separate encoder and decoder components. The watermark loading process involves retrieving the watermark from an array. To facilitate this process, the NI MyRIO device must be connected to a computer, as depicted in Figure 13.16.

13.7   Experimental results and interpretation

Ensuring the validity and robustness of our algorithm goes beyond testing it against various attack types. To achieve this, we subjected the watermarked and encrypted

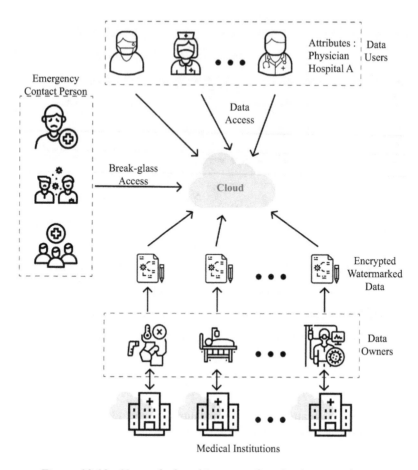

Figure 13.13   Networked architecture of medical image sharing

medical image to a range of attacks. Subsequently, we assessed the sensitivity of the embedded watermark and its ability to detect any changes in the image. Following the application of each attack, we extracted the entire embedded watermark and compared it with the original marks (i.e., the original watermark and the extracted watermark) to ensure that these marks remained undamaged despite the applied attacks. The validation of our system was conducted based on three factors:

1. Performance evaluation: This involves assessing the efficiency and effectiveness of the encryption algorithm in terms of computational speed, resource utilization, and resistance against cryptographic attacks.
2. Evaluation of psycho-visual image quality: We analyze the impact of the encryption process on the perceptual quality of the image. This assessment considers factors such as image fidelity, visual artifacts, and the preservation of important visual features.

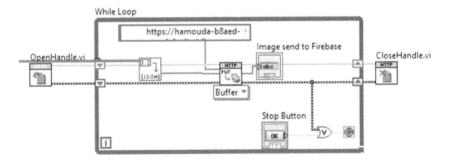

Figure 13.14   LabVIEW block for data sent to Cloud

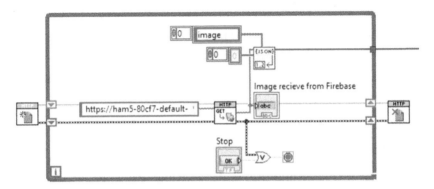

Figure 13.15   LabVIEW block for data received from Cloud

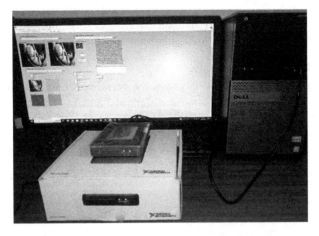

Figure 13.16   Real-time implementation

3. Evaluation of the inserted data: We examine the integrity and accuracy of the inserted data, ensuring that the encrypted image retains the embedded information without any loss or corruption.

13.7.1   Evaluation of the encryption process

The evaluation of the encryption algorithm involves the consideration of multiple criteria, among which the histogram and entropy play significant roles. These two factors are crucial in assessing the performance and quality of the encryption process. By incorporating the analysis of histogram and entropy as evaluation criteria, we gain valuable insights into the performance, fidelity, and security aspects of the encryption algorithm. These evaluations help us ensure the effectiveness and reliability of the encryption process in safeguarding multimedia data.

13.7.1.1   Histogram analysis

The histogram analysis provides insights into the distribution of pixel intensities in the encrypted image. By examining the histogram, we can evaluate the preservation of image details, such as contrast and brightness levels. A well-distributed histogram indicates that the encryption algorithm effectively maintains the original image characteristics (Figure 13.17).

13.7.1.2   Entropy

Entropy measures the randomness and uncertainty of the encrypted image. A high entropy value signifies a higher level of randomness, indicating a stronger encryption scheme. By analyzing the entropy, we can assess the robustness and security of the encryption algorithm against statistical attacks (Table 13.1).

13.7.1.3   Keys space

The proposed encryption technique employs a key space that can be calculated using the formula: $2^{n*c*p} = 2^{3*3*32}$. Following the condition stated by [22], the key size is greater than 2^{100}, ensuring resistance against brute force attacks. In this technique, the key generator consists of the Rossler Chaotic System, which has three parameters (p) and three initial conditions (c) encoded on 32 bits (n).

13.7.1.4   Differential analysis

Differential analysis is employed to assess the performance of the utilized cryptosystem in terms of its resistance against differential attacks. This analysis involves comparing the original image with its encrypted counterpart using metrics such as NPCR (Number of Pixels Change Rate) and UACI (Unified Average Changing Intensity). The obtained results, presented in Table 13.2, demonstrate excellent performance with a pixel change rate of up to 99.92% and an average changing intensity exceeding 33.81%.

13.7.2   Evaluation of the image quality: PSNR and WPSNR

To assess the effectiveness of a watermarking method, it is essential to consider various factors that influence the quality of the image. In previous studies [23],

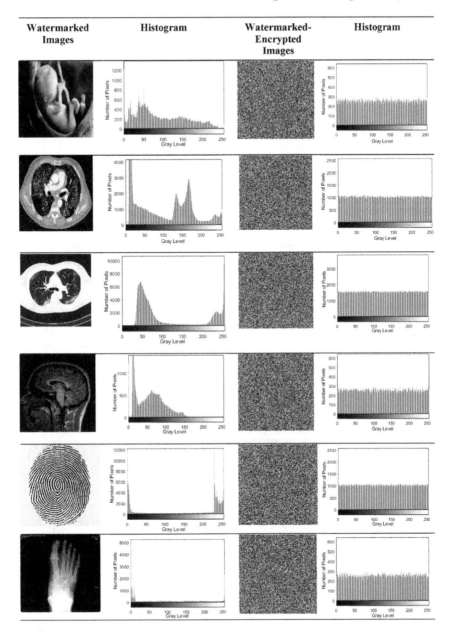

Figure 13.17   Histograms of different encrypted-watermarked medical images and their equivalent watermarked images.

significant attention has been given to the development of objective measures that aim to provide an accurate evaluation. These objective measures are derived from a comparison between the received watermarked image and the original image. The

Table 13.1   Entropy values of the watermarked and watermarked-encrypted
            images

Image	Watermarked image	Encrypted-watermarked image
Ultrasound-Baby	7.267972	7.996888
CT-Scan	7.368242	7.999219
Radio	4.729450	7.997245
Brain-MRI	6.649341	7.999231
Finger print	5.222935	7.999436
Covid pneumonia	6.402862	7.999533

Table 13.2   NPCR and UACI values watermarked-encrypted images

Image	NPCR %	UACI %
Ultrasound-Baby	99.91923	33.81259
CT-Scan	99.89258	33.79524
Radio	99.96120	33.80110
Brain-MRI	99.95136	33.80986
Finger print	99.87258	33.81965
Covid pneumonia	99.90012	33.75203

evaluation of image quality in our system involves the use of two important metrics: Peak Signal-to-Noise Ratio (PSNR) and Weighted Peak Signal-to-Noise Ratio (WPSNR). PSNR is a widely used metric that quantifies the difference between the original and reconstructed image. WPSNR, on the other hand, is an enhanced version of PSNR that takes into account the HVS's sensitivity to different image regions. By evaluating image quality using both PSNR and WPSNR, we gain a comprehensive understanding of the fidelity and perceptual quality of the reconstructed image. These metrics allow us to quantitatively measure the effectiveness of our watermarking and encryption techniques in preserving image quality and ensuring robust data protection. Through the evaluation of PSNR and WPSNR, we can validate the performance of our system and make informed decisions regarding the optimization and improvement of our crypto-watermarking algorithm.

13.7.2.1   Peak signal-to-noise ratio (PSNR)

PSNR measures the ratio of the peak signal power to the mean squared error (MSE) between the original and reconstructed image. To ensure a satisfactory embedding quality, a minimum PSNR value of 40 dBs is typically accepted. A higher PSNR value indicates a smaller difference between the two images, indicating better image quality (a higher level of embedding quality), meaning that the watermarked image experiences minimal distortion. On the other hand, a lower PSNR value suggests a more significant level of distortion, making the alterations noticeable to

Table 13.3   Variation of the PSNR and WPSNR in function of the visibility factor θ

θ	10		20		40	
Image	**PSNR (dB)**	**WPSNR (dB)**	**PSNR (dB)**	**WPSNR (dB)**	**PSNR (dB)**	**WPSNR (dB)**
Ultrasound-Baby baby	56.7895	58.0.215	46.0235	48.1000	42.9980	42.0018
CT-Scan	49.2586	51.0103	42.1526	41.2993	40.1012	40.0126
Radio	51.1256	52.9564	47.9206	48.1755	44.0010	43.9210
Brain-MRI	49.4931	50.0290	43.7981	43.4930	41.9586	41.3980
Finger print	53.2584	54.2569	48.0590	45.9125	43.2125	43.0009
Covid pneumonia	56.2589	56.0011	50.6584	49.0009	45.5569	44.9029

the HVS and easily detectable.

$$(PSNR)_{dB} = 10\log_{10}\left\{ N * M \left[\frac{MaxI^2_{(i,j)}}{\sum_{i,j}[I_{(i,j)} - W_{(i,j)}]} \right] \right\} \tag{13.4}$$

In the evaluation of the watermarking process, the grayscale intensity values of the pixels in the original and watermarked image denoted as I_{ij} and W_{ij}, respectively, are compared. In Equation (13.4), M and N represent the number of rows and columns in both the original and watermarked images. By considering the PSNR metric as shown in Table 13.3, we can assess the quality of the watermarking process and determine whether the distortion introduced during embedding remains within acceptable limits. Achieving a high PSNR value is desirable as it indicates a closer resemblance between the watermarked and original images, ensuring that the watermarking process preserves the visual integrity of the image.

13.7.2.2   Weighted peak signal-to-noise ratio (WPSNR)

Currently, the widely adopted metric for assessing embedding quality is WPSNR [13]. Unlike traditional PSNR, WPSNR takes into account the texture masking effect, making it a more accurate evaluation metric. This effect refers to the increased imperceptibility of noise-like secure data due to the presence of similar noise patterns in the cover image. Specifically, in regions with prominent textures, the embedded secure data becomes less noticeable. WPSNR is primarily calculated in the spatial domain and is not a feasible metric for frequency domain embedding. By incorporating this factor, WPSNR provides a more comprehensive assessment of the visibility and perceptibility of the embedded data in different regions of the image.

$$(WPSNR)_{dB} = 10\log_{10}\left(\frac{Max(I)^2_{(i,j)}}{\|NVF(W_{(i,j)} - I_{(i,j)}\|^2} \right) \tag{13.5}$$

Where I and W are the cover and watermarked images, respectively. Moreover, the noise visibility function (NVF) refers to the phenomenon where the visibility or perceptibility of noise-like secure data is influenced by the presence of similar noisy effects in the cover image [5]. In other words, the NVF describes how the visibility of embedded data is affected by the characteristics of the image, particularly in relation to the presence of texture or noise patterns. The best-known form of NVF is given as:

$$(NVF)_{(i,j)} = \left(\frac{1}{1 + \theta \sigma_x^2(i,j)} \right) \tag{13.6}$$

where $\sigma_x^2(i,j)$ denotes the local variance of the image in a window centered on the pixel with coordinates (i,j), $1 \leq i,j \leq M$ and θ is a tuning parameter corresponding to the particular image.

13.7.3 Effect of visibility factor

The impact of the visibility factor can be seen in Table 13.3, illustrating that as the value of (θ) increases, the watermark becomes more visible. This effect is further supported by the PSNR and WPSNR, where the PSNR decreases from 56.7895 dB to 42.0018 dB with an increasing visibility factor (from 10 to 40).

It is known that the PSNR and WPSNR values are considered good if they exceed 30 dB for ordinary images while they are considered good if they exceed 40 dB for medical images. Hence, it is noted that the results obtained by measuring PSNR and WPSNR between the original image and the watermarked image are highly favorable.

13.7.4 Evaluation of the watermarking algorithm

The evaluation of reliability or accuracy of the detected data is determined by calculating the distances between the inserted watermark and the detected watermark. This assessment is conducted using the Normalized Cross-Correlation (NCC) measure. The NCC measure allows for the comparison of the inserted watermark and the detected watermark, providing insights into the similarity or dissimilarity between the two. By quantifying the correlation between these two sets of data, the NCC measure enables the determination of the reliability of the detected watermark.

$$NCC_{(W,Wext)} = \frac{\sum_M \sum_N (W_{MN} - W_W)(Wext_{MN} - W_{Wext})}{\sigma_W \sigma_{Wext}} \tag{13.7}$$

With

$$\sigma_W = \sqrt{\sum_{M,N} (W_{MN} - W_W)^2}$$
$$\sigma_{Wext} = \sqrt{\sum_{M,N} (W_{MN} - W_{Wext})^2} \tag{13.8}$$

By employing the NCC measure, researchers and practitioners can assess the performance of watermarking algorithms in terms of the accuracy of watermark detection. This measure plays a crucial role in validating the robustness and effectiveness of watermarking techniques, ensuring that the embedded data can be reliably retrieved and identified from the watermarked content.

Simulated results of WPSNR, PSNR, and NC values between the Watermarked Ultrasound-Baby Image, Encrypted Watermarked Image, and Decrypted Watermarked Image before applying any attacks are depicted in Figure 13.18. To thoroughly analyze the robustness of our system, we have chosen to apply commonly encountered attacks such as JPEG attacks, Gaussian noise, and Cropping [24]. After subjecting the Ultrasound-Baby medical image to these attacks, our objective is to extract the watermark and calculate the NC value. This calculation enables us to assess the algorithm's ability to withstand multiple attacks (Table 13.4).

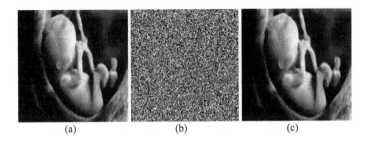

(a)　　　　　　　　(b)　　　　　　　　(c)

Figure 13.18　Evaluation of imperceptibility and robustness of watermark without attacks for θ = 10. (a) Watermarked Ultrasound-Baby Image, (b) Encrypted Watermarked Image, and (c) Decrypted Watermarked Image.

Table 13.4　Evaluation of the NC values of the encrypted, watermarked, and attacked Ultrasound-Baby image by JPEG, Gaussian noise, and Cropping attacks

Image	Ultrasound-Baby					
Attack	*JPEG Gaussian noise Cropping*					
	Rate %	**NCC**	**Variance**	**NCC**	**Windowsize**	**NCC**
	10	1	0.001	1	[2*2]	1
	20	1	0.002	1	[4*4]	1
	30	1	0.003	1	[16*16]	1
	40	1	0.004	1	[32*32]	1
	50	1	0.005	1	[64*64]	1
	60	1	0.006	1	[128*128]	0.82
	70	0.85	0.007	0.91	[256*256]	0.42
	80	0.6	0.008	0.89		
	90	0.4	0.009	0.35		

In the existing literature, a NCC value equal to or greater than 0.75 is considered acceptable for the extracted watermark [25]. In the field of medical imaging, the watermark embedded in the image should be imperceptible. The watermarked image should closely resemble the original host image. The significance of our algorithm lies in its ability to withstand various types of attacks, ensuring the extracted watermark remains unmodified. After each attack is applied, we extract the embedded watermark and compare it with the original watermark. The objective is to verify that the watermark remains unchanged despite the attacks imposed on the watermarked image. Hence, regardless of the watermarking system used, achieving excellent values of PSNR, WPSNR, and an NCC of 1 is of utmost importance [26].

13.8   Conclusion

In this study, a combined approach involving watermarking and encryption systems was proposed for embedding patient information into medical images. The primary objective of the watermarking technique is to ensure the integrity and traceability of the medical image, while cryptography is employed to safeguard the confidentiality of patient data. By integrating these two systems, the proposed approach exhibits enhanced robustness against various types of attacks. To achieve this robustness, several techniques are employed. The Haar DWT is utilized to improve the integrity of the watermark, while the SHA-2 hash function and chaos are employed to strengthen the encryption process and enhance the security of the watermark against different attack scenarios. The combination of these techniques provides a comprehensive solution that meets the requirements of medical imaging, as it leverages multiple algorithms to enhance image quality and ensure the successful extraction of all patient data. By adopting this approach, the study aims to overcome the limitations of existing methods and provide an effective solution for embedding patient information into medical images. The successful implementation of the proposed system using LabVIEW on the MyRIO board, along with its integration with cloud storage and retrieval, underscores its effectiveness in preserving the integrity, confidentiality, and accessibility of medical images. The combination of watermarking, encryption, and cloud-based storage offers a comprehensive solution for safeguarding sensitive medical data.

References

[1]   Abu-Faraj, M., Al-Hyari, A., Altaharwa, I., Alqadi, Z., and Ali, B. (2023). Increasing the security of transmitted text messages using chaotic key and image key cryptography. *International Journal of Data and Network Science*, 7(2), 809–820.

[2]   Şahin, M. E. (2023). Memristor-based hyperchaotic system and DNA encoding based image encryption application on LabVIEW. *International Journal of Engineering Research and Development*, 15(1), 269–276.

[3] Arumugham, S., Rajagopalan, S., Rayappan, J. B. B., and Amirtharajan, R. (2018). Networked medical data sharing on secure medium: A web publishing mode for DICOM viewer with three layer authentication. *Journal of Biomedical Informatics*, *86*, 90–105.

[4] Amdouni, R., Gafsi, M., Abbassi, N., Hajjaji, M. A., and Mtibaa, A. (2023). Robust hardware implementation of a block-cipher scheme based on chaos and biological algebraic operations. *Multimedia Tools and Applications*, 1–34.

[5] Levický, D., and Foriš, P. (2004). "Human visual system models in digital image watermarking." *Radioengineering* 13.4 38–43.

[6] Ajili, S., Hajjaji, M. A., and Mtibaa, A. (2015). "Hybrid SVD-DWT watermarking technique using AES algorithm for medical image safe transfer." In: *2015 16th International Conference on Sciences and Techniques of Automatic Control and Computer Engineering (STA)*. Piscataway, NJ: IEEE, p. 69–74.

[7] Aparna, P. and Kishore, P. V. V. (2019). "A blind medical image watermarking for secure E-healthcare application using crypto-watermarking system." *Journal of Intelligent Systems* 29.1 1558–1575.

[8] Bhat, B., Ali, A. W. and Gupta, A. (2015). "DES and AES performance evaluation." *International Conference on Computing, Communication & Automation*. Piscataway, NJ: IEEE.

[9] Huang, L-C., Feng, T-H. and Hwang, M-S. (2017). "A new lossless embedding techniques based on HDWT." *IETE Technical Review* 34.1 40–47.

[10] Hamidi, M., El Haziti, M., Cherifi, H., *et al.* (2021). A hybrid robust image watermarking method based on DWT-DCT and SIFT for copyright protection. *Journal of Imaging*, 7.10, 218.

[11] Şahin, M. E., Bulut, G. G. and Güler, H. (2018). An implementation of chaotic circuits with Multisim-LabVIEW. *International Advanced Researches and Engineering Journal*, 2.3, 304–308.

[12] Yadav, D. K., Singh, S., Pujari, S. and Mishra, P. (2015). Fingerprint based attendance system using microcontroller and LabView. *International Journal of Advanced Research in Electrical, Electronics and Instrumentation Engineering*, 4.6, 5111–5121.

[13] Hosam, O. and Halima, N. B. (2016). "Adaptive block-based pixel value differencing steganography." *Security and Communication Networks* 9.18 5036–5050.

[14] Stanković, R. S. and Bogdan J. F. (2003). "The Haar wavelet transform: Its status and achievements." *Computers & Electrical Engineering* 29.1 25–44.

[15] Zhang, Y. (2009). "Blind watermark algorithm based on HVS and RBF neural network in DWT domain." *WSEAS Transactions on Computers* 8.1 174–183.

[16] Sundara Krishnan, K., Suhaila, S. and Raja, S. P. (2022). "A novel medical image encryption using Rössler system." *Intelligent Automation & Soft Computing* 33.2 1081–1101.

[17] Li, C. and Chen, G. (2004). "Chaos and hyperchaos in the fractional-order Rössler equations." *Physica A: Statistical Mechanics and its Applications* 341, 55–61.

[18] Mandal, M. K., Kar, M., Singh, S. K., *et al.* (2014). "Symmetric key image encryption using chaotic Rossler system." *Security and Communication Networks*, 7.11, 2145–2152.

[19] Odema, M., Adly, I. and Ghali, H. A. (2019). "LabVIEW-based interactive remote experimentation implementation using NI myRIO." *2019 International Conference on Innovative Trends in Computer Engineering (ITCE)*. Piscataway, NJ: IEEE.

[20] Klinger, Thomas. (2003). *Image Processing with LabVIEW and IMAQ Vision.* Prentice-Hall Professional.

[21] Yang, Y., Zheng, X., Guo, W., Liu, X. and Chang, V. (2019). "Privacy-preserving smart IoT-based healthcare big data storage and self-adaptive access control system." *Information Sciences*, 479, 567–592.

[22] Sirichotedumrong, W. and Kiya, H. (2019). "Grayscale-based block scrambling image encryption using ycbcr color space for encryption-then-compression systems." *APSIPA Transactions on Signal and Information Processing* 8 e7.

[23] Hajjaji, M. A., Gafsi, M. and Mtibaa, A. (2019). "Discrete cosine transform space for hiding patient information in the medical images." *2019 IEEE International Conference on Design & Test of Integrated Micro & Nano-Systems (DTS)*. Piscataway, NJ: IEEE.

[24] Singh, P., and Chadha, R. S. (2013). "A survey of digital watermarking techniques, applications and attacks." *International Journal of Engineering and Innovative Technology (IJEIT)* 2.9 165–175.

[25] Hajjaji, M. A., Albouchi, A. and Mtibaa, A. (2019). "Combining DWT/KLT for secure transfer of color images." 2019 *IEEE International Conference on Design & Test of Integrated Micro & Nano-Systems (DTS)*. Piscataway, NJ: IEEE.

[26] Ajili, S., Hajjaji, M. A., Bouallegue, B. and Mtibaa, A. (2014). "Joint watermarking\encryption image for safe transmission: Application on medical imaging." In *2014 Global Summit on Computer & Information Technology (GSCIT)* (pp. 1–6). Piscataway, NJ: IEEE.

Chapter 14
Conclusion
Zhihan Lyu[1]

The digitization of data brings increasing importance to multimedia digital security How, current technology faces challenges such as increased data volume and resource demands Future research should focus on intelligent and adaptable solutions, as well as protecting privacy Practical and comprehensive approaches are needed to address these challenges and ensure the reliability of multimedia security technology.

14.1 The development and future trend of multimedia watermarking technology

Recent studies have shown significant progress in the development of multimedia watermarking technology, which has broad application value in protecting digital copyright and multimedia content. Agarwal *et al.* [1] proposed a digital watermarking algorithm based on discrete cosine transform and genetic algorithm to improve the robustness of color images in multimedia applications and concealment. Gutub [2] proposed a semi-authenticated multimedia audio watermarking technique based on counting key sharing to improve audio robustness and concealment. Moad *et al.* [3] proposed a wavelet transform-based digital watermarking scheme for medical images to improve the concealment and robustness of images in telemedicine applications. Al-Otum *et al.* [4] designed a multimedia double watermarking scheme based on multi-threshold segmentation and local quantization to protect the copyright of multimedia. Dzhanashia *et al.* [5] proposed a low-complexity digital watermarking method based on neural networks and multiple embedding templates to improve the robustness and concealment of multimedia. Yang *et al.* [6] summarized the research development and future challenges in multimedia security and privacy protection in the Internet of Things, proposing some solutions and future research directions.

Sahu *et al.* [7] provided a comprehensive overview of digital watermarking technology, including its basic concepts, existing technologies, research

[1]Department of Game Design, Faculty of Arts, Uppsala University, Sweden

opportunities, and challenges. Alshathri *et al.* [8] proposed an audio water-marking scheme based on mirrored electronically stored medical images, which showed high concealment and robustness. Amine *et al.* [9] developed a digital watermarking scheme based on wavelet transform to improve the security of remote transmission of medical images, demonstrating improved image robust-ness and concealment while maintaining image quality. Pal *et al.* [10] designed a medical image watermarking method based on a support vector machine (SVM) and wavelet transform, which showed good robustness and concealment. Sayahi *et al.* [11] proposed a multi-resolution three-dimensional (3D) grid digital watermarking scheme based on spherical harmonic functions and wavelet transform to improve the robustness and concealment of 3D models. Verma *et al.* [12] proposed a digital image watermarking scheme based on important block selection, which demonstrated good robustness and concealment and can effectively protect image data.

Figure 14.1 illustrates the structural relationship between multimedia encryp-tion algorithms and multimedia digital security.

In conclusion, diverse digital watermarking schemes have been extensively investigated and employed in medical images, 3D models, and IoT applications. These schemes leverage advanced techniques, including wavelet transform, SVM, and spherical harmonic function, to improve the concealment and robustness of images and to safeguard image data from tampering. Nevertheless,

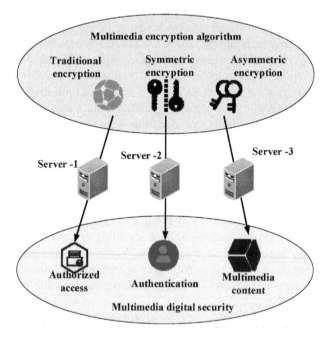

Figure 14.1   The relationship structure of the multimedia encryption algorithm and multimedia digital security

digital watermarking technology still confronts challenges when faced with distinct application scenarios and attack methods. Consequently, future research endeavors should delve deeper into the technical issues in the digital watermarking domain and formulate more efficient and resilient digital watermarking schemes.

14.2   The development and future trend of multimedia encryption technology

Jayapandian [13] proposed a cloud-based dynamic scheduling system for multimedia data encryption using the Tabu search algorithm. The study aimed to analyze the progress of digital multimedia encryption technology by modeling the algorithm abstractly and conducting numerical experiments to compare and analyze the performance of different algorithms. The results demonstrated that the encryption system designed could efficiently carry out encryption tasks in the field of cloud computing, indicating the potential of using the Tabu search algorithm for dynamic scheduling in multimedia encryption. Roy *et al.* [14] proposed a novel image encryption technique based on the Von-Neumann method for computer vision and IoT applications. The authors implemented this technique in MATLAB® and conducted experimental tests on various aspects of image encryption. The results demonstrated that the proposed technique has high practical value in image encryption. Faragallah *et al.* [15] presented a novel encryption framework that combines watermarking and selective encryption to enhance communication security. The authors explored the encryption algorithm using air domain and transform domain methods and demonstrated the implementation of the results in the field of secure communication. Naik *et al.* [16] reviewed the application of chaotic maps in the fields of pseudo-random number generators and encryption. The author discusses the development of chaotic maps in encryption technology, applies it to stream cipher storage, and evaluates the simulation experiments. The results indicated that applying it to the encryption field can greatly improve the efficiency of the algorithm. In their recent study, Srinivasan *et al.* [17] have introduced a novel approach to multimedia data security processing in medical applications, which is of great significance in protecting the confidentiality and privacy of sensitive medical data. By exploring encryption technology, the authors proposed an efficient and fast encryption scheme and evaluated its effectiveness through experimental tests on actual medical data. The proposed approach has potential applications in various fields where multimedia data security is crucial. Nassar *et al.* [18] discussed confidentiality considerations and effective security models when transmitting multimedia signals under different wireless channels. Experimental results demonstrate that the prototype model can provide better security performance and confidentiality.

Erkan *et al.* [19] introduced an image encryption technology that is based on the double Schaffer functions and employs a 2D chaotic map model for basic operations. They have applied this technology in the field of image encryption and tested the results using numerical experiments to demonstrate their safety and practicality. Li [20] proposed an optimized network information security communication encryption algorithm that aims to improve data transmission efficiency by optimizing the algorithm and applying it to network communication. The performance of the encryption algorithm has been explored through experiments, and the results indicate that the algorithm has a high success rate and practicality in network communication. In the realm of cryptography, recent research efforts have been devoted to enhancing the security of multimedia data. Srinivasan *et al.* introduced a novel approach to multimedia data encryption in medical applications, which employs fast encryption techniques. Meanwhile, Ullah *et al.* [21] conducted a comprehensive review of elliptic curve cryptography, analyzing its history, development, and technical challenges and providing insights into the future prospects of this field. In terms of image encryption, Hebbale *et al.* [22] proposed an encryption method that uses Tuna Swarm Optimization, 3D chaotic mapping, and DNA encoding to achieve efficient image compression while maintaining high levels of security. Trung *et al.* [23], on the other hand, designed an encryption system based on elliptic curve cryptography and Vigenère symmetric keys, which demonstrated superior performance in security and practicality. Saleem *et al.* [24] proposed a secure information processing method for multimedia forensics, based on the zero-trust security model, which is applicable to large-scale data analysis in a SaaS cloud computing environment. The experimental results indicate that the proposed method can effectively ensure the security and reliability of data.

These studies have contributed to the understanding and development of current security technology applications and trends. Each study proposes a unique method for ensuring secure data transmission and examines its performance. These methods include image encryption techniques utilizing chaotic maps and Schaffer functions, optimized communication encryption algorithms for network information security, comprehensive research on elliptic cryptography, and multimedia forensics methods based on zero-trust security models. By improving the efficiency of data transmission while maintaining communication data security, these methods showcase the vast potential and applicability of current security technologies.

14.3   Conclusion

As the digitization of data continues to expand and be utilized in various fields, the issue of multimedia digital security is becoming increasingly critical. Security issues such as copyright protection, identity verification, data tampering, and data forgery have become more prevalent. However, current multimedia digital security technology faces challenges and shortcomings, such as digital watermarking technology leading to increased data volume and quality degradation. Certain technologies have high computing resource demands that could affect system speed and efficiency. These limitations highlight the need for more efficient and flexible multimedia security solutions that can meet the diverse needs and applications of different scenarios, prompting further research in this area.

As the use of digitized data continues to expand across various fields, it is imperative to address the challenges and shortcomings of multimedia digital security technology. One promising research direction is to develop more intelligent and adaptive multimedia digital security technology. Achieving this goal requires the integration of artificial intelligence and machine learning to automate multimedia digital security and make it adaptable to different scenarios and needs. Another crucial research direction is to protect the privacy of multimedia data. In the era of big data, where the leakage of personal information and privacy is a growing concern, the prevention of misuse or leakage of multimedia data becomes a crucial research area. Finally, future research needs to consider practical application scenarios and develop more comprehensive and feasible solutions to address the challenges faced by multimedia digital security technology. This approach will ensure the reliability and practicability of multimedia digital security technology and enable it to continue to adapt and evolve in an ever-changing information security environment.

References

[1]   Agarwal, N., Singh, PK: 'Discrete cosine transforms and genetic algorithm based watermarking method for robustness and imperceptibility of color images for intelligent multimedia applications', *Multimedia tools and applications*, 2022, 81(14), pp. 19751–19777.

[2]   Gutub, A.: 'Regulating watermarking semi-authentication of multimedia audio via counting-based secret sharing', *Pamukkale Üniversitesi Mühendislik Bilimleri Dergisi*, 2022, 28(2), pp. 324–332.

[3]   Moad, MS, Kafi, MR, Khaldi, A.: 'A wavelet based medical image watermarking scheme for secure transmission in telemedicine applications', *Microprocessors and Microsystems*, 2022, 90, pp. 104490.

[4]   Al-Otum, HM: 'Dual image watermarking using a multi-level thresholding and selective zone-quantization for copyright protection, authentication and recovery applications', *Multimedia Tools and Applications*, 2022, 81(18), pp. 25787–25828.

[5]   Dzhanashia, K., Evsutin, O.: 'Low complexity template-based watermarking with neural networks and various embedding templates', *Computers and Electrical Engineering*, 2022, 102, pp. 108194.

[6]   Yang, W., Wang, S., Hu, J., *et al.*: 'Multimedia security and privacy protection in the internet of things: research developments and challenges', *International Journal of Multimedia Intelligence and Security*, 2022, 4(1), pp. 20–46.

[7]   Sahu, AK, Umachandran, K., Biradar, VD, *et al.*: 'A Study on Content Tampering in Multimedia Watermarking', *SN Computer Science*, 2023, 4(3), pp. 1–11.

[8]   Alshathri, S., Hemdan, EED: 'An efficient audio watermarking scheme with scrambled medical images for secure medical internet of things systems', *Multimedia Tools and Applications*, 2023, pp. 1–19.

[9]   Amine, K., Redouane, KM, Sayah, MM: 'A wavelet-based watermarking for secure medical image transmission in telemedicine application', *Multimedia Tools and Applications*, 2023, pp. 1–17.

[10]   Pal, P., Chowdhuri, P., Si, T.: 'A novel watermarking scheme for medical image using support vector machine and lifting wavelet transform', *Multimedia Tools and Applications*, 2023, pp. 1–20.

[11]   Sayahi, I., Jallouli, M., Mabrouk, AB, *et al.*: 'Robust hybrid watermarking approach for 3D multiresolution meshes based on spherical harmonics and wavelet transform', *Multimedia Tools and Applications*, 2023, pp. 1–26.

[12]   Verma, VS, Gupta, S., Gupta, P.: 'Image data protection in IoT applications using significant block selection based image watermarking', *Multimedia Tools and Applications*, 2023, 82(4), pp. 5073–5090.

[13]   Jayapandian, N.: 'Cloud dynamic scheduling for multimedia data encryption using Tabu search algorithm', *Wireless Personal Communications*, 2021, 120(3), pp. 2427–2447.

[14]   Roy, S., Shrivastava, M., Pandey, CV, *et al.*: 'IEVCA: An efficient image encryption technique for IoT applications using 2-D Von-Neumann cellular automata', *Multimedia Tools and Applications*, 2021, 80, pp. 31529–31567.

[15]   Faragallah, OS, El- Shafai, W., Sallam, AI, *et al.*: 'Cybersecurity framework of hybrid watermarking and selective encryption for secure HEVC communication', *Journal of Ambient Intelligence and Humanized Computing*, 2022, pp. 1–25.

[16]   Naik, RB, Singh, U.: 'A review on applications of chaotic maps in pseudo-random number generators and encryption', *Annals of Data Science*, 2022, pp. 1–26.

[17]   Srinivasan, K., Rathee, G., Raja, MR, *et al.*: 'Secure multimedia data processing scheme in medical applications', *Multimedia Tools and Applications*, 2022, pp. 1–12.

[18]   Nassar, SS, El- Bendary, MAM: 'Confidentiality considerations: multimedia signals transmission over different wireless channels utilized efficient secured model', *Multimedia Tools and Applications*, 2022, 81(18), pp. 25707–25744.

[19]   Erkan, U., Toktas, A., Lai, Q.: '2D hyperchaotic system based on Schaffer function for image encryption', *Expert Systems with Applications*, 2023, 213, pp. 119076.

[20]   Li, J.: 'Research on an optimized encryption algorithm for network information security communication', *International Journal of Communication Networks and Distributed Systems*, 2023, 29(1), pp. 31–46.

[21]   Ullah, S., Zheng, J., Din, N., *et al.*: 'Elliptic Curve Cryptography; Applications, challenges, recent advances, and future trends: A comprehensive survey', *Computer Science Review*, 2023, 47, pp. 100530.

[22]   Hebbale, SB, Akula, VS, Baraki, P.: 'Tuna Swarm Optimization with 3D-chaotic map and DNA encoding for image encryption with lossless image compression based on FPGA', *International Journal of Electrical and Computer Engineering Systems*, 2023, 14(1), pp. 59–72.

[23]   Trung, MM, Do, TT, Van Tanh, N., *et al.*: 'Design a cryptosystem using elliptic curves cryptography and Vigenère symmetry key', *International Journal of Electrical and Computer Engineering*, 2023, 13(2), pp. 1734.

[24]   Saleem, M., Warsi, MR, Islam, S.: 'Secure information processing for multimedia forensics using zero-trust security model for large scale data analytics in SaaS cloud computing environment', *Journal of Information Security and Applications*, 2023, 72, pp. 103389.

Index

Printed in the USA
CPSIA information can be obtained
at www.ICGtesting.com
LVHW011819041124
795688LV00003B/272